Table of Contents

What You'll Find in
The Ultimate Shape Book

Teacher resource page for each of the 50 topics:

Prewriting Activities
Read aloud from the resources suggested to enrich language and develop new concepts. Plan real-life experiences to increase vocabulary and reinforce the relationship between the spoken and written word.

Let the Writing Begin
Here are suggestions for using this book simultaneously with students of varying writing levels—emergent writers, beginning writers, and independent writers. (See description of the writing forms on page 3.)

Five reproducible forms including the following for each topic:

Front Cover
Students color and cut out the cover. You may wish to reproduce this on heavy paper and/or laminate it.

Back Cover
The back cover includes a poem. Read the poem with students. Encourage students to add a new stanza.

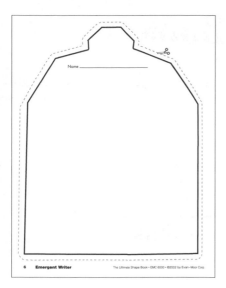

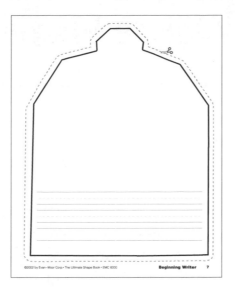

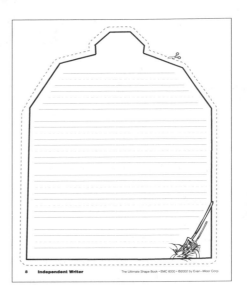

Emergent Writers Form

Students use this blank shape form to tell a story in pictures. Below the pictures, write a description dictated by students. This is a valuable task for an aide, parent volunteer, or cross-age tutor.

Beginning Writers Form

Students use this draw-and-write form and the short writing prompts provided on the teacher resource page to move from picture stories to written stories. Writing lines are always at the bottom of the shape.

Independent Writers Form

Students use this lined form to write about one of the topics suggested on the teacher resource page. Reproduce as many copies as students need to write their stories.

• •

Finishing Touches

Put Books Together

The books may be put together in one of these ways:

- Staple and cover with book tape.
- Punch holes and lace up. Lace down through end holes, up through middle hole; tie.
- Punch holes and use metal rings.

Share Books

Provide opportunities for students to share their stories with others. Read books to the whole class, send books home to share, and put student-authored books in your class library.

I like to sit in my favorite chair and read a book.

Big Barn

Literature Connections

Barn Cat: A Counting Book by Carol P. Saul; Little, Brown and Company Inc., 1998.
Barn Dance by Bill Martin, Jr. and John Archambault; Henry Holt, 1988.
Barn Kitty by June Kirkpatrick; Gently Worded Books, 1999.
Big Red Barn by Margaret Wise Brown; HarperCollins Publishers, 1995.
Once upon MacDonald's Farm by Stephen Gammell; Simon & Schuster, 2000.

Concrete Experiences

Visit a barn or view a video about a barn. Name the parts of the barn. List the animals that live in the barn. Talk about the different jobs that are done in the barn.

Let the Writing Begin

Emergent Writers

- **Animal Babies**
  Students draw and describe an animal baby.

- **B is for Barn**
  Students draw something that begins with the sound the letter *b* stands for.

Beginning Writers

- **Who Lives in the Barn?**
  Students draw animals that live in the barn and copy the sentence, adding the name of the animals they have drawn.

  _____ *lives in the barn.*

- **Look Inside**
  Students draw pictures to show what might be hiding in the barn, and copy and complete the couplet.

  Open the barn door and look inside.
  See a _____ trying to hide.

Independent Writers

- **The Day the Door Was Left Open**
  Students plan and write a story that tells what happens the day the barn door was left open.

- **Who Is in the Barn?**
  Students write *Who Am I?* riddles on the lined pages, and draw and write the answers on the picture pages.

Front Cover

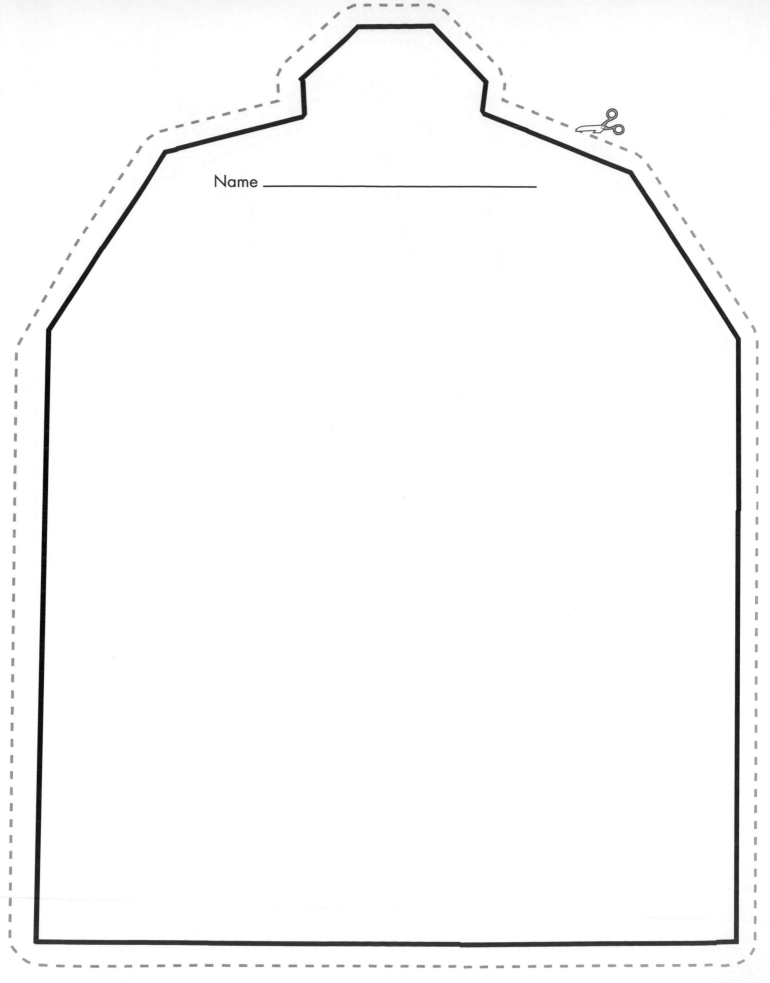

Name _____

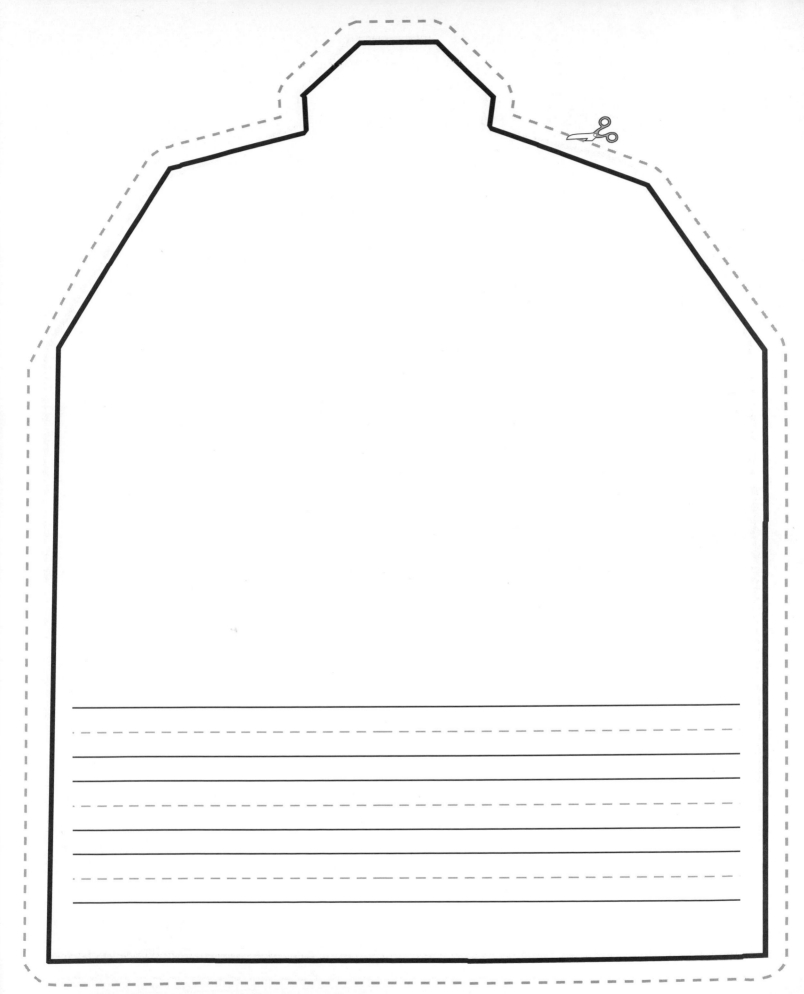

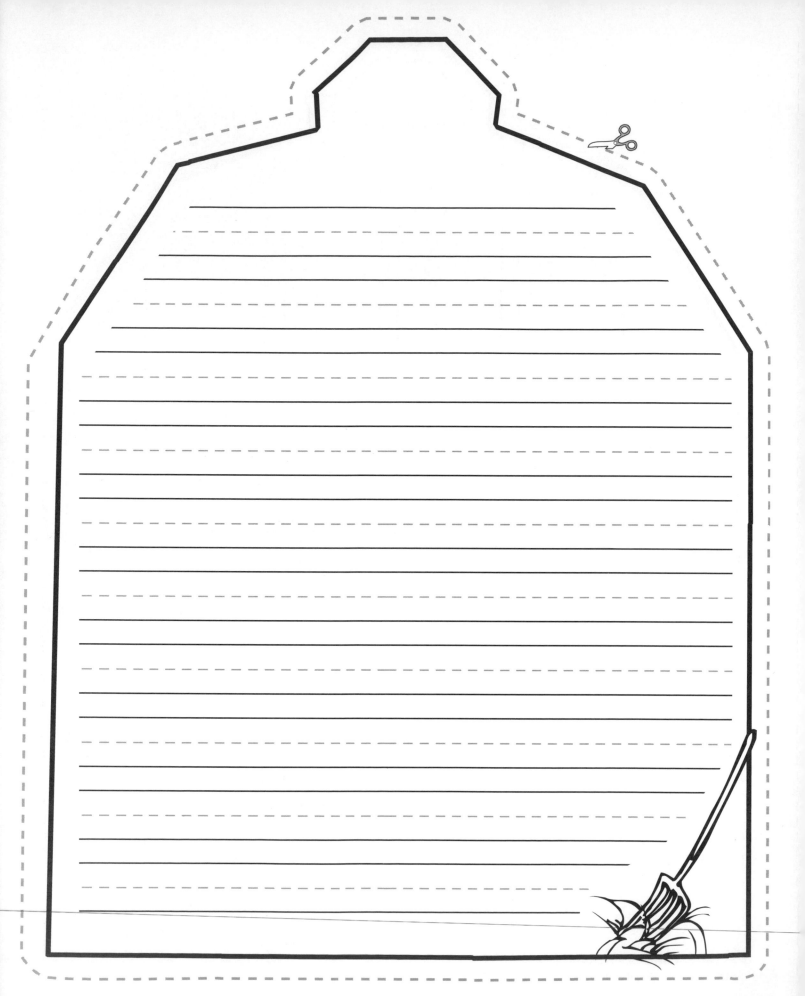

There's a big barn on the farm.

Animals live there safe from harm.

Inside the barn are oats and hay

With warm, dry places for animals to stay.

Back Cover 9

Penguin

Literature Connections

Antarctic Antics: A Book of Penguin Poems by Judy Sierra; Harcourt Brace & Co., 1998.
Busy Penguins by John Schindel; Tricycle Press, 2000.
Penguin (Photobook) by Frans Lanting and Christine K. Eckstrom; TASCHEN America, 1999.
Penguin Pete by Marcus Pfister; North-South Books, 1997.
Penguins! by Gail Gibbons; Holiday House, 1999.
The Puzzled Penguin: A Pop-Up Book by Keith Faulkner; Millbrook Press Trade, 1999.
Tacky the Penguin by Helen Lester; Houghton Mifflin Company, 1988.

Concrete Experiences

Discuss how living in a very cold climate is different than living in the climate where you live. How are penguins usually characterized? How is this different than birds living in the area where you live?

Let the Writing Begin

Emergent Writers

- **Penguins Play**
  Students draw penguins playing and tell about the game the penguins are playing.

- **The Penguin Counting Book**
  Students draw a designated number of penguins and write the numerals.

Beginning Writers

- **Percy Penguin's Travels**
  Students draw a place that Percy Penguin might visit. Then they copy the sentences.

  Percy Penguin visited _____.

  It was _____.

- **A Penguin Couplet**
  Students draw pictures to show how a penguin might travel across the ice. Then they copy or complete the couplet.

  Penguin _____ *across the ice.*
  Its black-and-white feathers look very nice.

Independent Writers

- **My Black-and-White World**
  Students imagine how it would feel to be a yellow polka-dotted penguin in the midst of its black-and-white world. They write a story from the viewpoint of the penguin.

- **The Adventures of Super Penguin**
  Students plan and write a story that describes one adventure of the superhero—Super Penguin.

Front Cover **11**

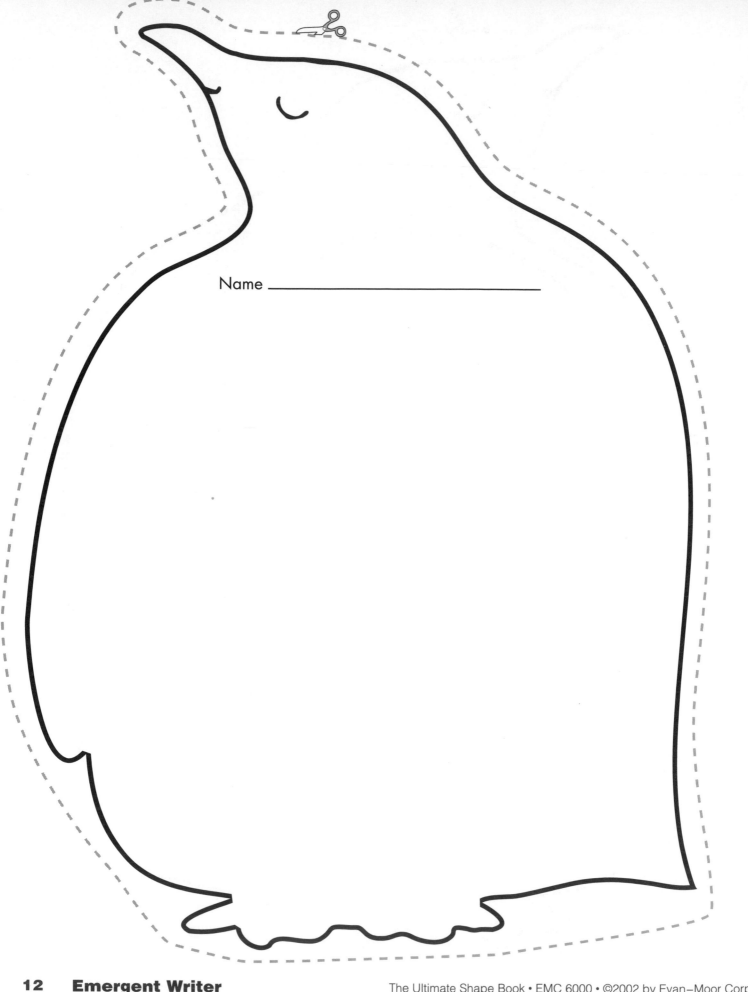

Name _____

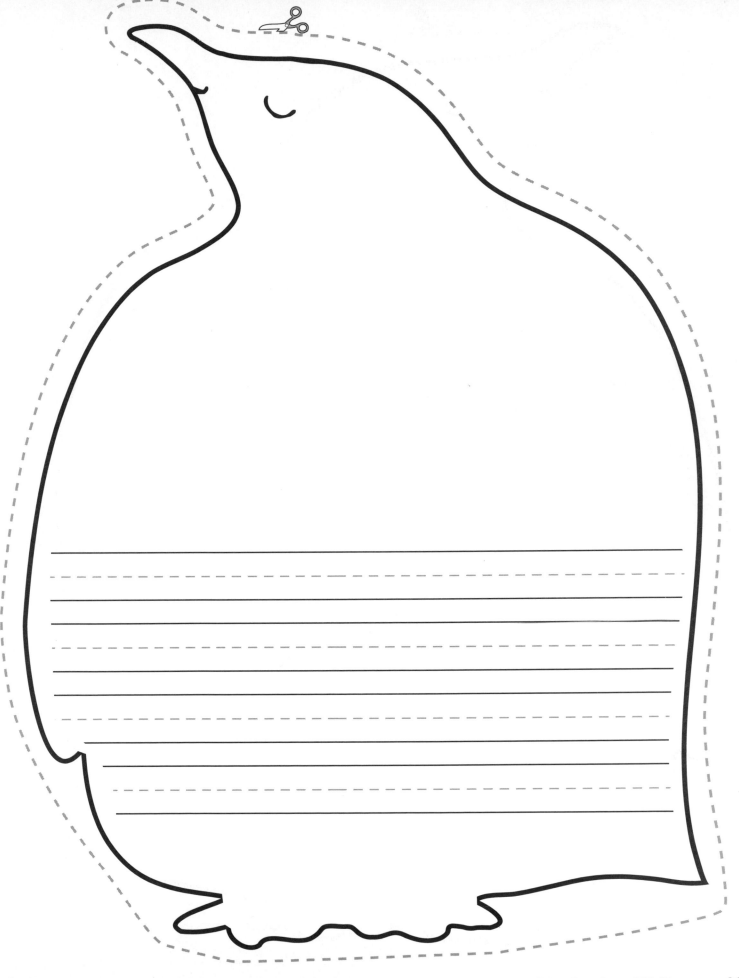

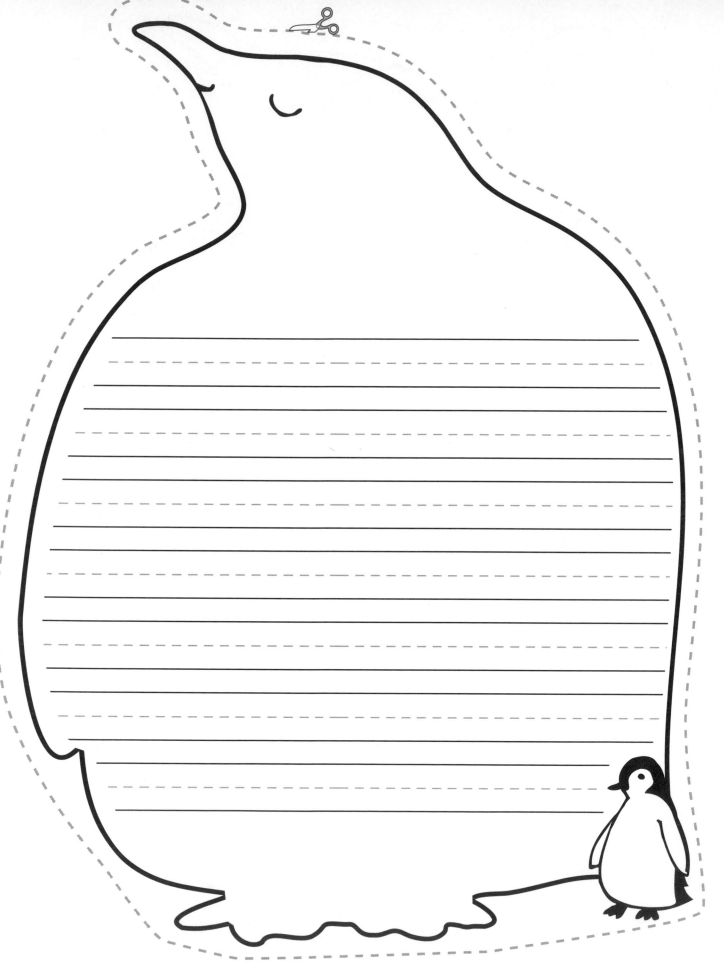

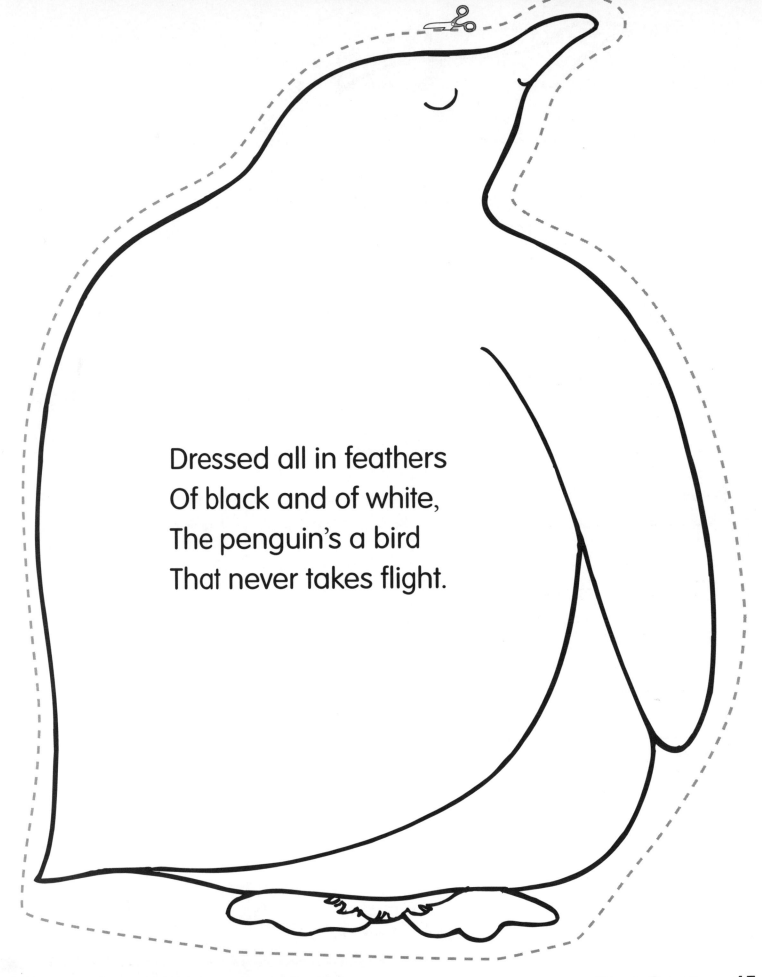

Dressed all in feathers
Of black and of white,
The penguin's a bird
That never takes flight.

Chair

Literature Connections

A Chair for My Mother by Vera B. Williams; Greenwillow, 1984.
Granny's Wonderful Chair by Frances Browne; Antique Collectors Club, 1999.
Little Fox by Marilyn Janovitz; North-South Books, 1999.
The Morning Chair by Barbara M. Joosse; Clarion Books, 1995.
Mrs. Piccolo's Easy Chair by Jean Jackson; Dorling Kindersley Publishing Inc., 1999.
Peter's Chair by Ezra Jack Keats; Puffin Books, 1998.

Concrete Experiences

Have students sit in several different chairs—a wooden chair, a padded chair, a rocking chair.
Discuss the differences.

Let the Writing Begin

Emergent Writers

• **My Favorite Chair**
Students draw their favorite chairs and describe them.

• **What Can You Do in a Chair?**
Students draw themselves doing something in a chair and then tell what they drew.

Beginning Writers

• **Who Is Sitting in My Chair?**
Students draw a picture of someone or something sitting in the chair. Then they copy and complete the sentence.
A(n) _____ is sitting in my chair.

• **Color Chairs**
Students draw and color chairs on several pages, using a different color on each page. Then they copy and complete the sentences.

This chair is _____.

(It's fun to make the last chair a combination of all the colors.)

This chair is _____ and _____ and _____ and _____ and _____.

Independent Writers

• **The Flying Chair**
Students plan and write a story that tells what happens when they sit in a chair that spreads its wings and flies away.

• **Where's the Chair?**
Students write riddles that describe places on the lined pages, and then draw and write the answers on the emergent writer pages provided.

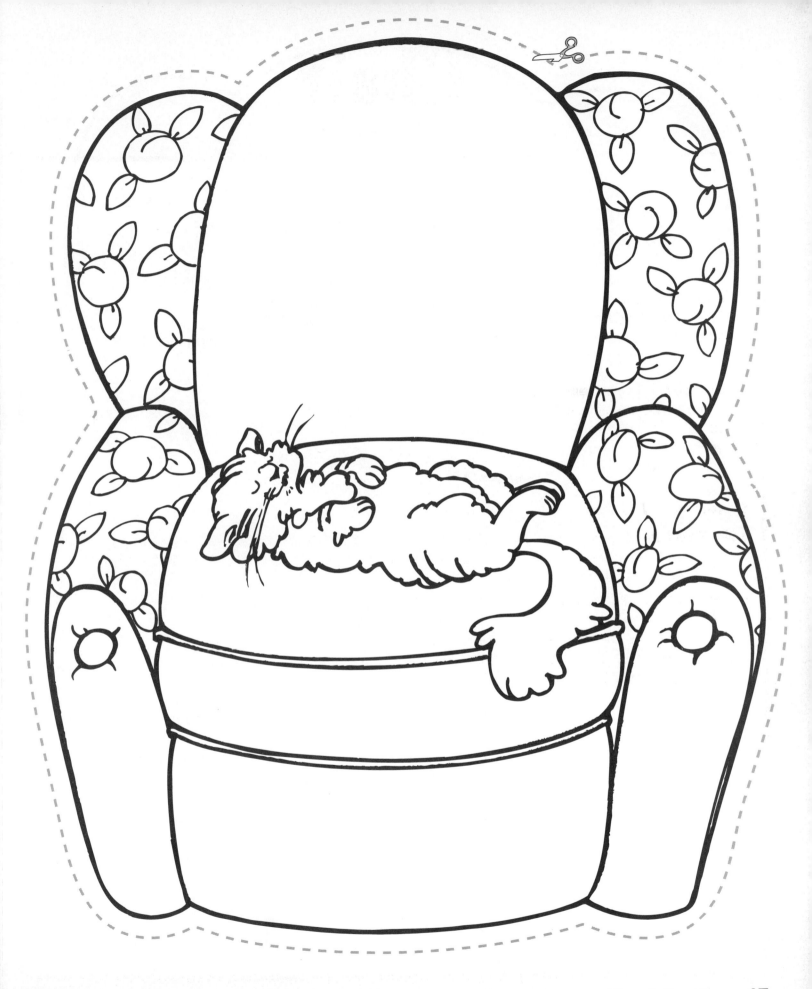

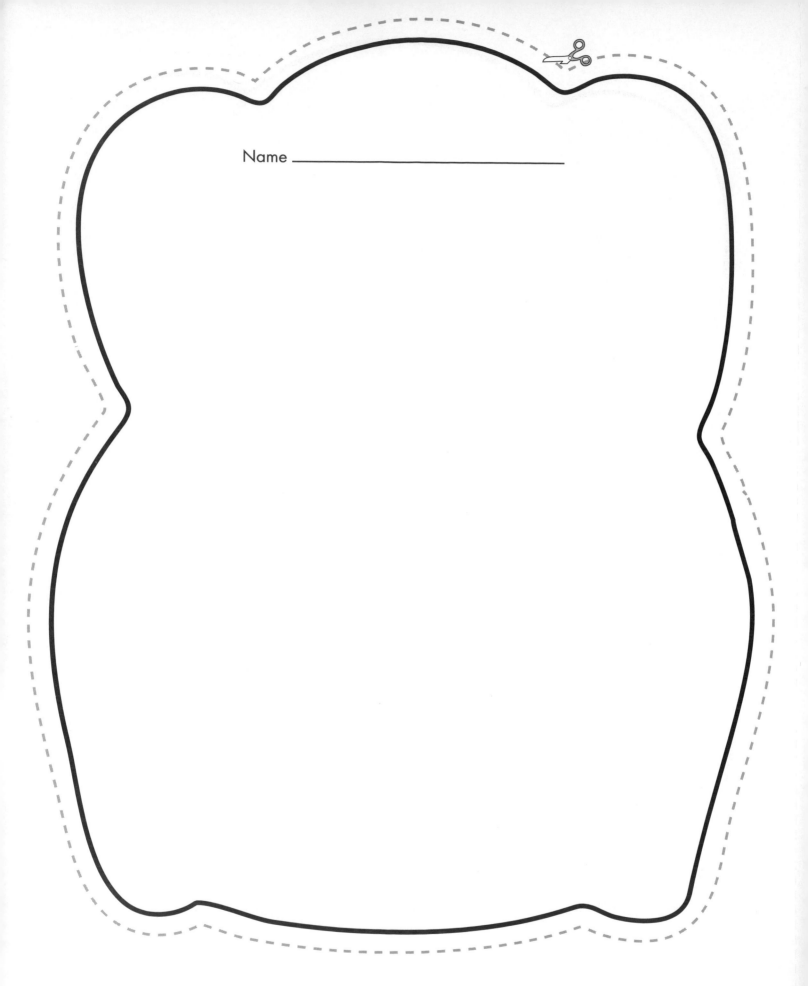

Name _____

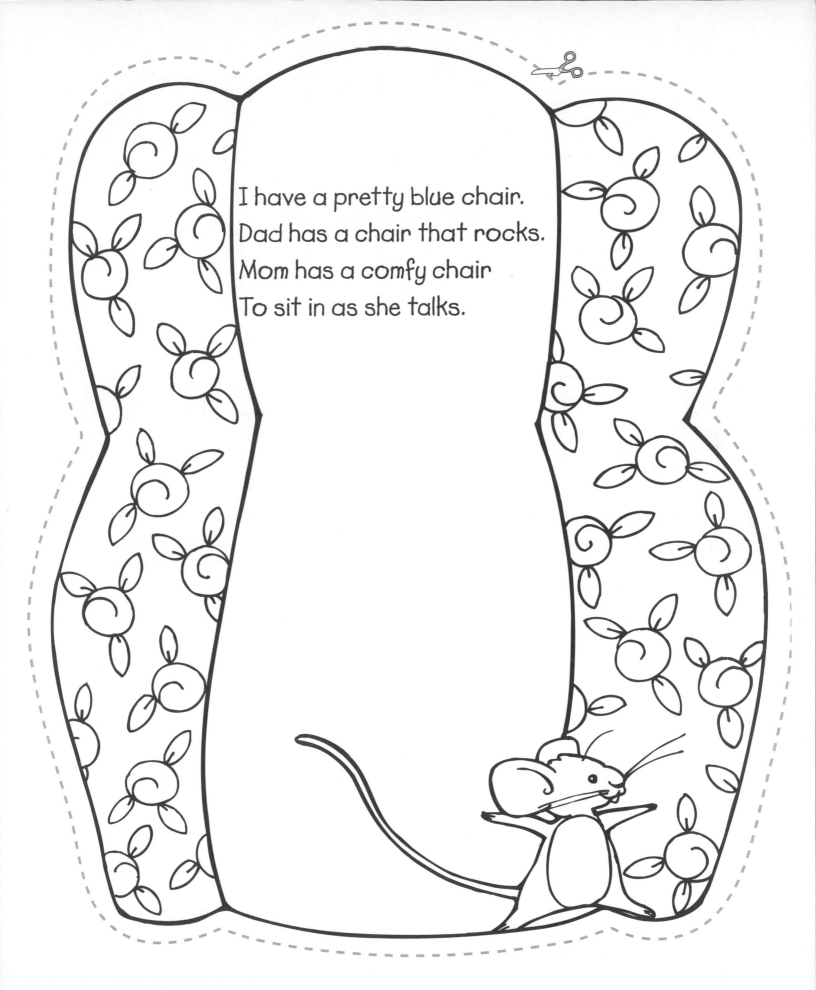

I have a pretty blue chair.
Dad has a chair that rocks.
Mom has a comfy chair
To sit in as she talks.

©2002 by Evan–Moor Corp • The Ultimate Shape Book • EMC 6000

Snail

Literature Connections

The Biggest House in the World by Leo Lionni; Pantheon Books, 1968.
Mr. Carey's Garden by Jane Cutler; Houghton Mifflin Company, 1996.
The Snail House by Allan Ahlberg; Candlewick Press, 2001.
Snails by Kevin J. Holmes; Bridgestone Books, 1998.
The Snail's Spell by Joanne Ryder; Viking Press, 1988.

Concrete Experiences

Observe a snail moving. Brainstorm and list words that could be used to describe the movement *(dawdle, slink, pokey, amble, creep, crawl, slide)*. Draw a large picture of a snail. Talk about the different parts of the snail and label them.

Let the Writing Begin

Emergent Writers

- **Big, Bigger, Biggest**
  Students draw three snails—one with a big shell, one with a bigger shell, and the third with the biggest shell. Write the words *big, bigger, biggest* under the snails.

- **A Beautiful Shell**
  Students draw snails, coloring their shells to make them beautiful, and then describe what makes the shells beautiful.

Beginning Writers

- **As Slow As**
  Students draw a snail. Then they copy and complete the sentence.

  The snail moves as slow as _____.

- **Snail Snacks**
  Students draw a snack that a snail might enjoy, and then copy and complete this verse.

  A snail likes to eat _____ so sweet.

Independent Writers

- **Home Sweet Home**
  Students write from a snail's viewpoint to describe how always carrying a house along can be good and bad.

- **If I Were as Small as a Snail**
  Students write a story about what might happen if they were as small as a snail.

Front Cover 23

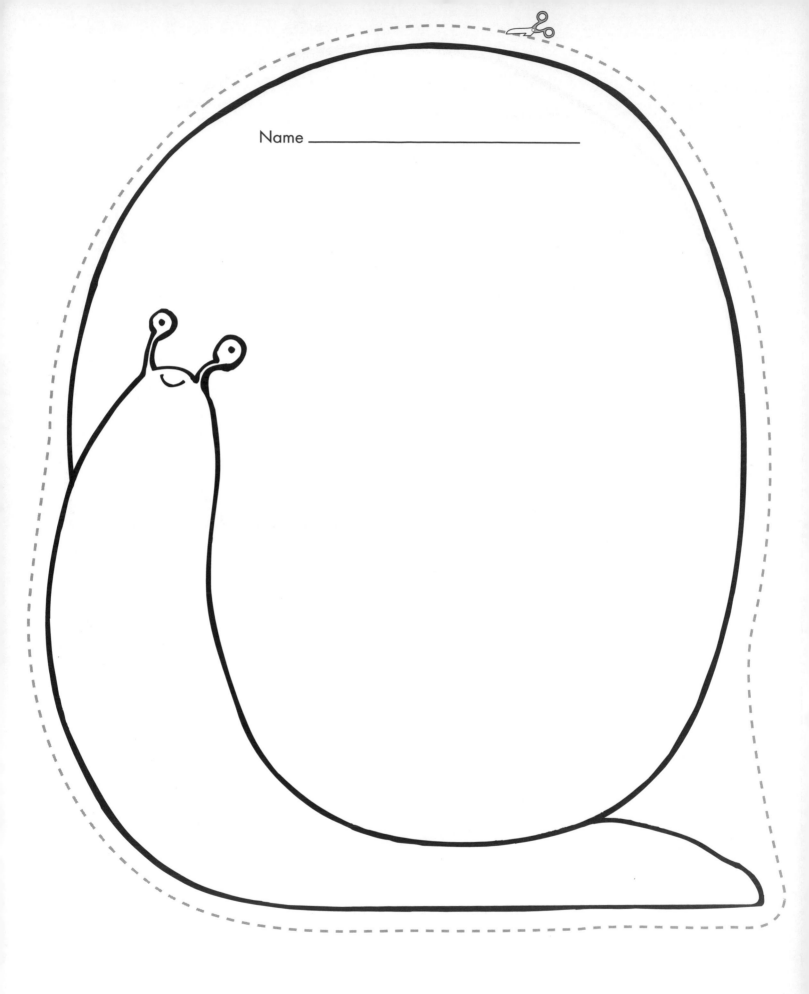

Name _____

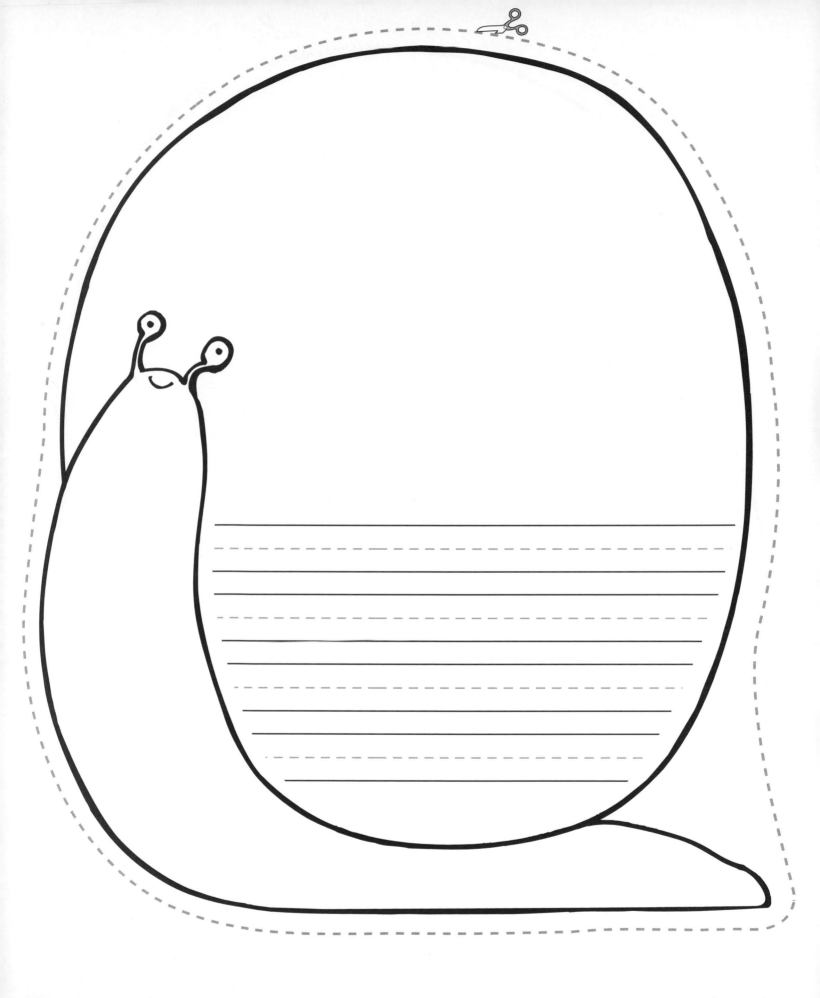

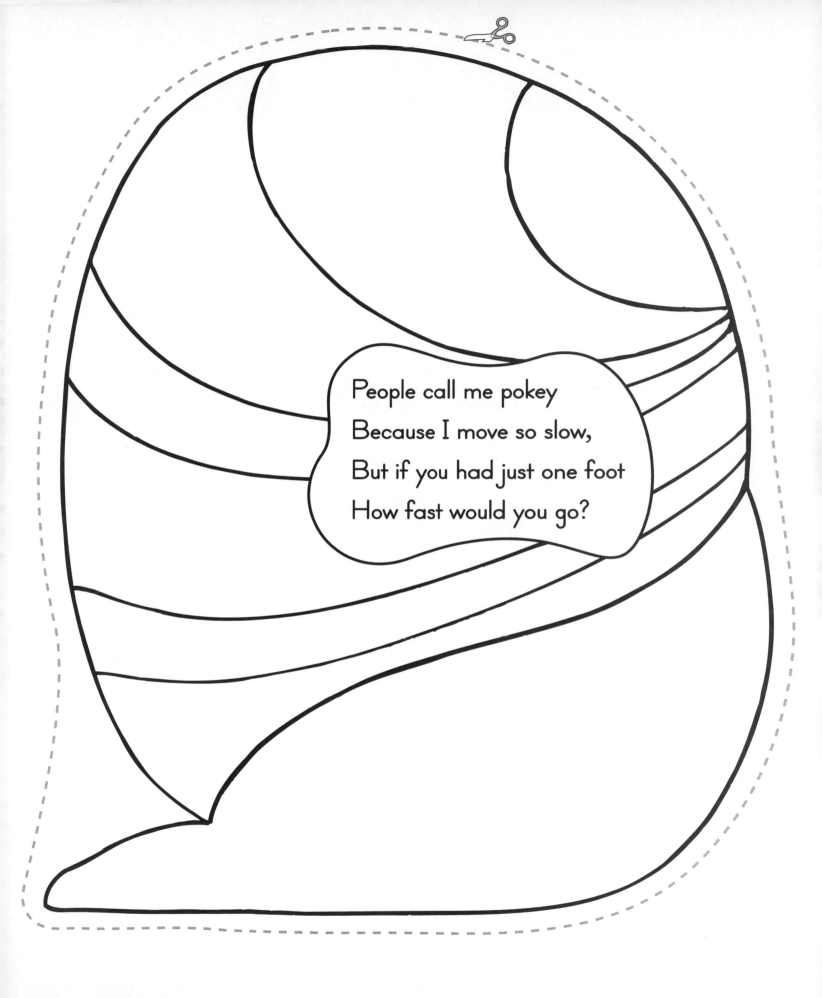

Refrigerator

Literature Connections
Note: Picture books featuring refrigerators are in short supply. Here are some good kitchen and food books that reference refrigerators.

The Children's Kitchen Garden: A Book of Gardening, Cooking, and Learning by Georgeanne Brennan et al.; Ten Speed Press, 1997.

Ice Cream Larry by Daniel Manus Pinkwater; Marshall Cavendish Corp., 1999.

In My Momma's Kitchen by Jerdine Nolen; Lothrop, Lee & Shepard Books, 1999.

Isaac the Ice Cream Truck by Scott Santoro; Henry Holt, 1999.

Simply Delicious by Margaret Mahy; Orchard Books, 1999.

Concrete Experiences
Visit the refrigerator in the school cafeteria or a local grocery store. List words that describe how it feels to be cold *(chilly, shivery, cool, frostbitten)*. List the things that are kept in a refrigerator.

Let the Writing Begin

Emergent Writers

- **A Surprise in the Refrigerator**
  Students draw a surprising object in their refrigerators. Then they tell how the surprise got into the refrigerator.

- **Can You Guess?**
  Students draw an item of food that might be found in a refrigerator. They think of three clues that identify the food. Students share the clues and have others guess what's inside.

Beginning Writers

- **Put It Inside**
  Provide five of the forms on page 31 for each student. Students choose five things to put in their refrigerators. On the first page, they draw one of the first item. On the second page, they draw two of the second item, and so on for the five items. On the lines, they complete the sentences.
  Here is one (two, three, etc.) _____. Put it inside.

- **A Treat to Eat**
  Students draw a treat in the refrigerator. Then they copy and complete the couplet.

  I open the door to get a treat.
  I take out some _____ to eat.

Independent Writers

- **The Day I Did the Grocery Shopping**
  Students plan and write an adventure about an imagined trip to the grocery store.

- **Why Refrigerators Are Important**
  Students write a persuasive paragraph explaining why refrigerators are important.

The list on the refrigerator reads:

honey
bread
dog food
bones

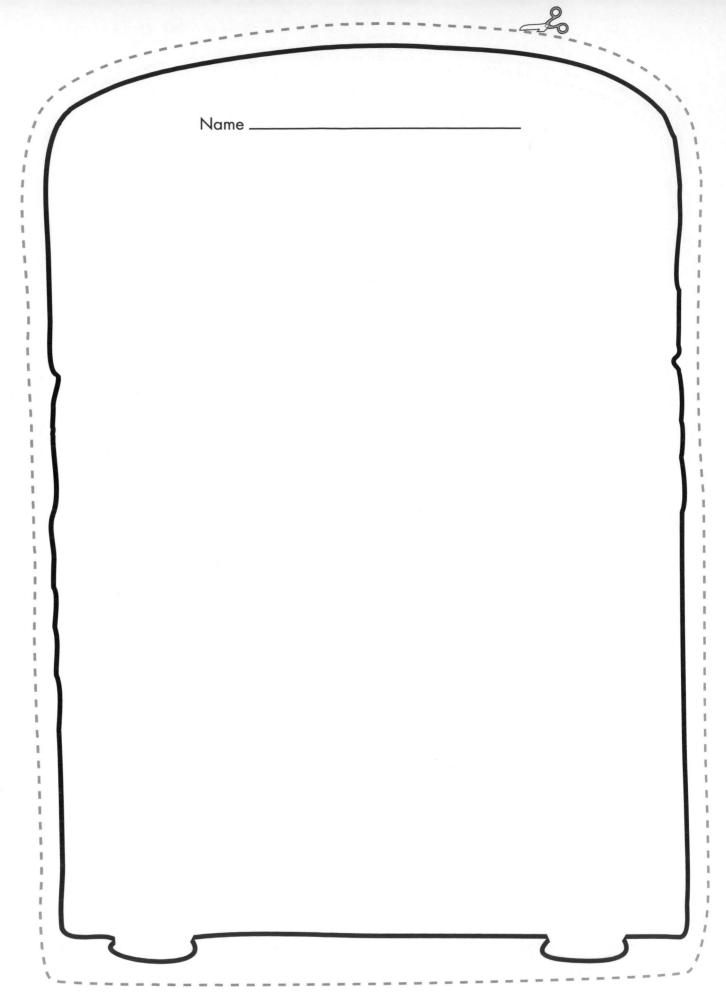

Name _____

The Ultimate Shape Book • EMC 6000 • ©2002 by Evan-Moor Corp

Open up its big, wide door.
The refrigerator is my grocery store.

Crocodile

Literature Connections

Bill and Pete to the Rescue by Tomie dePaola; Puffin Books, 2001.
The Christmas Crocodile by Bonny Becker; Simon & Schuster Children's Books, 1998.
Counting Crocodiles by Judy Sierra; Harcourt Brace & Company, 1997.
Crocodile Listens by April Pulley Sayre; Greenwillow, 2001.
Crocodiles & Alligators by Seymour Simon; HarperCollins Children's Books, 1999.
The Enormous Crocodile by Roald Dahl; Knopf, 2000.
Five Little Monkeys Sitting in a Tree by Eileen Christelow; Clarion Books, 1993.
The Gator Girls by Joanna Cole et al.; William Morrow & Co., Inc., 1995.

Concrete Experiences

Show pictures of crocodiles and alligators. Note the differences in their appearances. List similarities in their appearances as well.

Let the Writing Begin

Emergent Writers

- **A Crocodile Smile**
  Students draw a crocodile smiling and then tell a story about what made the crocodile smile.

- **A Crocodile Counting Book**
  Students write numbers on the blank pages and then draw crocodiles to match the numbers.

Beginning Writers

- **Crocodiles Can...**
  Students draw a crocodile doing something. Then they copy and complete the sentence.

  A crocodile can _____.

- **A Crocodile in My Bathtub**
  Students draw a scene with a crocodile in their bathtubs. Then they copy and complete the sentences.

  There's a crocodile in my bathtub. What will I do? I'll _____.

Independent Writers

- **Why Crocodile Has a Long Tail**
  Students write a tale explaining why crocodile has a long tail.

- **Crocodile Is Missing**
  Students imagine what might happen when a crocodile is found missing from the zoo.

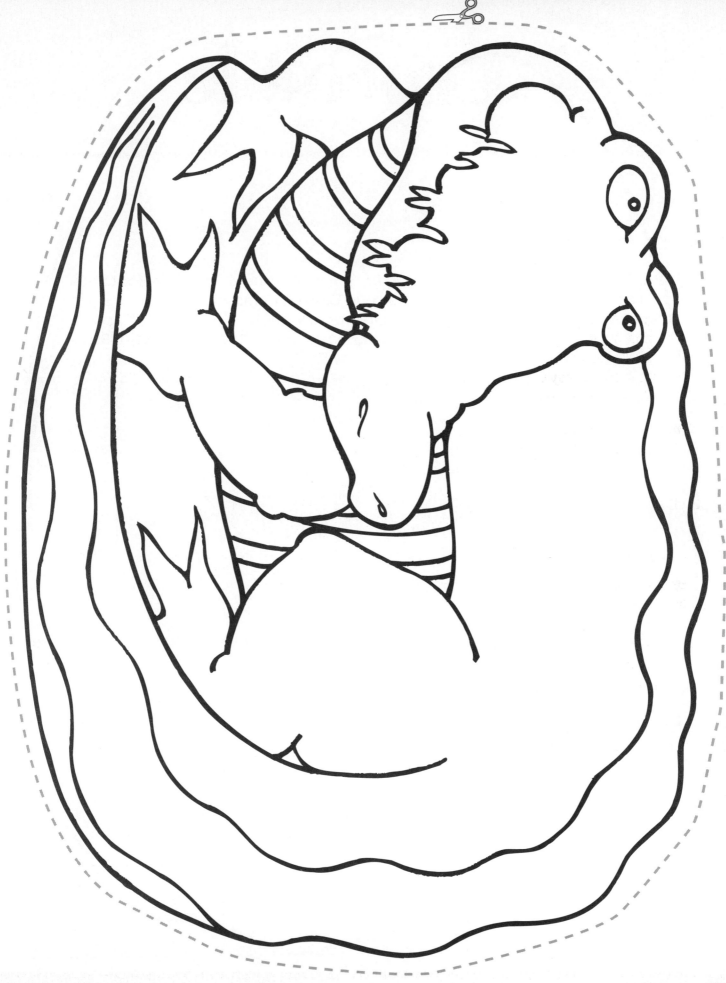

Front Cover 35

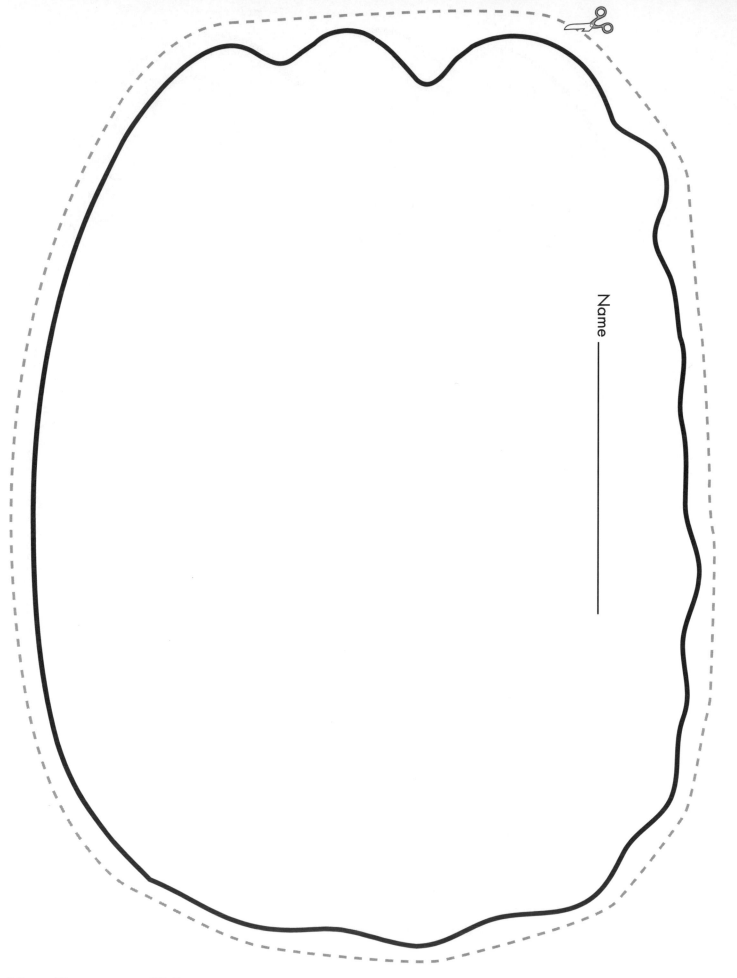

Name _____

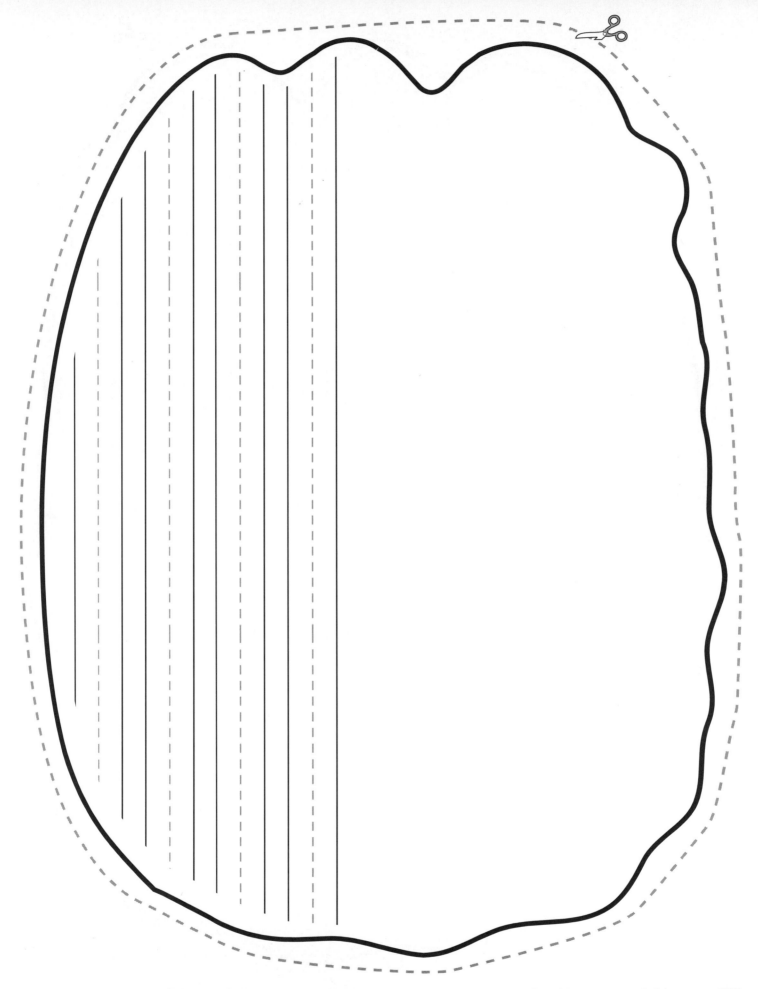

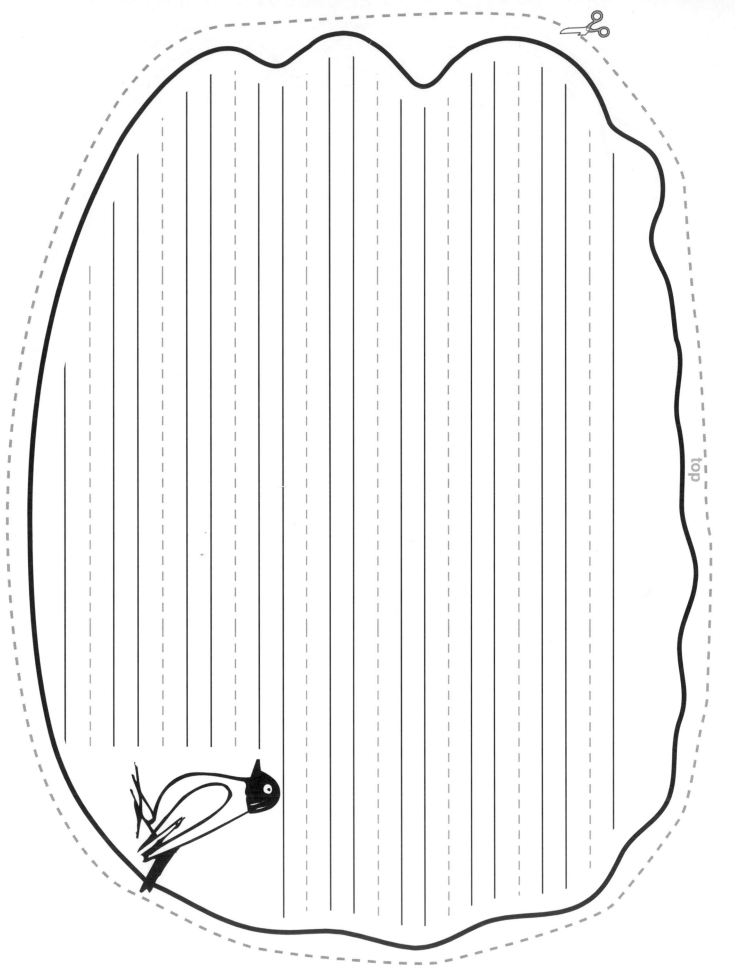

top

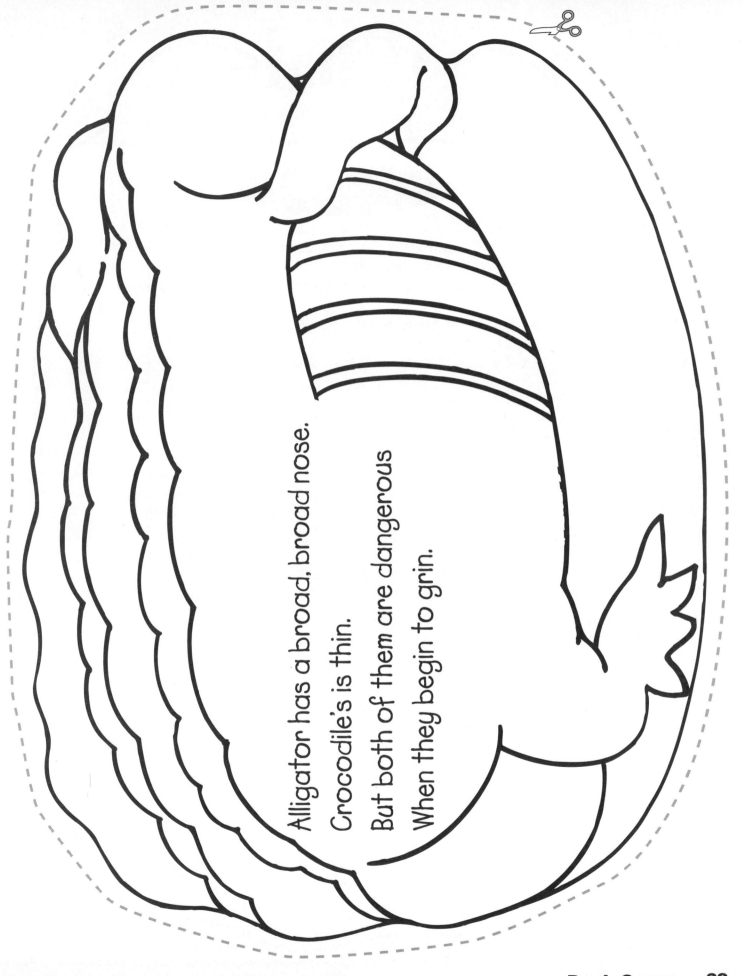

Alligator has a broad, broad nose.
Crocodile's is thin.
But both of them are dangerous
When they begin to grin.

Whale

Literature Connections

Amos and Boris by William Steig; Farrar, Straus & Giroux Inc., 1971.

Baby Beluga by Raffi; Crown Publishing, 1997.

Splash! A Book About Whales and Dolphins by Melvin Berger and Gilda Berger; Cartwheel Books, 2001.

A Symphony of Whales by Steve Schuch; Harcourt Brace & Co., 1999.

The Whales by Cynthia Rylant; Blue Sky Press, 2000.

Whales, Dolphins, and Porpoises by Mark Carwardine; Dorling Kindersley Publishing Inc., 1995.

The Whales' Song by Dyan Sheldon; Puffin Books, 1997.

Concrete Experiences

On the playground or play field, mark the length of several different whales. *(killer whale = 25 ft [8 m], sperm whale = 60 ft [18 m], fin whale = 80 ft [24 m], blue whale = 100 ft [31 m])* Have students compare the sizes of the whales to the equipment on the playground. For example, *"The blue whale is bigger than the whole sandbox and swing area."*

Let the Writing Begin

Emergent Writers

- **Where Is the Whale?**
  Students draw pictures to show where the whale is and then tell about their pictures.

- **A _____ Whale**
  Students draw whales in action—swimming, diving, spouting, eating. Then they tell about what the whales are doing.

Beginning Writers

- **Whale Facts**
  Students draw a whale and then list facts about whales.

  Whales _____.

- **I Spy a Whale**
  Students draw themselves with binoculars looking out across the water. Then they copy the verse, filling in the blank.

  I spy a big whale in the sea. That big whale is _____ at me. (looking, smiling, waving, winking, etc.)

Independent Writers

- **If I Were a Whale**
  Students imagine what life would be like if they were whales.

- **Wee Willie, the Littlest Whale**
  Students tell a tale about the littlest whale in the sea— Wee Willie.

The Ultimate Shape Book • EMC 6000 • ©2002 by Evan–Moor Corp.

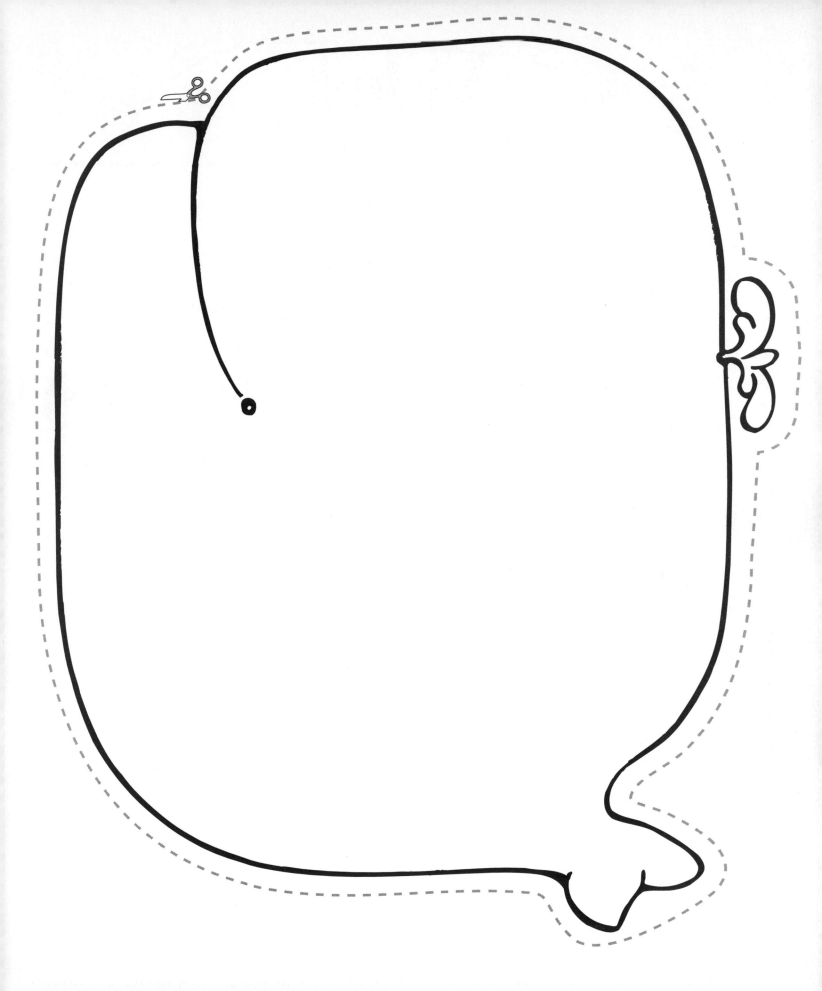

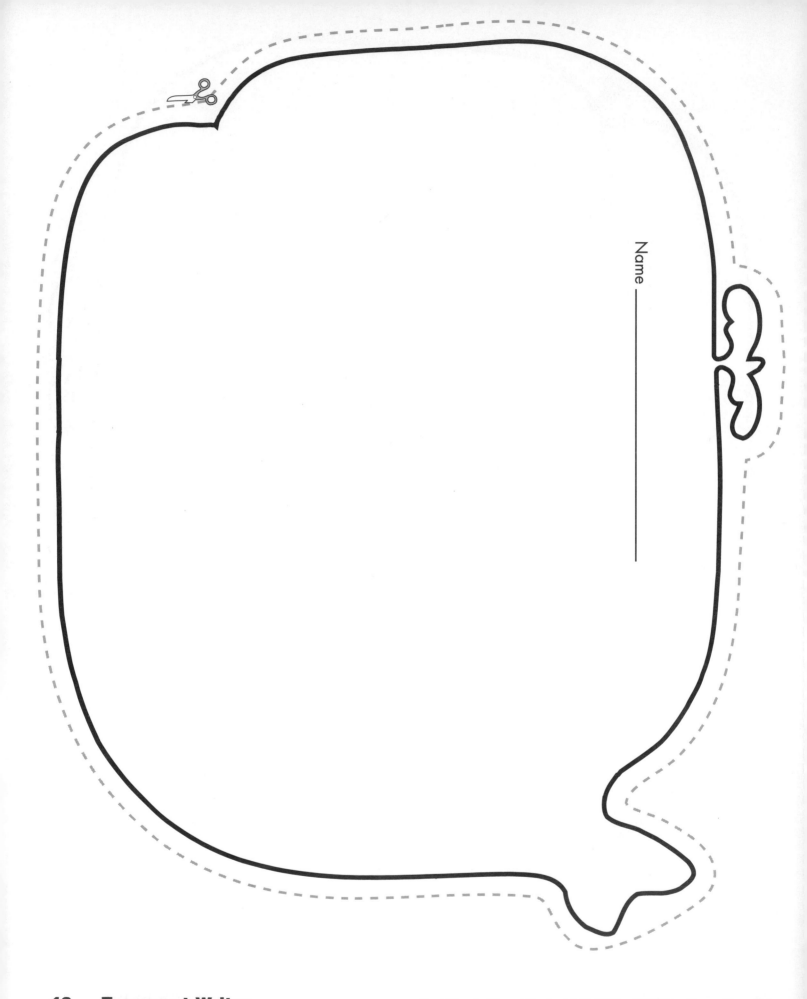

Name _____

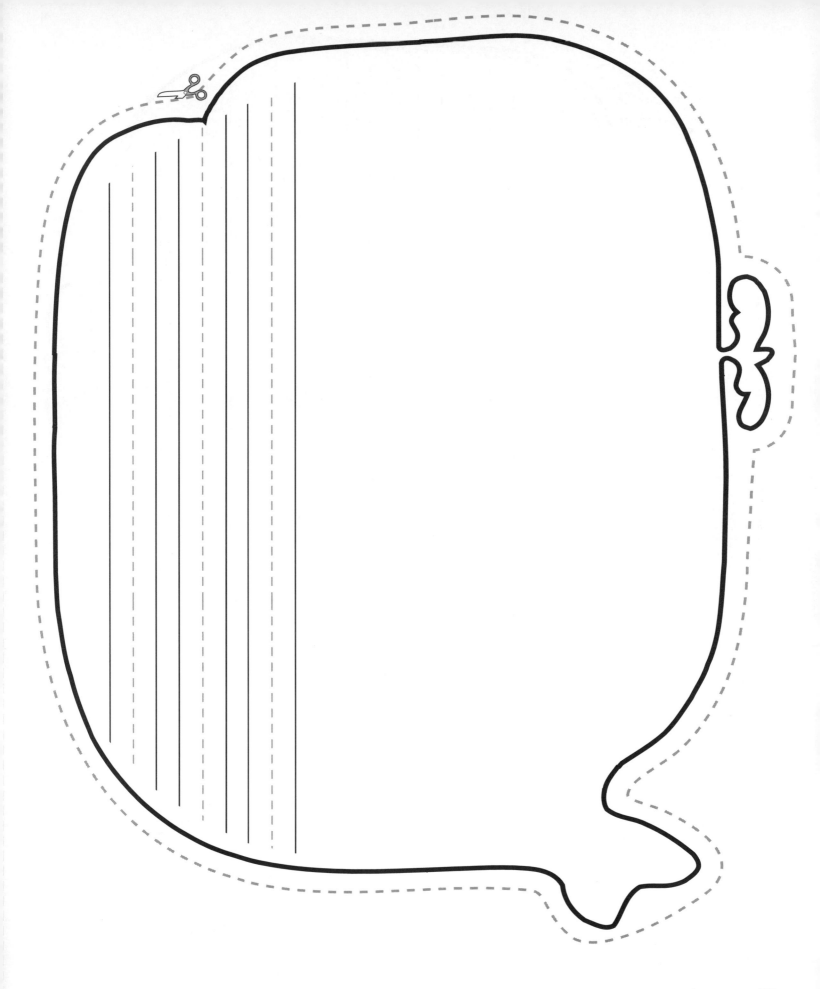

Beginning Writer **43**

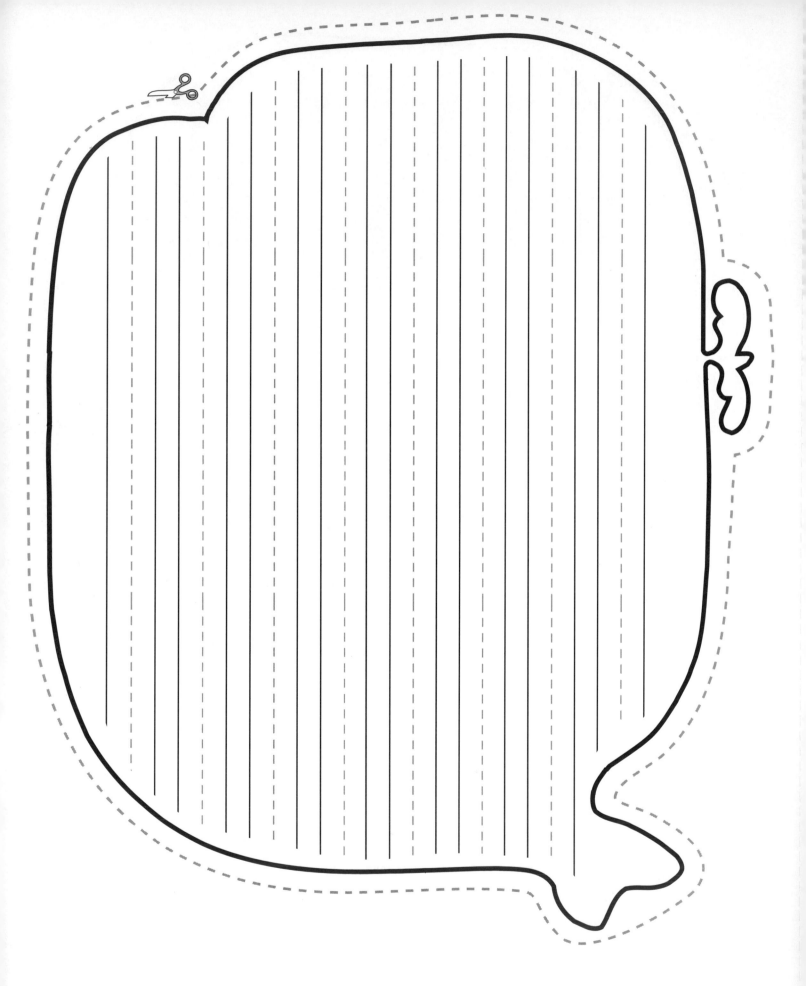

The Ultimate Shape Book • EMC 6000 • ©2002 by Evan-Moor Corp

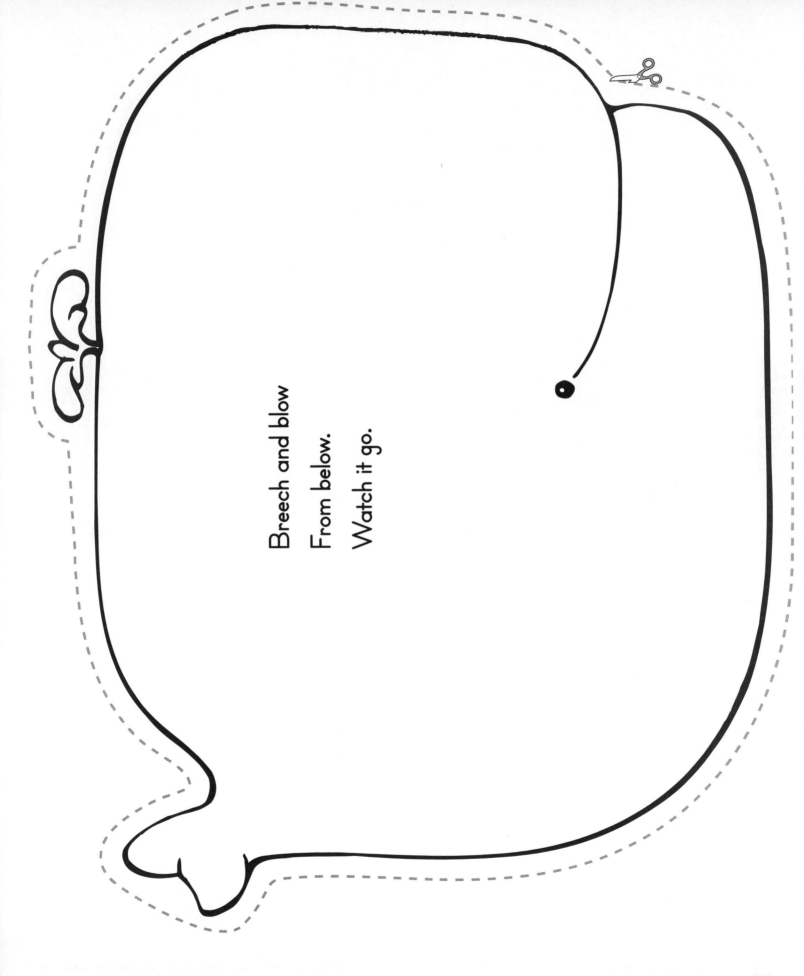

Breech and blow

From below.

Watch it go.

Cow

Literature Connections

Blossom Comes Home by James Herriot; St. Martin's Press, 1993.

Click, Clack, Moo: Cows That Type by Doreen Cronin; Simon & Schuster Children's Books, 2000.

The Complete Cow by Sara Rath; Voyageur Press, 1998.

The Cows Are in the Corn by James Young; Penguin USA, 1996.

Milk from Cow to Carton by Aliki; HarperCollins Children's Books, 1992.

Minnie and Moo Go to Paris by Denys Cazet; Dorling Kindersley Publishing Inc., 1999.

Concrete Experiences

Visit a dairy farm or view the *Reading Rainbow* feature on visiting a dairy. Have students note the journey milk takes on its way to their breakfast tables.

Let the Writing Begin

Emergent Writers

• **Milk and _____**
Students draw a picture of what they like to eat with a glass of cold milk.

• **In the Pasture**
Students think of something that the cows might be doing in the pasture and draw it.

Beginning Writers

• **Colorful Cows**
Recite "The Purple Cow" by Frank Gelett Burgess. Have students draw a colorful cow on their pages and then copy the sentence.

"I've never seen a _____ cow."

• **Moo Says the Cow**
Students draw cows conversing with other animals and write the sounds that they make.

Moo says the cow. Woof! Woof! says the dog.

Independent Writers

• **The Cow That Made Chocolate Milk**
Imagine the commotion when Farmer Ted milked Old Bessie and the milk was chocolate!

• **Made from Milk**
Students research products that are made from milk and write a report about them.

Front Cover 47

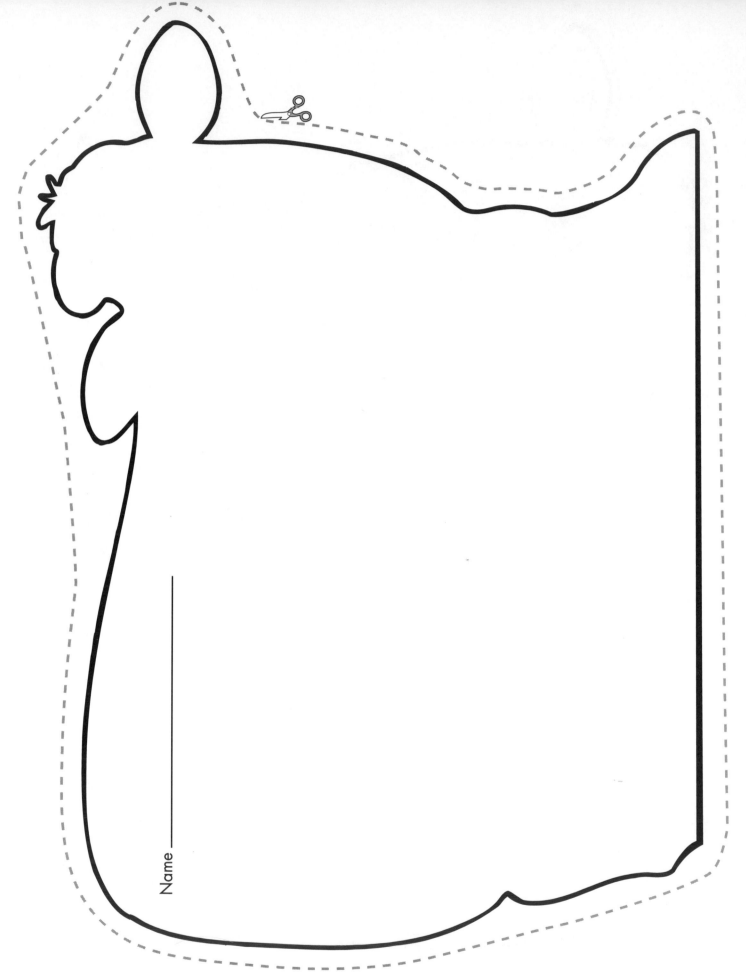

Name _____

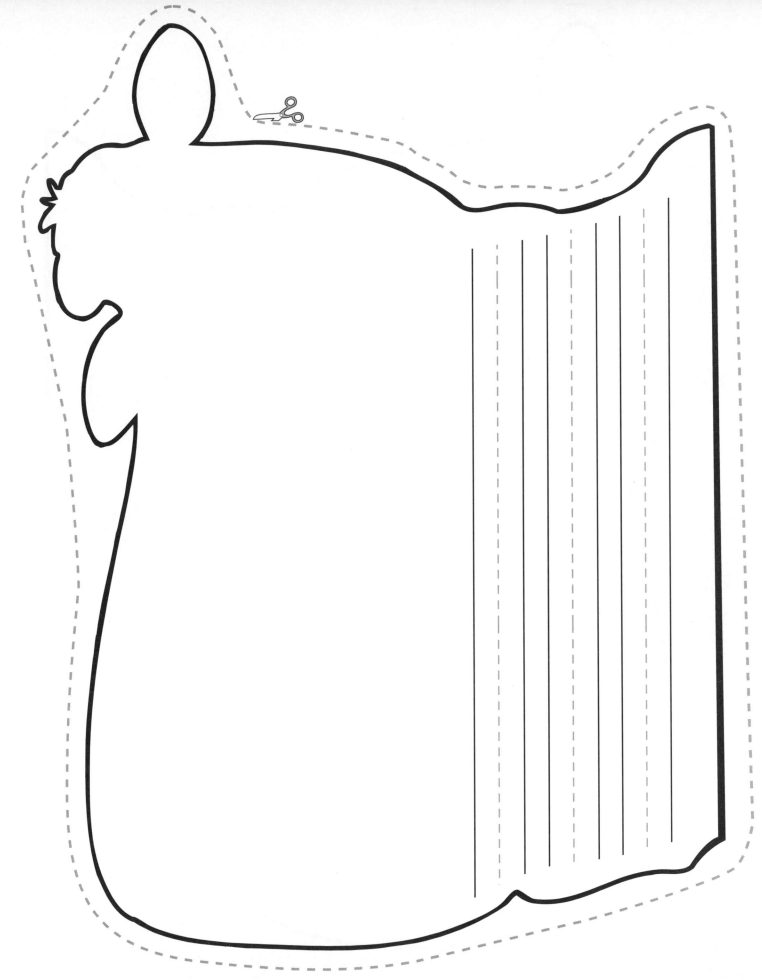

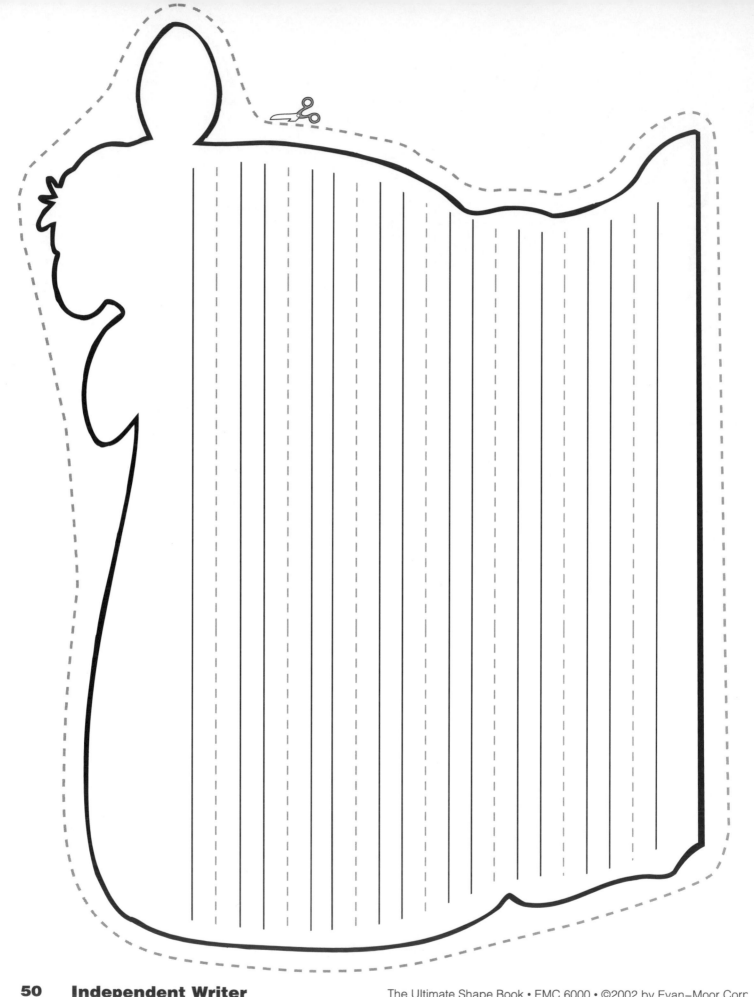

A cow, you see, is a wonderful creature.
For she has a most unusual feature.
She eats grass and munches hay
And turns them into milk each day.
What a marvelous barnyard creature!

©2002 by Evan-Moor Corp • The Ultimate Shape Book • EMC 6000

Back Cover 51

Lizard

Literature Connections

The Iguana Brothers: A Tale of Two Lizards by Tony Johnston; Cartwheel Books, 1995.

Komodo! by Peter Sis; Mulberry Books, 1999.

Lizards, Frogs, and Polliwogs: Poems and Paintings by Douglas Florian; Harcourt Brace & Co., 2001.

Lizards! (Know-It-Alls) by Christopher Nicholas; Learning Horizons, 2000.

The Mixed-up Chameleon by Eric Carle; Crowell Junior Books, 1984.

Concrete Experiences

Invite someone from your local pet store to bring a lizard to your classroom and talk about lizard habits.

Let the Writing Begin

Emergent Writers

- **Lizard on the Path**
  Students draw a lizard on a path and show what other creatures or vehicles are using the road. Their oral stories might include an explanation about what happens.

- **Changing Colors**
  Students draw a chameleon in several settings and color it differently to match the object it is sitting on each time.

Beginning Writers

- **The Lizard Climbed over the Fence**
  Students draw a picture to show what the lizard saw when it climbed over the fence. Then they copy and complete the sentences.

  The lizard climbed over the fence to see what it could see. And all that it could see was _____.

- **I Saw a Lizard**
  Students draw a picture to show what happened when they saw a lizard under a tree. Then they copy and complete this couplet.

  I saw a lizard under a tree. He _____ when he saw me.

Independent Writers

- **How Lizard Lost His Tail**
  Students imagine and write an adventure in which a lizard loses its tail.

- **Lovely Little Lizards**
  Students write alliterative sentences about lizards.

Front Cover 53

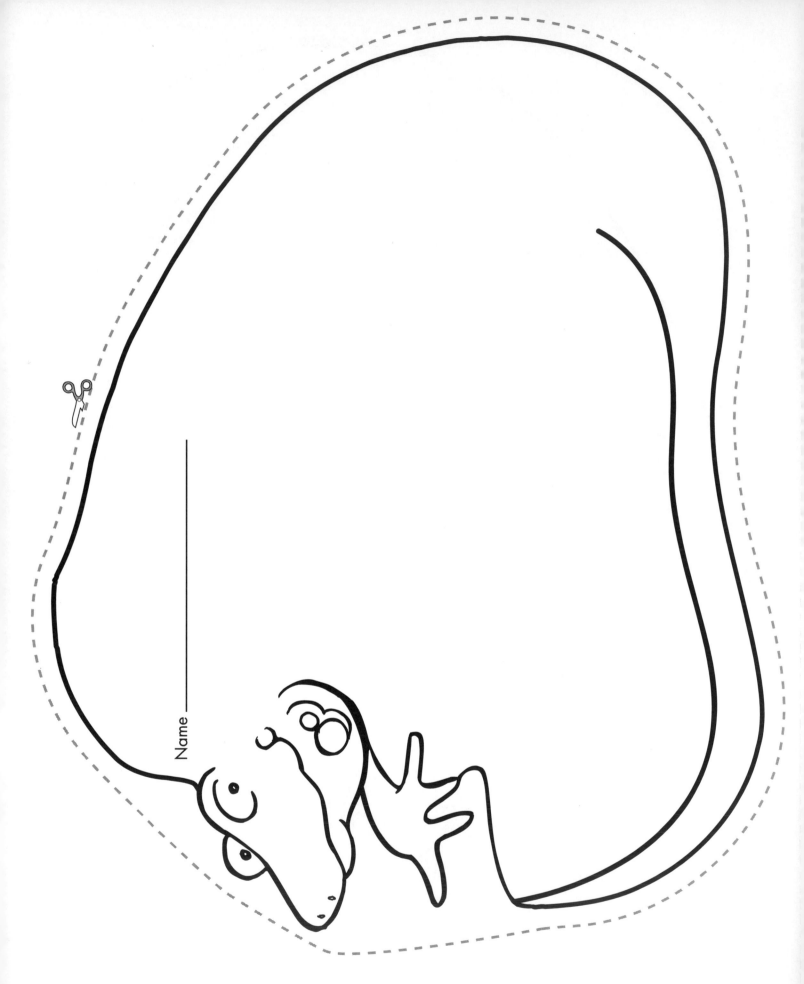

Name

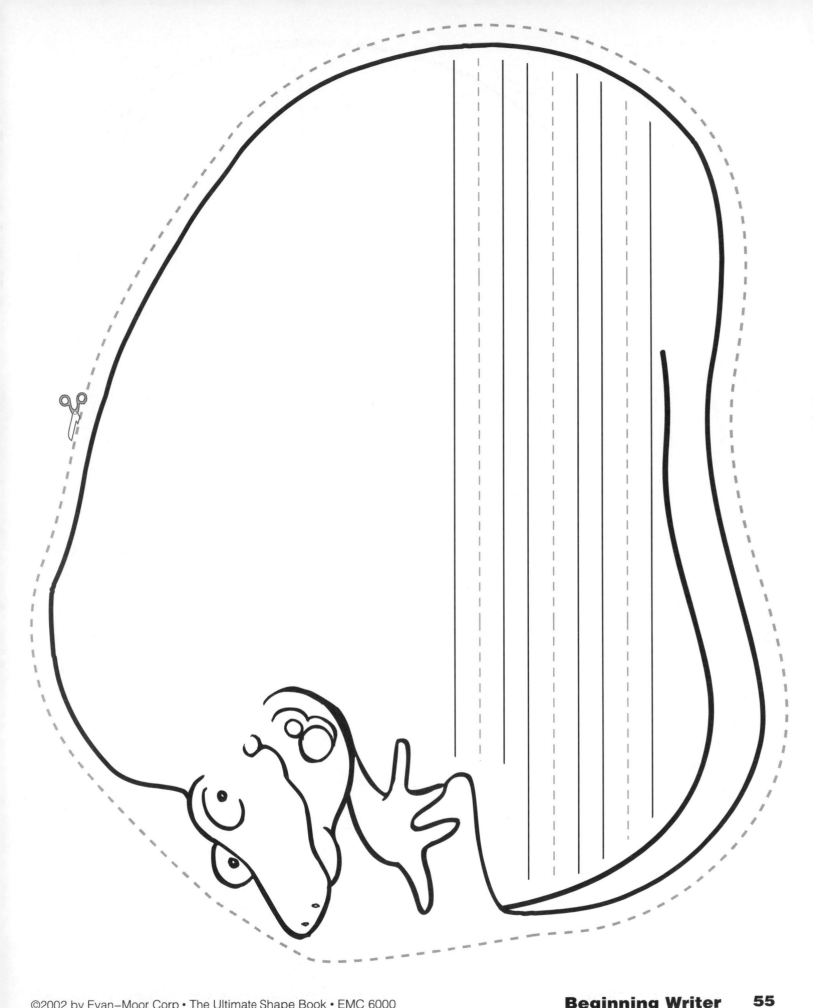

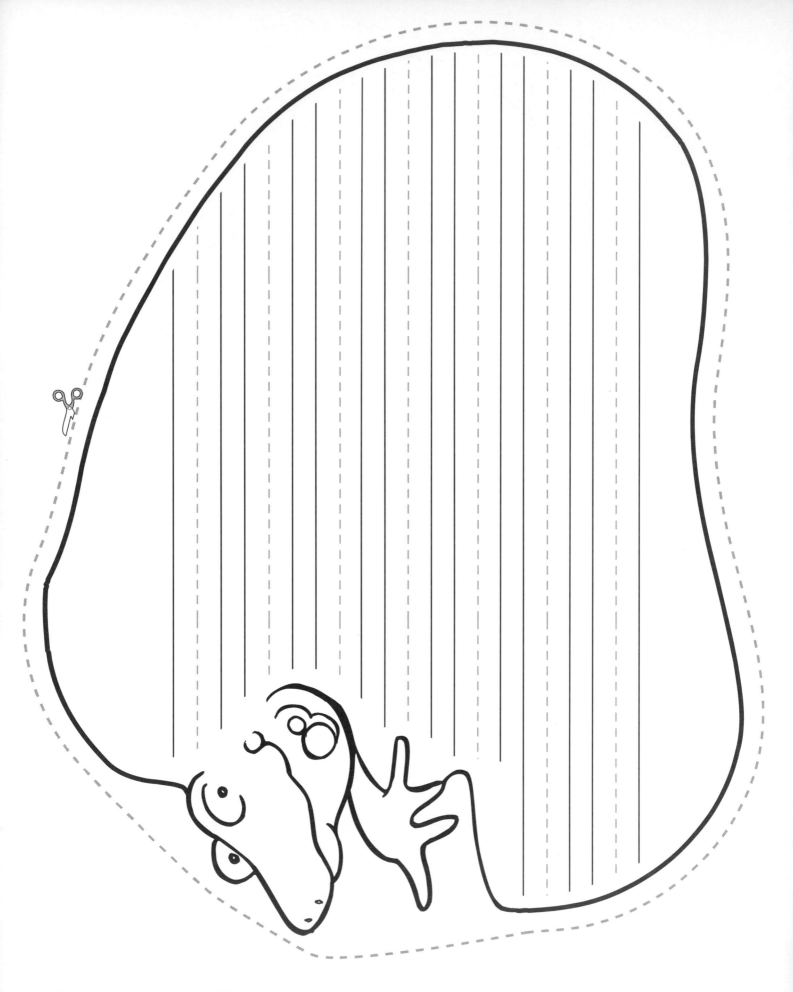

Independent Writer

The Ultimate Shape Book • EMC 6000 • ©2002 by Evan–Moor Corp

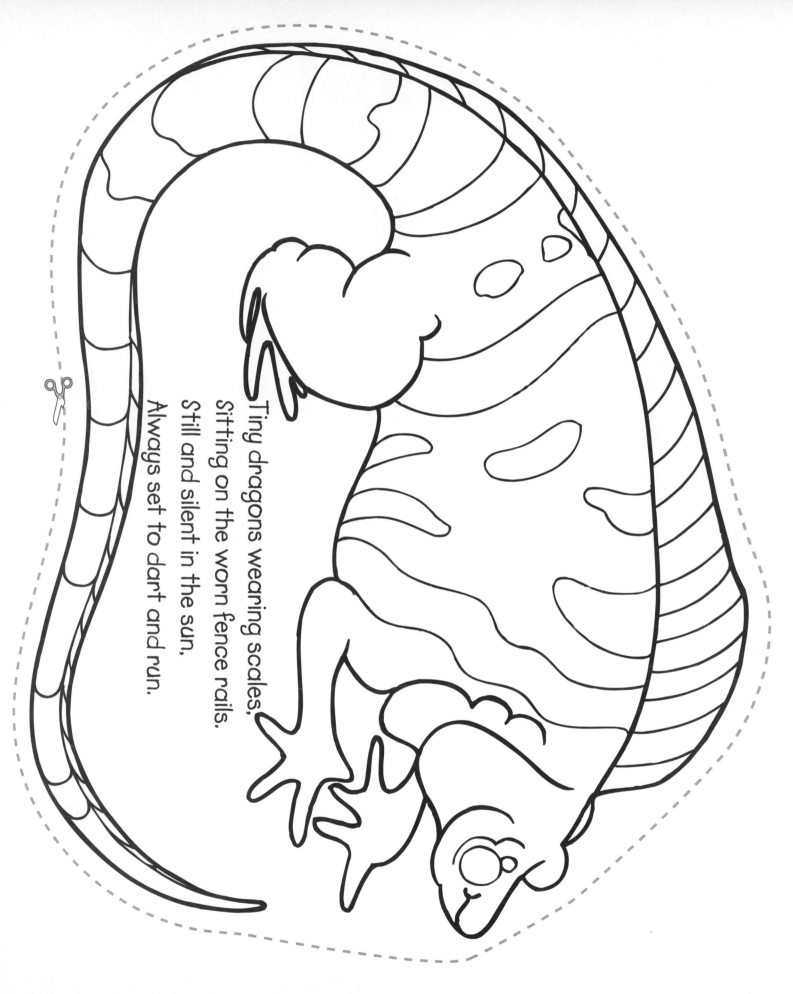

Tiny dragons wearing scales,
Sitting on the worn fence rails.
Still and silent in the sun.
Always set to dart and run.

Goat

Literature Connections

Beatrice's Goat by Page McBrier; Atheneum, 2001.

Three Billy Goats Gruff by Janet Stevens; Econo-Clad Books, 1999.

The Three Billy Goats Gruff by Paul Galdone; Houghton Mifflin Company, 1981.

Three Billy Goats Gruff by Peter Christen Asbjrnsen et al.; Harvest Books, 1991.

The Three Billy Goats Gruff/Just a Friendly Old Troll (Another Point of View) by Alvin Granowsky; Raintree/Steck-Vaughn, 1996.

The Trees of the Dancing Goats by Patricia Polacco; Simon & Schuster Children's Books, 1996.

Concrete Experiences

Discuss with students what goats eat and where they live. Several good nonfiction books are referenced in the literature connections. If a goat farmer is available in your area, enjoy a visit with actual goats.

Let the Writing Begin

Emergent Writers

- **A Goat in the Garden**
  Students draw pictures to show what might happen if a goat was loose in the garden. Then they describe the scene.

- **Goats at Play**
  Students draw goats playing and describe their games.

Beginning Writers

- **Who's That Tripping Across the Bridge?**
  Students draw a goat crossing a bridge. Then they copy and complete the sentences.

  "It's I. I am _____."

- **Goat's Lunch**
  Students draw to show what Goat is eating for lunch, then copy and complete the couplet.

  Greedy Goat eats _____ for lunch.

  Nibble, nibble. Munch, munch, munch.

Independent Writers

- **The Goat Ate My Homework**
  Students write about a goat that eats their homework and what happens when they tell the story at school.

- **A Cart for a Goat**
  Students write about a boy who builds a cart for his goat, and explain what the boy and the goat do once the cart is built.

©2002 by Evan-Moor Corp • The Ultimate Shape Book • EMC 6000

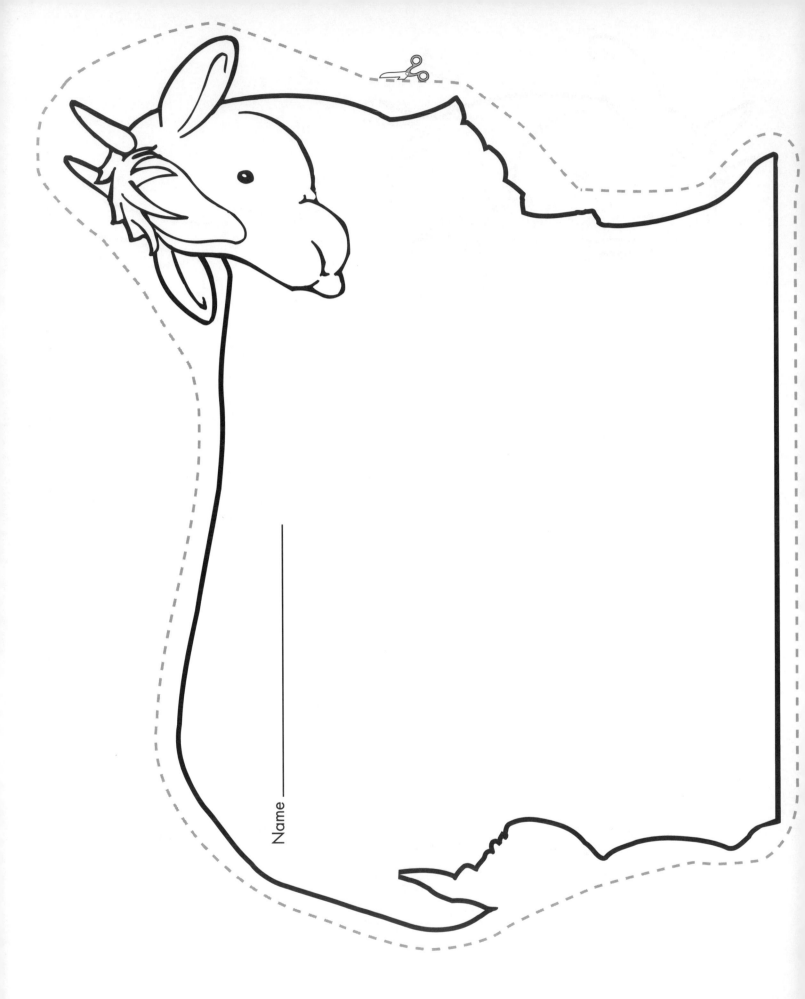

Name _____

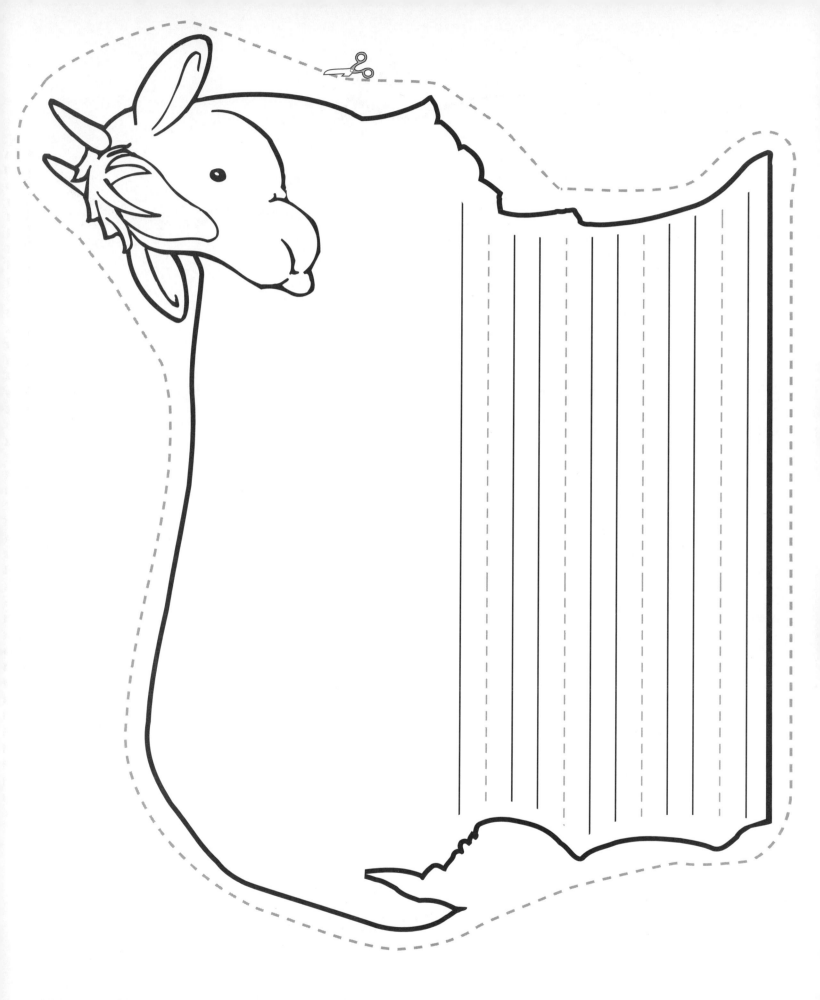

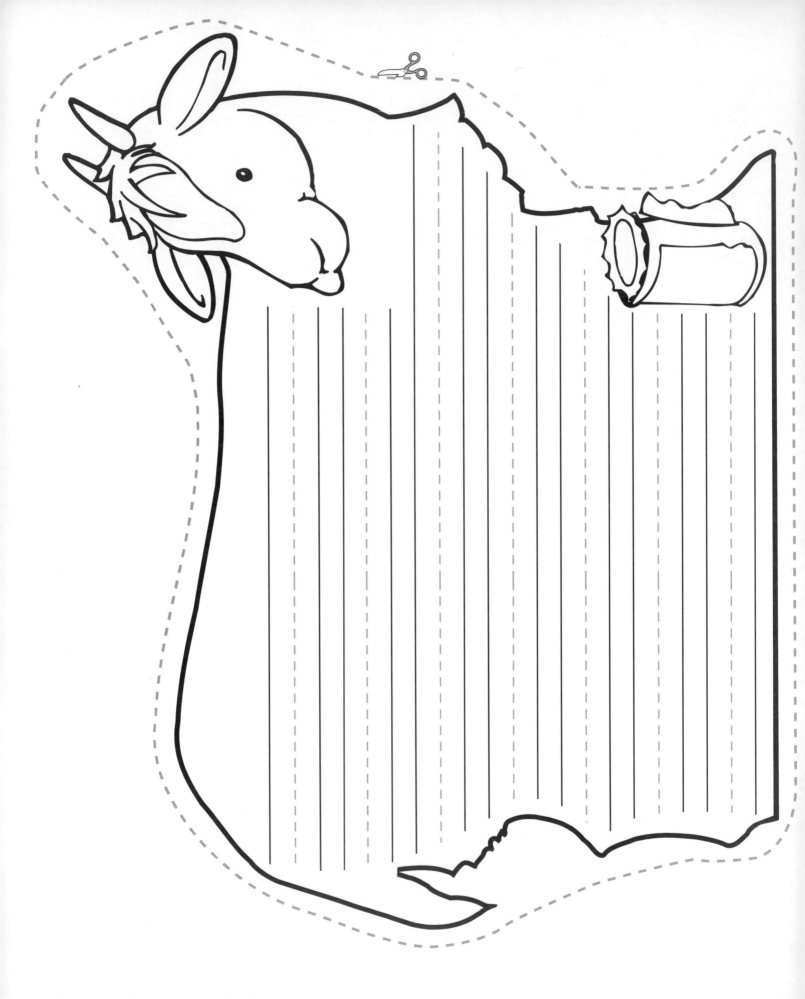

The Ultimate Shape Book • EMC 6000 • ©2002 by Evan-Moor Corp.

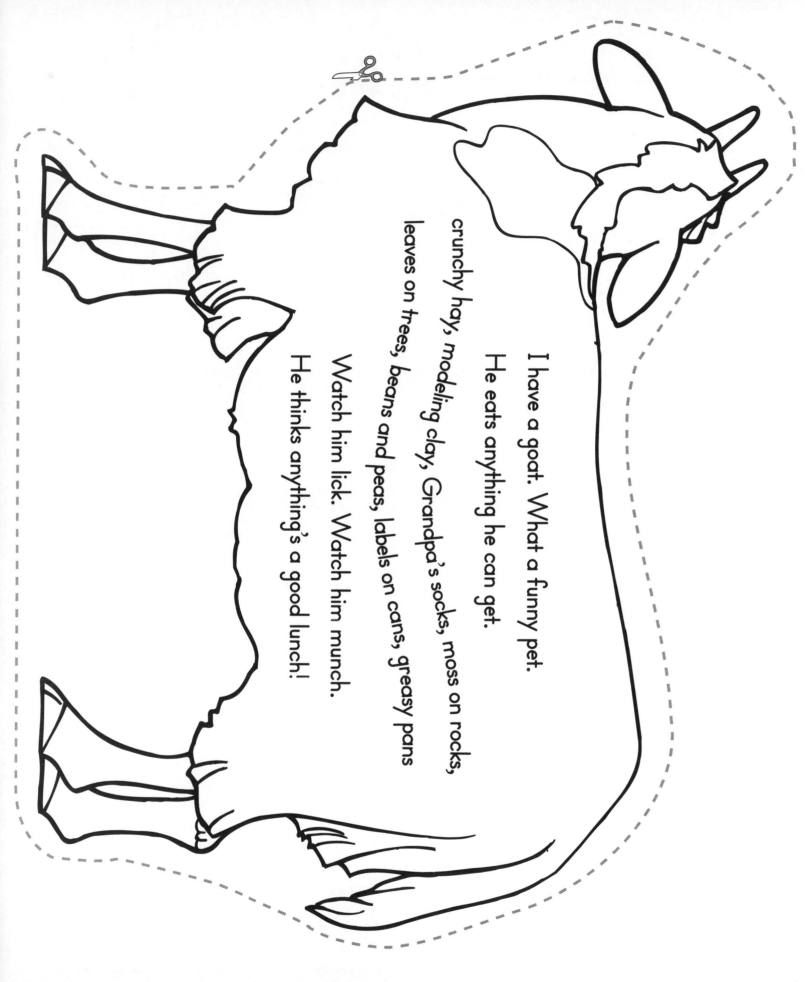

I have a goat. What a funny pet.
He eats anything he can get.
crunchy hay, modeling clay, Grandpa's socks, moss on rocks,
leaves on trees, beans and peas, labels on cans, greasy pans
Watch him lick. Watch him munch.
He thinks anything's a good lunch!

Bat

Literature Connections

Amazing Bats by Frank Greenaway; Knopf, 1991.
Bat: In the Dining Room by Crescent Dragonwagon; Marshall Cavendish Corp., 1997.
Bats by Gail Gibbons; Holiday House, 1999.
Desert Song by Tony Johnston; Sierra Club Books for Children, 2000.
Night Creatures by Gallimard Jeunesse; Scholastic Trade, 1998.
Stellaluna by Janell Cannon; Harcourt Brace & Co., 1993.
When Birds Could Talk & Bats Could Sing by Virginia Hamilton; Scholastic Trade, 1996.

Concrete Experiences

Invite a "bat expert" to your classroom to talk about the special characteristics of bats. Turn out the lights and listen to a recording of night sounds.

Let the Writing Begin

Emergent Writers

- **Sleeping Upside Down**
  Students draw a picture of a bat sleeping upside down and tell how it would feel to sleep in that position.

- **One Word, Two Meanings**
  Students draw pictures of the mammal bat and the bat used in baseball. Then they tell about the two different meanings.

Beginning Writers

- **Think of That!**
  Students draw pictures that combine two words that rhyme with *bat.* Then they copy and complete the sentences.

  Think of That!
  A _____. (A bat that is fat. A cat with a hat. A very flat mat.)

- **A Bat Counting Book**
  Students draw a cave, write a number in the cave, and draw that number of bats in the cave. Then they copy and complete the sentence.

  _____ bats in a cave.

Independent Writers

- **A Night Flight**
  Students write about what it would be like to fly when everything is dark. Encourage them to write about sounds and smells, as well as the things they might see.

- **In the Bat Cave**
  Students use what they know about bats to write a description of a bat cave.

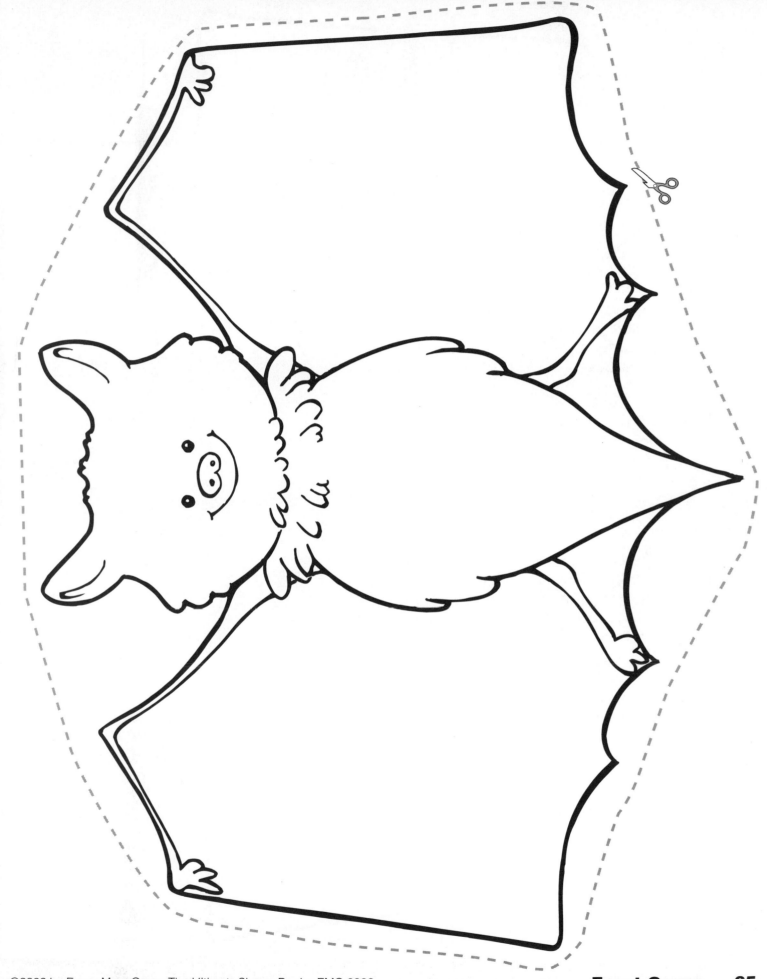

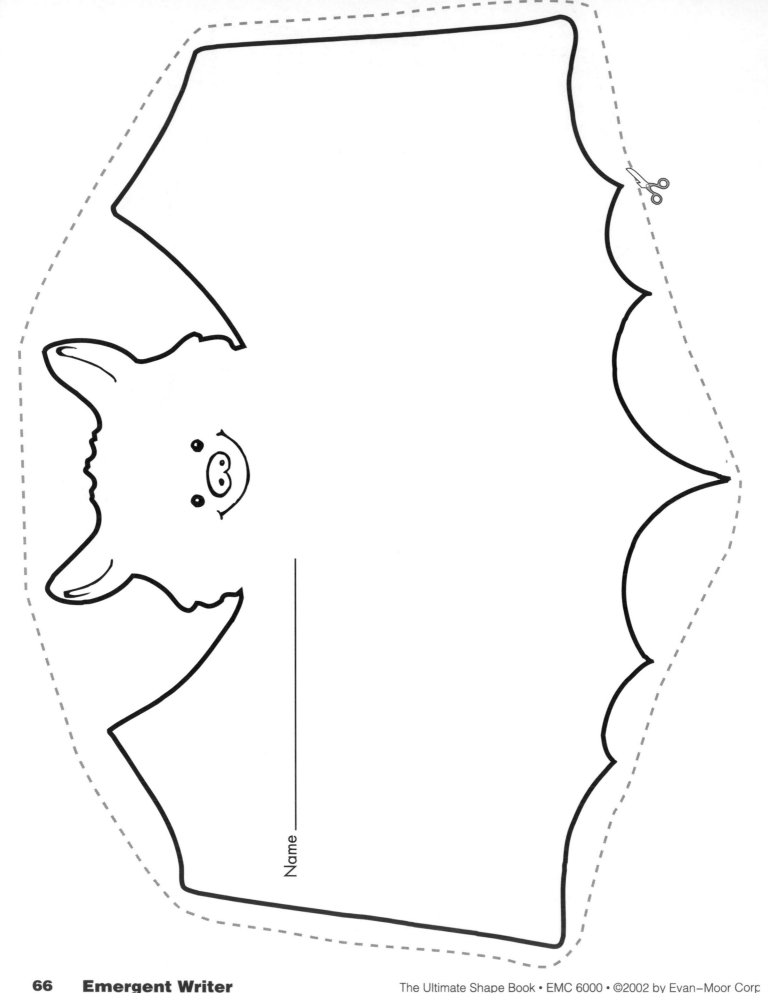

Name

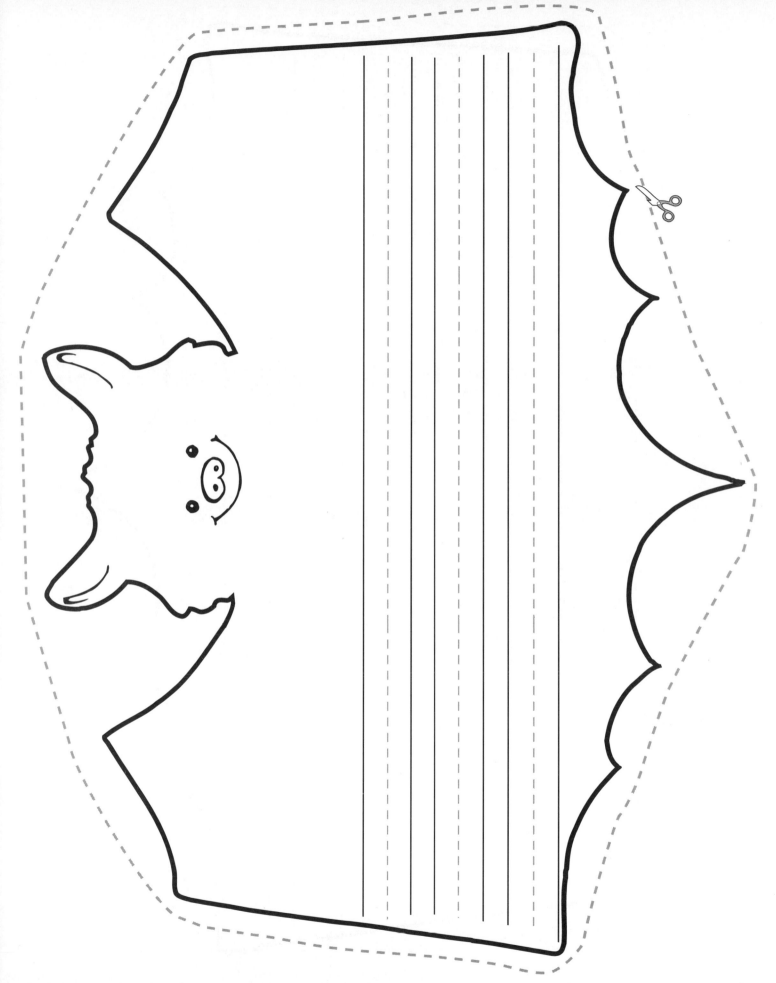

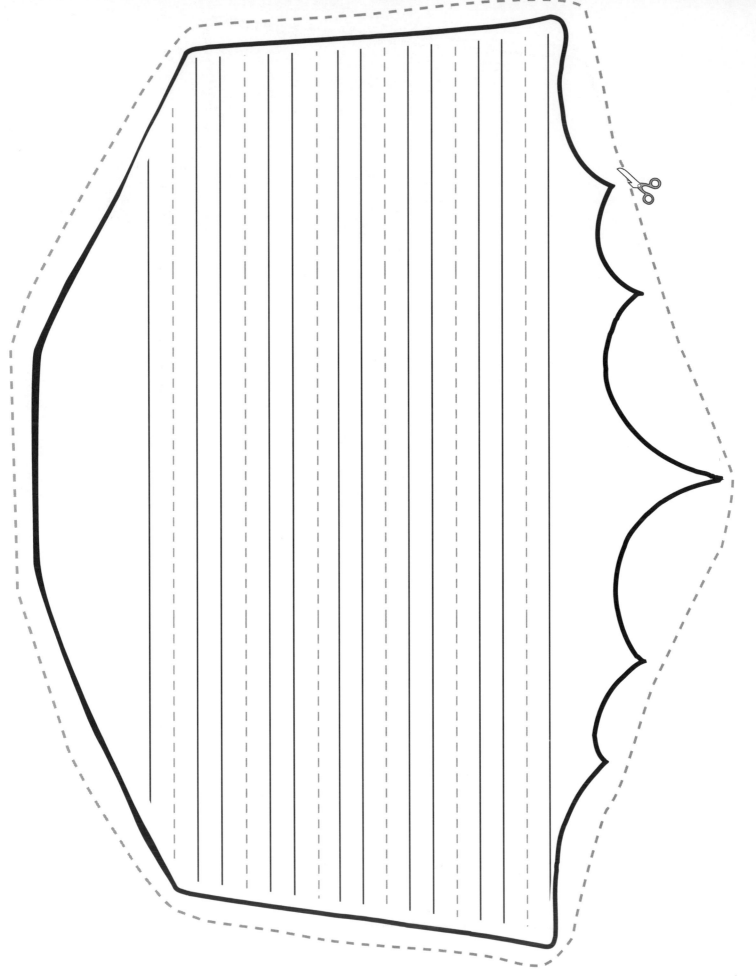

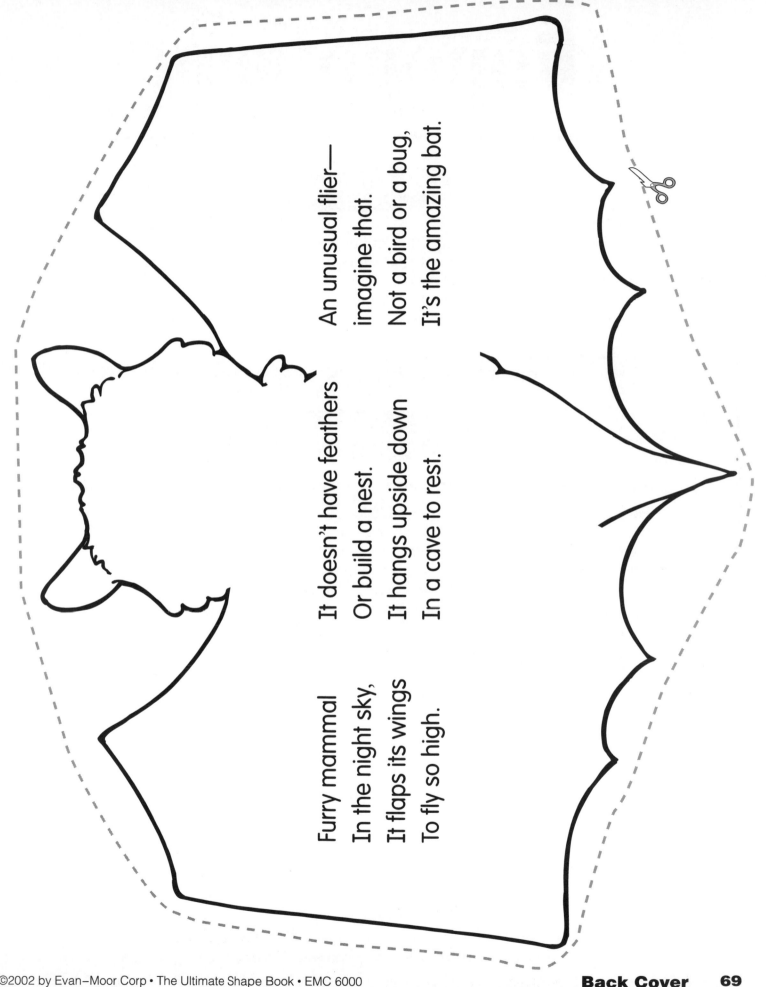

An unusual flier—
imagine that.
Not a bird or a bug,
It's the amazing bat.

It doesn't have feathers
Or build a nest.
It hangs upside down
In a cave to rest.

Furry mammal
In the night sky,
It flaps its wings
To fly so high.

Hippopotamus

Literature Connections

George and Martha by James Marshall; Houghton Mifflin Company, 1974.
The Happy Hippopotami by Bill Martin, Jr.; Harcourt Brace & Co., 1992.
Hippos by Jenny Markert; Child's World, 2001.
Hippos Go Berserk! by Sandra Boynton; Simon & Schuster Children's Books, 1996.
Ten Little Hippos: A Counting Book by Bobette McCarthy; Macmillan, 1992.

Concrete Experiences

Help students understand how heavy a hippopotamus is by making comparisons with familiar items.

Let the Writing Begin

Emergent Writers

- **Happy Hippo**
  Students draw a picture to show a happy hippo. Then they explain why the hippo is happy.

- **Hippo's Friend**
  Students draw a picture of Hippo with a friend. Then they tell about who the friend is and why the two friends like each other.

Beginning Writers

- **Big and Little**
  Students draw a big hippo with little ears and little eyes and a little tail. Then they copy and complete the sentences.

  Hippo is big. He has a big head and a big body. But Hippo has little _____ and little _____ and a little _____.

- **Hippo Fun**
  Students draw a picture of hippos having fun in the water. Then they copy and complete this couplet.

  Hippos _____, and hippos swim.
  They have fun. Just look at them.

Independent Writers

- **With a Twitch of Its Ear**
  Students write a fairy tale about a hippo that could grant wishes with a twitch of its ear.

- **Humongous and Miniscule**
  Students list synonyms for *big* and *little,* and then use the words listed to write sentences that compare the hippopotamus to smaller creatures.

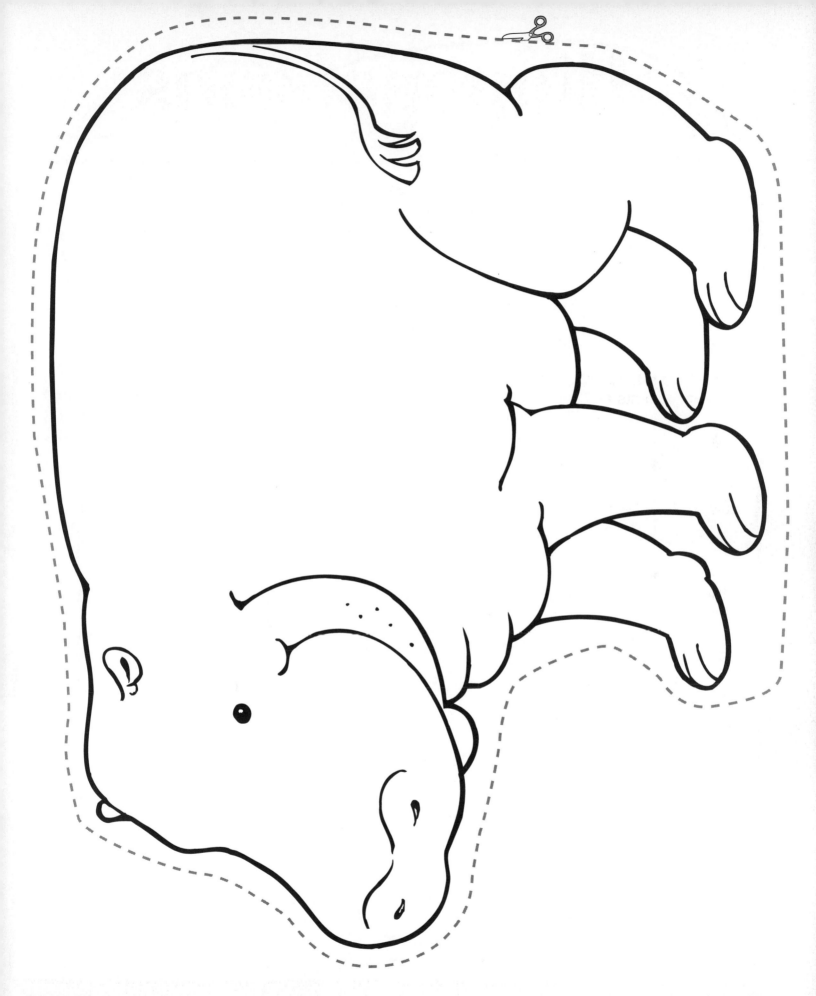

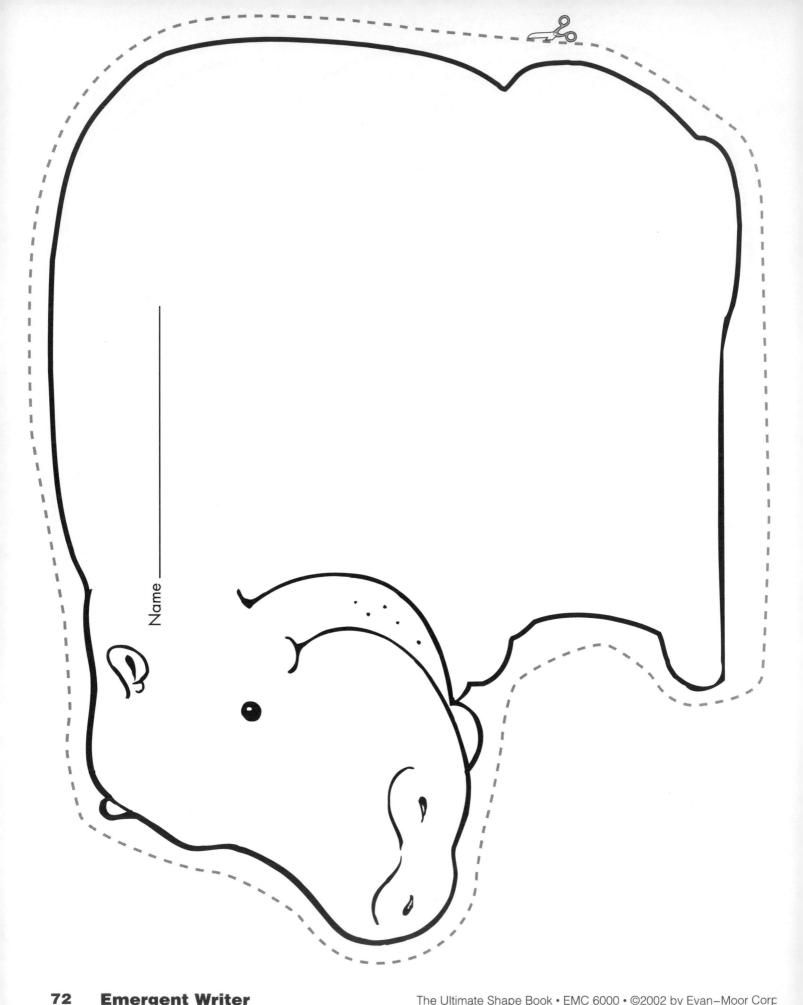

Name

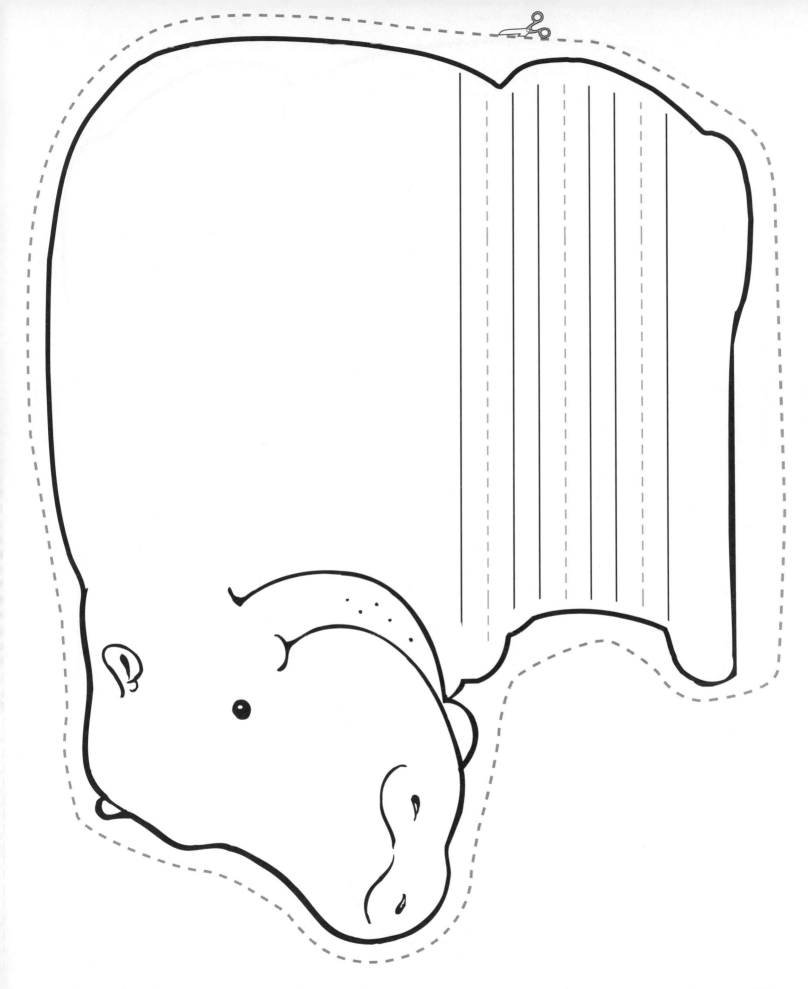

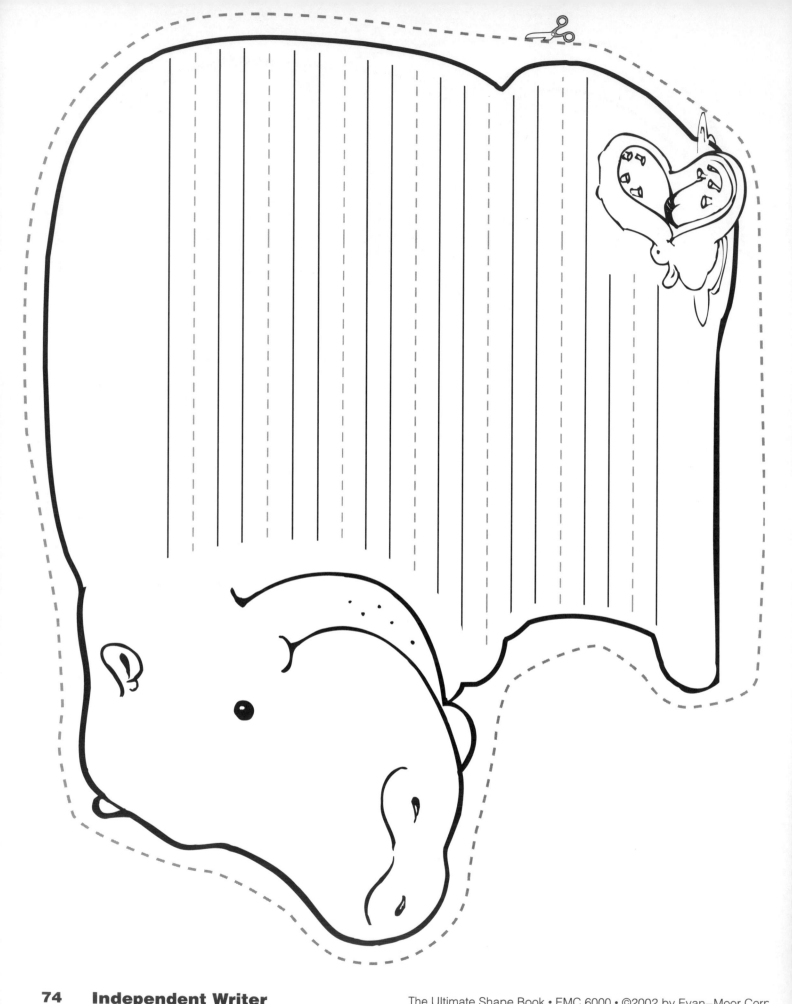

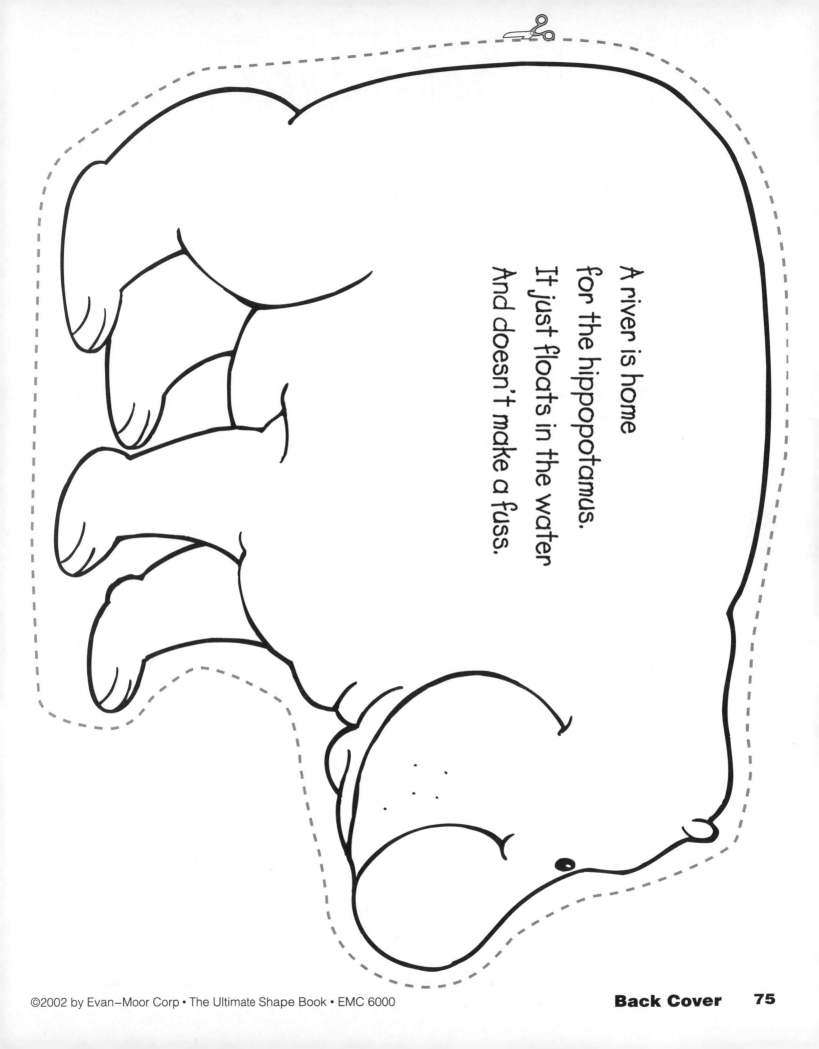

A river is home
for the hippopotamus.
It just floats in the water
And doesn't make a fuss.

Back Cover 75

Octopus

Literature Connections

Herman the Helper by Robert Kraus; Aladdin Paperbacks, 1987.
An Octopus Followed Me Home by Dan Yaccarino; Viking Children's Books, 1997.
An Octopus Is Amazing by Patricia Lauber; Thomas Y. Crowell, 1990.
Octopus by Carol Carrick; Houghton Mifflin Company, 1991.
Polkabats and Octopus Slacks: 14 Stories by Calef Brown and Daniel Manus Pinkwater; Houghton Mifflin Company, 2001.

Concrete Experiences

List words that describe an octopus.

Let the Writing Begin

Emergent Writers

- **Squeezing Inside**
  On a plain piece of drawing paper, students draw places where an octopus might squeeze inside. The drawing is cut out and glued as a flap to the blank shape page. Then the students draw what's under the flap.

- **1, 2, 3, 4, 5, 6, 7, EIGHT**
  Students draw an octopus showing its eight tentacles. They number each tentacle to count to eight.

Beginning Writers

- **If I Had Eight Arms…**
  Students draw to show what they could do with eight arms. Then they copy and complete the sentence.

  If I had eight arms, I could _____.

- **Hold It!**
  Students draw a picture that answers the question, "What is Octopus holding?" Then they copy and complete the sentence.

  Octopus is holding _____.

Independent Writers

- **A Narrow Escape**
  Students describe a dangerous situation for an octopus and tell how the octopus escapes.

- **Colorful Thoughts**
  Students write thoughts that reflect different moods, match the thoughts to colors, and then use the thoughts and colors in a series of couplets about a colorful octopus.

  Octopus dons a coat of sad gray-blue.
  It mopes underwater missing you.
  Octopus shines a bold, brilliant green,
  As it remembers tasty treats it's seen.

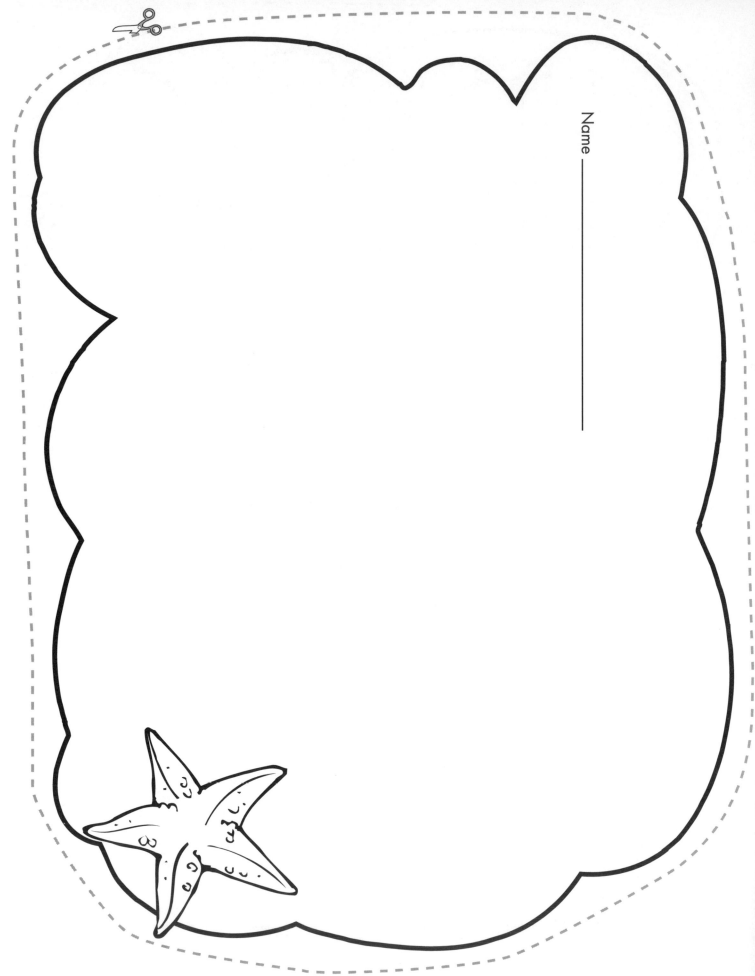

Name _____

The Ultimate Shape Book • EMC 6000 • ©2002 by Evan-Moor Corp.

Octopus lives in the salty sea.

Octopus is as smart as can be.

Eight tentacles grab prey to eat.

A cloud of ink hides her retreat.

Hen

Literature Connections

Big Fat Hen by Keith Baker; Red Wagon, 1997.
Emma's Eggs by Margriet Ruurs; Stoddart Publishers, 1999.
Henny Penny by Paul Galdone; Clarion Books, 1968.
Hilda Hen's Happy Birthday by Mary Wormell; Harcourt Brace & Co., 1995.
The Little Red Hen by Paul Galdone; Houghton Mifflin Company, 1985.
Mrs. Hen's Big Surprise by Christel Desmoinaux; Margaret McElderry, 2000.
Rosie's Walk by Pat Hutchins; Aladdin Paperbacks, 1983.

Concrete Experiences

Observe or read about chickens. List words that describe how a hen looks. List sounds that a hen makes.

Let the Writing Begin

Emergent Writers

- **A Surprise in Hen's Nest**
  Students draw a surprise that Hen found in her nest. Then they tell about the surprise.

- **Cluck, Cluck, Cluck**
  Students draw a noisy hen in a quiet place. They tell about the problem caused by the noise.

Beginning Writers

- **How Many Chicks?**
  Students draw a mother hen with several chicks. They copy and complete the sentence.

  Mother Hen has _____ chicks.

  Encourage students to write what the hen and chicks are doing.

- **Ten Hens in a Pen**
  Students draw ten hens doing various things in the pen. Then they write about what the hens are doing, ending with the sentence.

  There are ten hens in the pen.

Independent Writers

- **"That's Not My Egg!" by Mrs. Hen**
  Students write a note from Mrs. Hen to the farmer explaining a strange egg that she has found in her nest.

- **Little Hen**
  In the style of "The Little Red Hen," students write a tale about an ambitious hen who does a job by herself and then has to decide whether to share the rewards of the completed job with others.

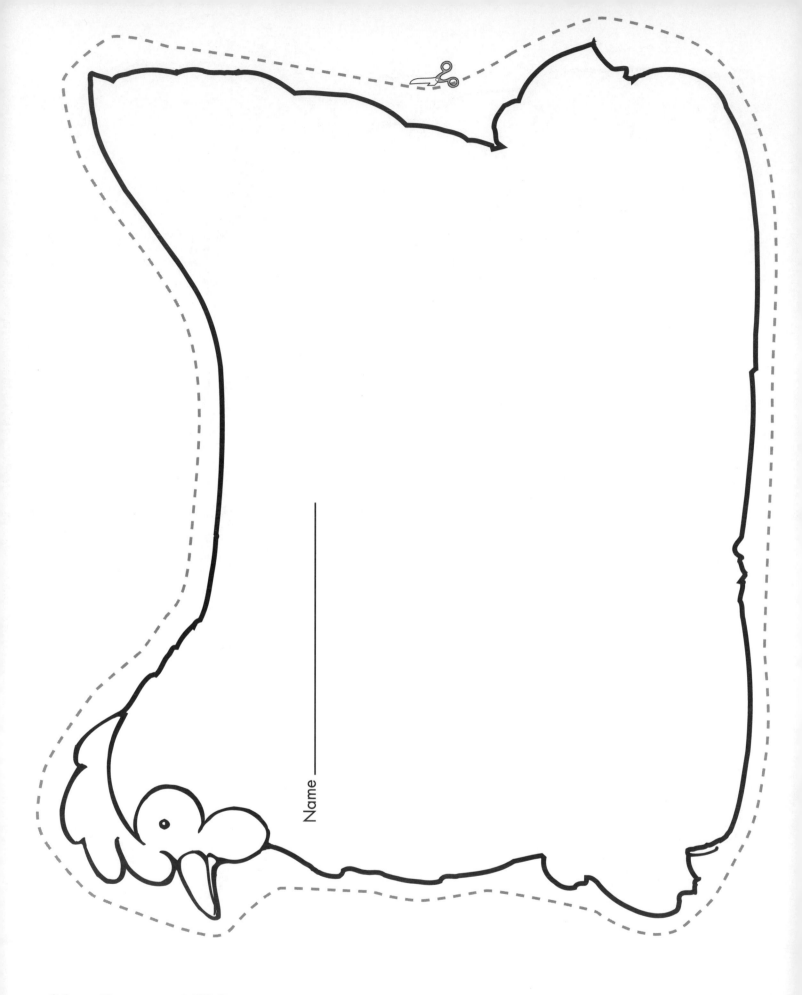

Name

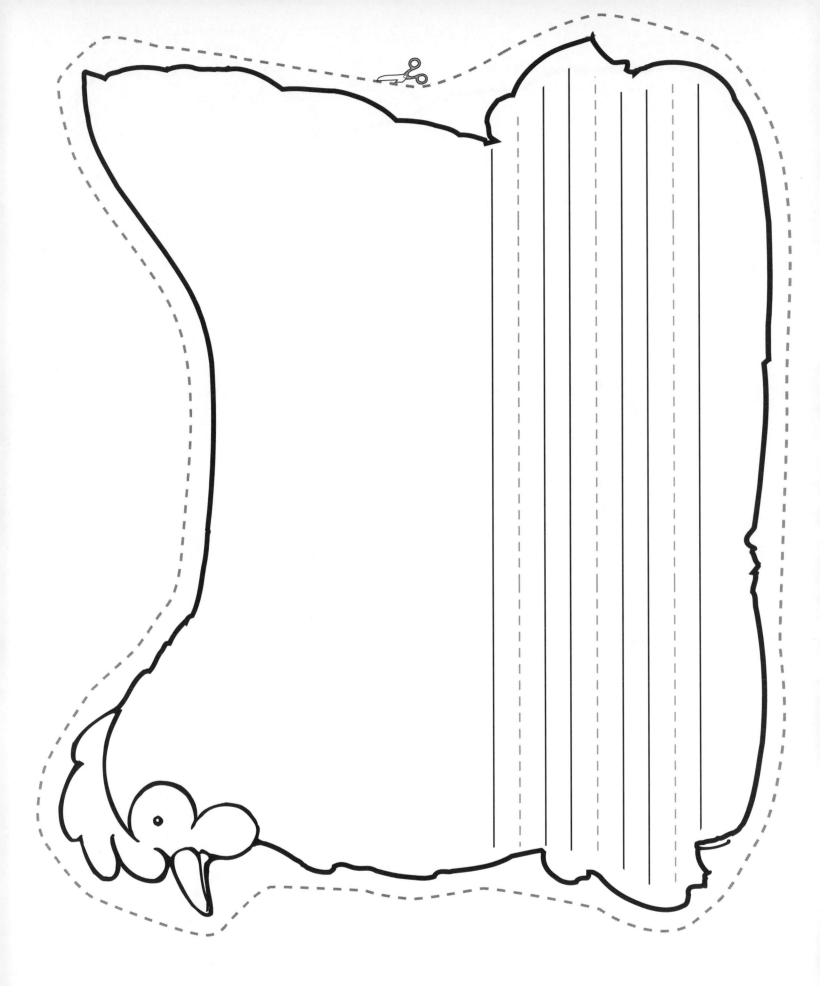

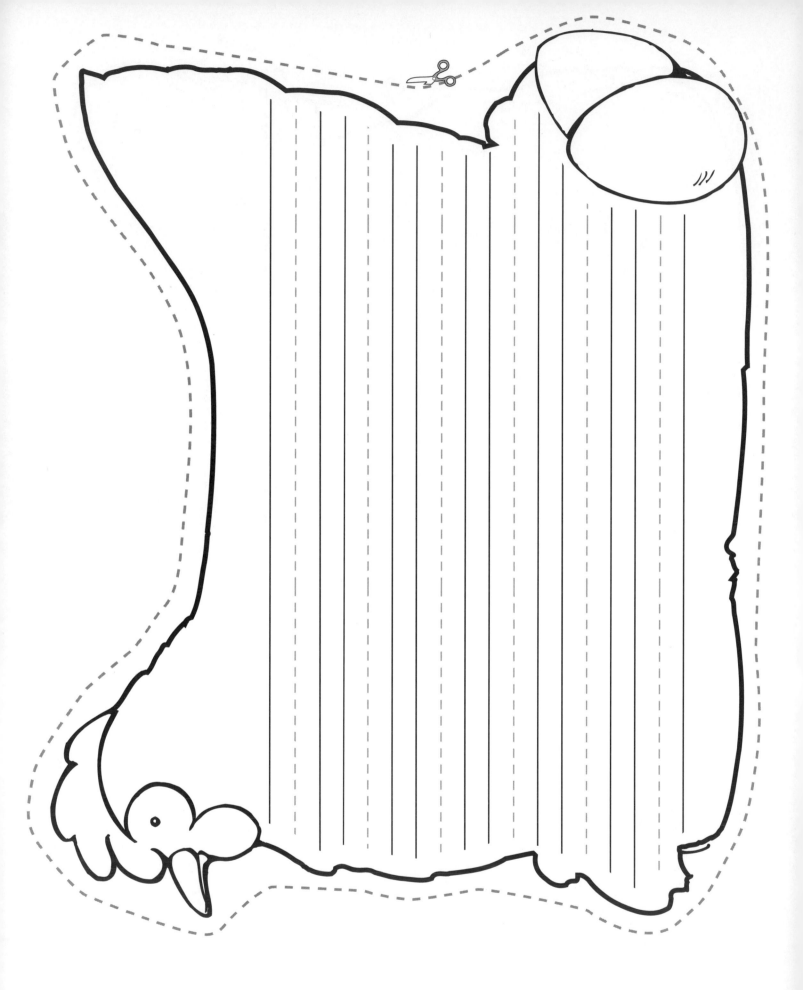

The Ultimate Shape Book • EMC 6000 • ©2002 by Evan-Moor Corp

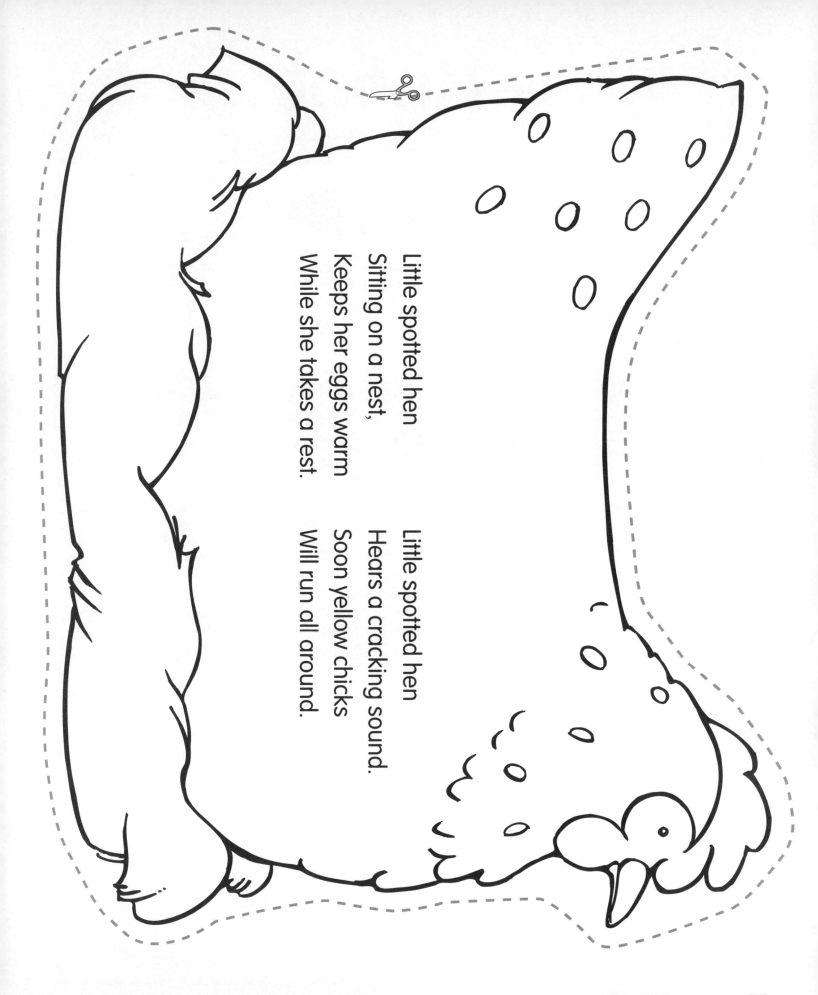

Little spotted hen
Sitting on a nest,
Keeps her eggs warm
While she takes a rest.

Little spotted hen
Hears a cracking sound.
Soon yellow chicks
Will run all around.

Robot

Literature Connections

Benjamin McFadden and the Robot Babysitter by Timothy Bush; Crown Publishing, 1998.
Cosmo and the Robot by J. Brian Pinkney; Greenwillow, 2000.
The Iron Giant: A Story in Five Nights by Ted Hughes; Alfred A. Knopf Inc., 1999.
Robobots by Matt Novak; Dorling Kindersley Publishing Inc., 1999.
Robots by Darcy Lockman; Marshall Cavendish Corp., 2000.

Concrete Experiences

Watch a mechanical or remote control toy. List words that describe the way it moves and the sounds it makes. Brainstorm a list of things a robot might do.

Let the Writing Begin

Emergent Writers

- **My Robot Can…**
  Students draw a picture to show something a robot can do.

- **Robot Noises**
  Students draw robots moving and think of the noises that they would make. Write down the dictated noises. Students will enjoy reading this onomatopoetic page.

Beginning Writers

- **Color'bots**
  Create lists of words that rhyme with different color words. Students choose a color, draw and color a robot, and then copy and complete the couplets.

  This robot is _____.
  It _____.

  This robot is red.
  It makes my bed.

- **Interview with a Robot**
  Students draw themselves talking to a robot. Then they copy the questions below and write the robot's answers.

  What is your name?
  Where are you from?
  What do you do?

Independent Writers

- **Life with My Robot**
  Students create an imaginary robot companion and write a story about an adventure they have together.

- **Inside the Robot**
  Students draw a view of the inside of a robot, label the parts, and then write a paragraph telling how the parts work together.

Front Cover **89**

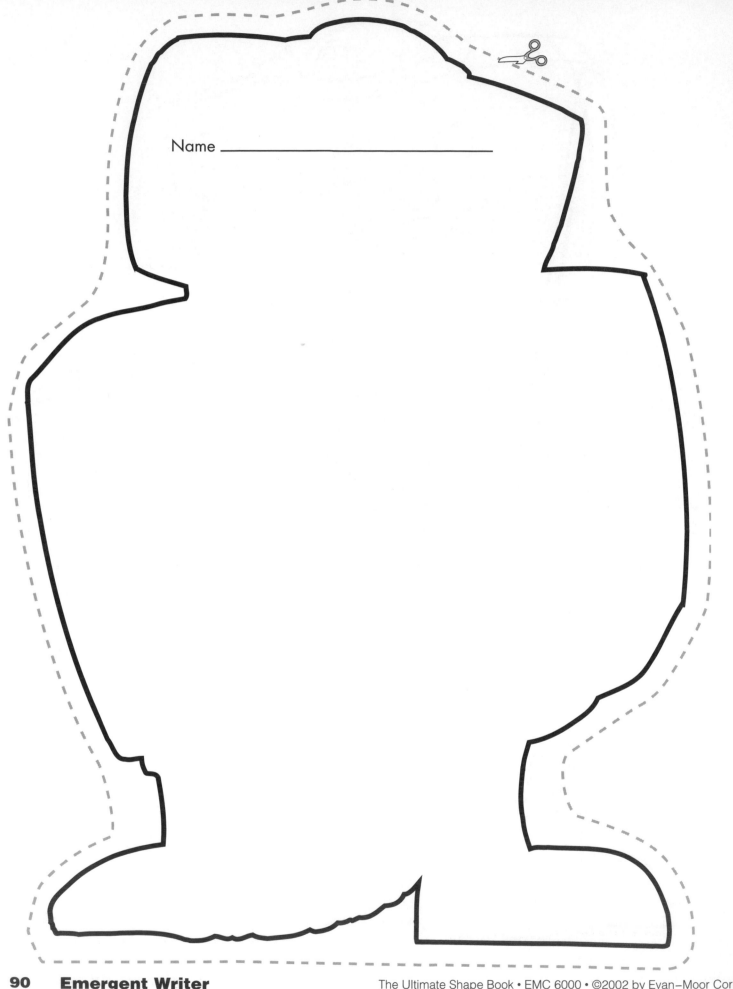

Name _____

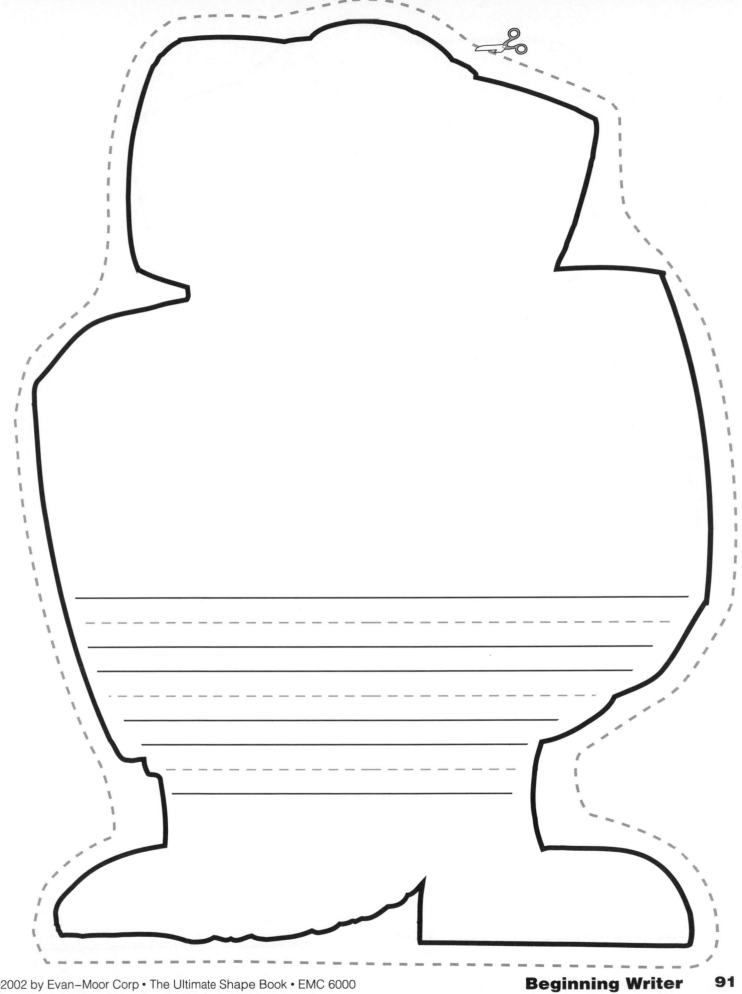

©2002 by Evan-Moor Corp • The Ultimate Shape Book • EMC 6000

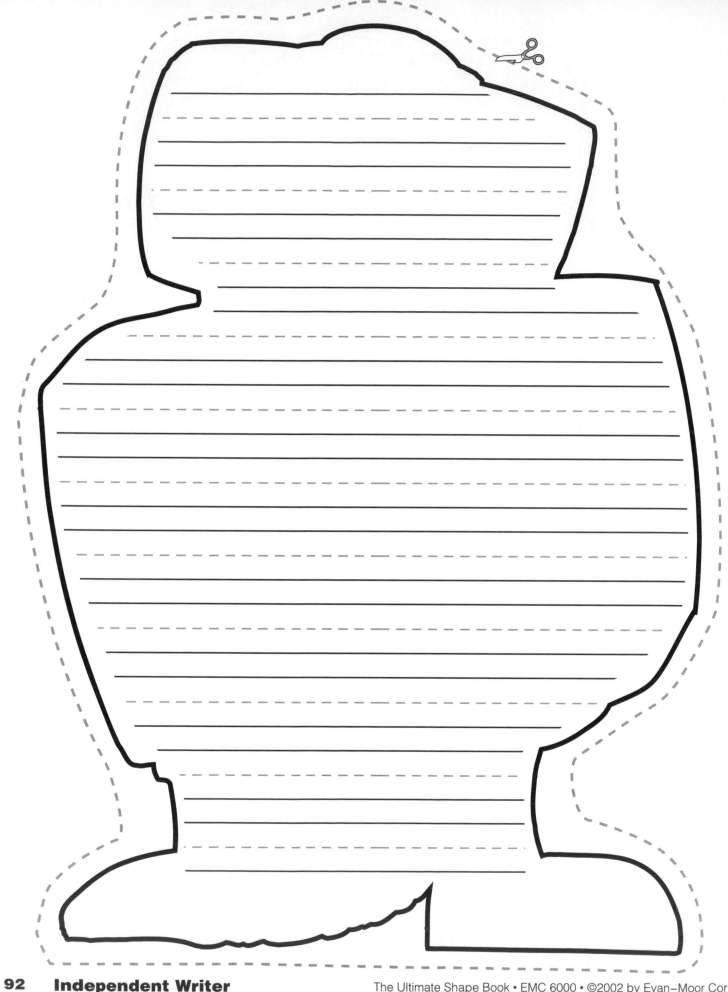

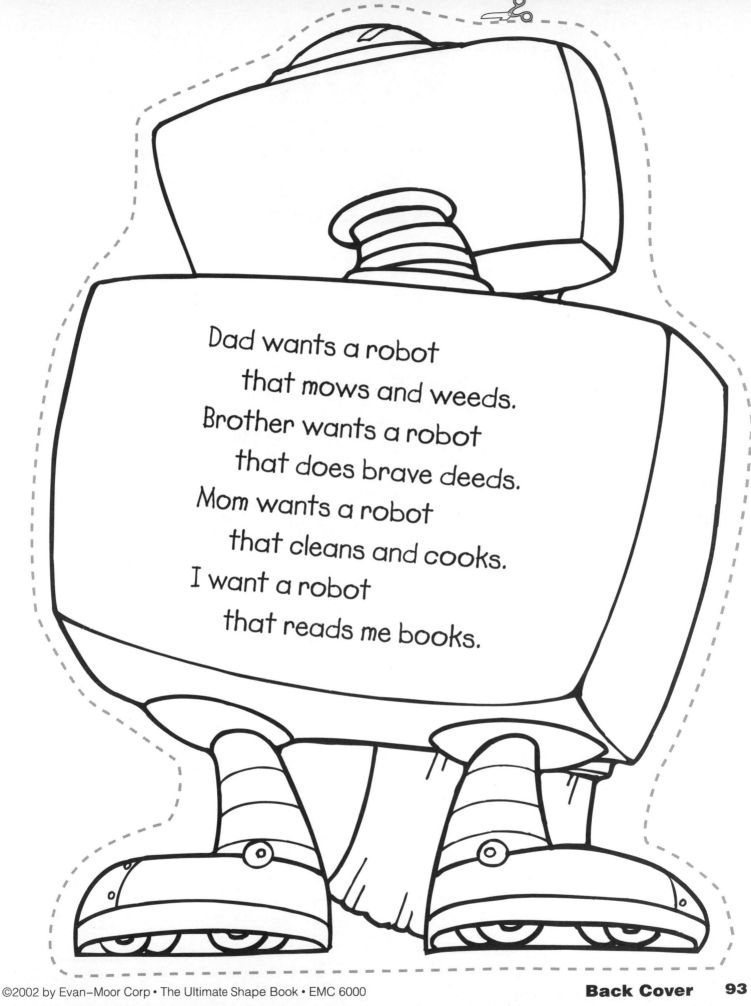

Dad wants a robot
    that mows and weeds.
Brother wants a robot
    that does brave deeds.
Mom wants a robot
    that cleans and cooks.
I want a robot
    that reads me books.

Crow

Literature Connections

As the Crow Flies: A First Book of Maps by Gail Hartman; Aladdin Paperbacks, 1993.
Clever Crow by Cynthia DeFelice; Atheneum, 1998.
Crows: An Old Rhyme by Heidi Holder; Farrar, Straus & Giroux Inc., 1990.
A Crow's Journey by David Cunningham; Albert Whitman & Co., 1996.
Pig and Crow by Kay Chorao; Henry Holt, 2000.

Concrete Experiences

Discuss the reason that farmers put up scarecrows. Make a list of exclamations you might make if you wanted to scare someone.

Let the Writing Begin

Emergent Writers

• **Black as a Crow**
Students draw things that are black like crows and then name the things that they have drawn.

• **Three Crows in a Row**
Students draw three crows in a row. They count the crows aloud ("one, two, three") and say, "Three crows in a row."

Beginning Writers

• **Down in the Cornfield**
Students draw four pictures of the cornfield—the first shows four crows; the second, three crows; the third, two crows; and the fourth, one crow. Then they copy and complete the sentences.

_____ black crows in the corn.
One flew away.
Now there are _____.

• **The Crow Flies**
Where would you fly to if you were a crow? Students draw a destination and then copy and complete this question and answer.

Mr. Crow, where will you go?
I'll fly to _____.

Independent Writers

• **The Crow Who Couldn't Fly**
Imagine the everyday routine of a crow that couldn't fly. Students write from the crow's point of view.

• **The Lonely Scarecrow**
The scarecrow stands all alone in the field. Where have all the crows gone? Students write to explain what happened to cause this dilemma.

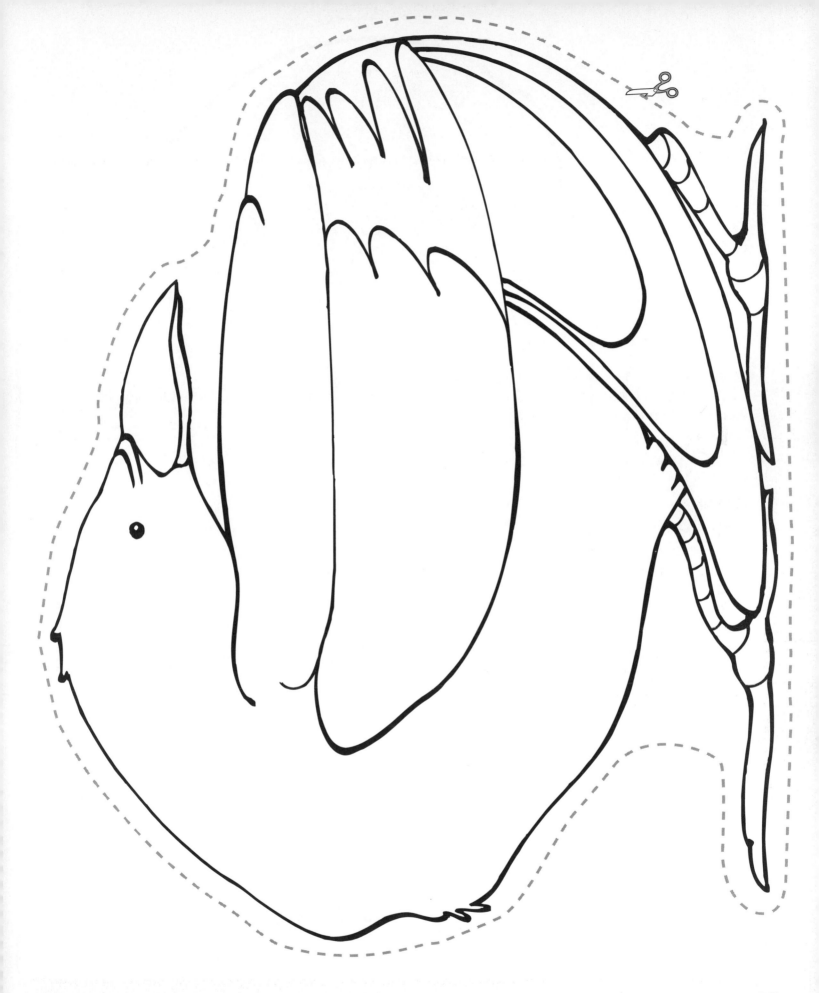

©2002 by Evan-Moor Corp • The Ultimate Shape Book • EMC 6000

Front Cover   95

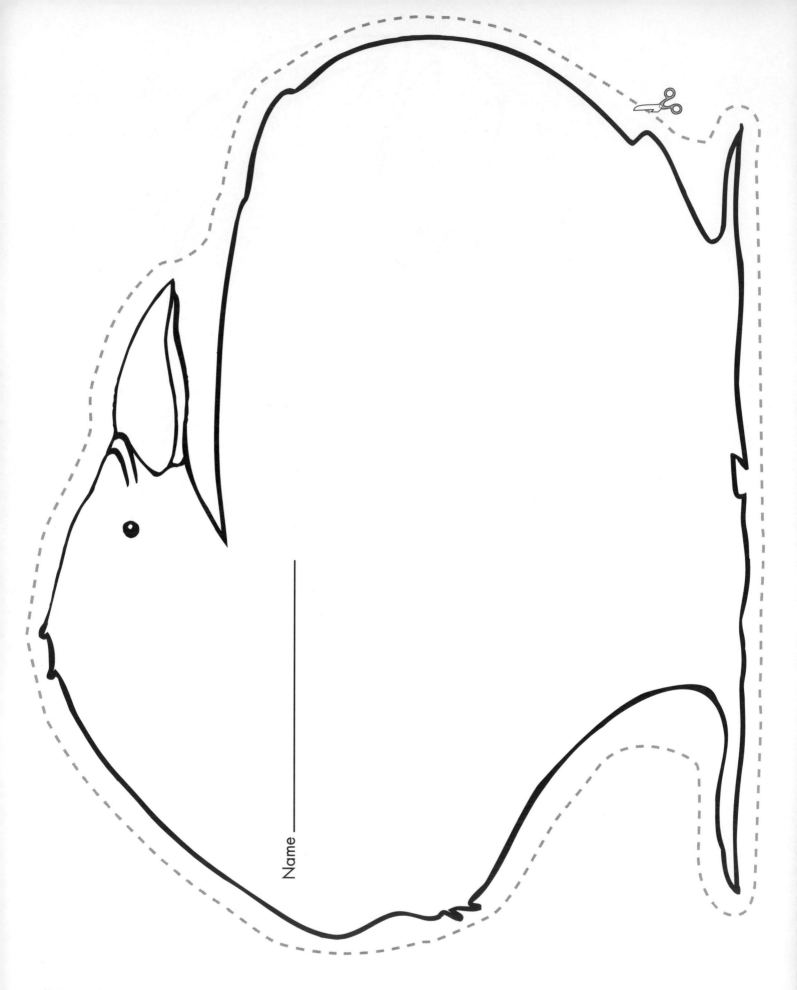

Name

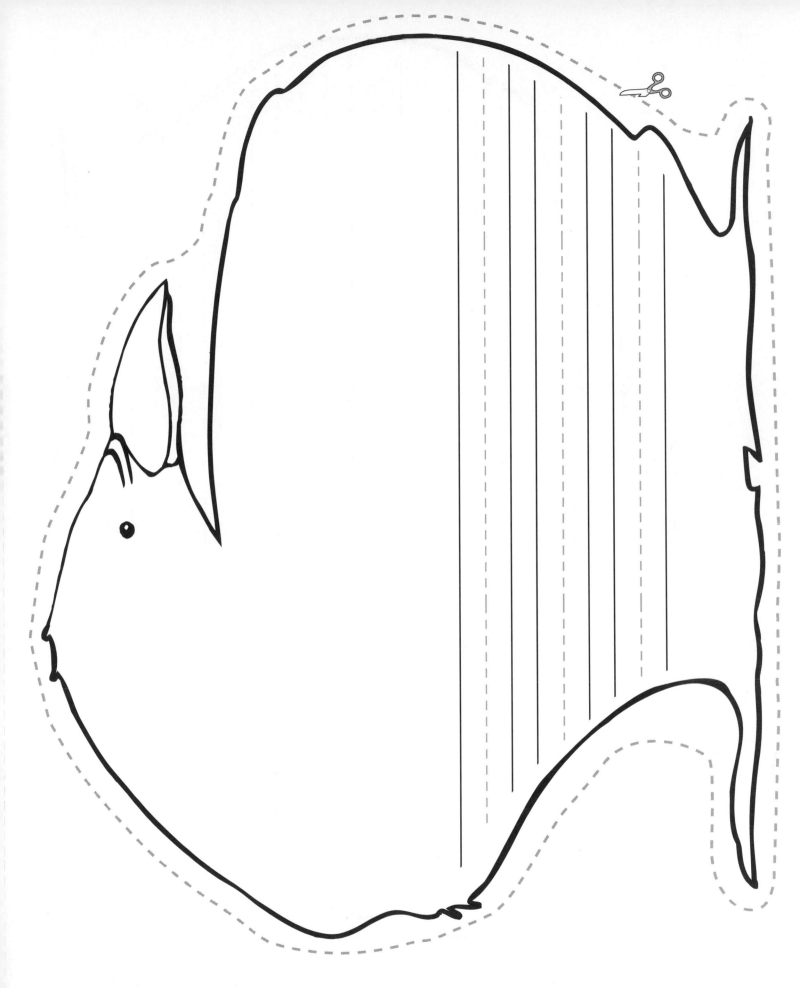

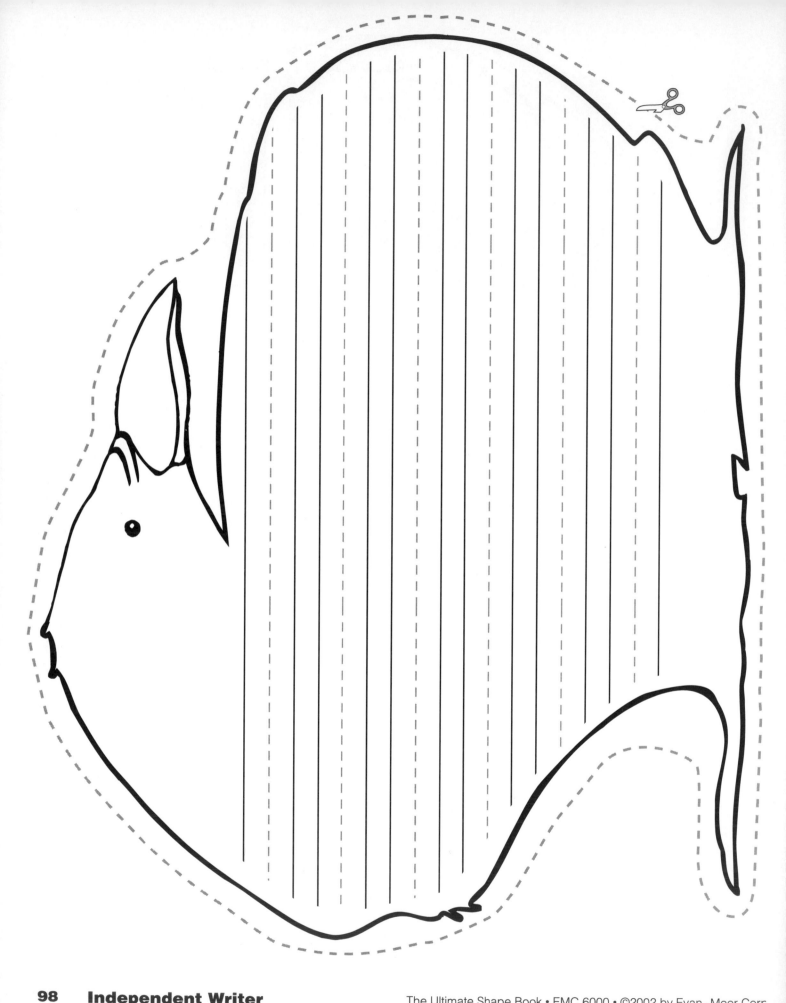

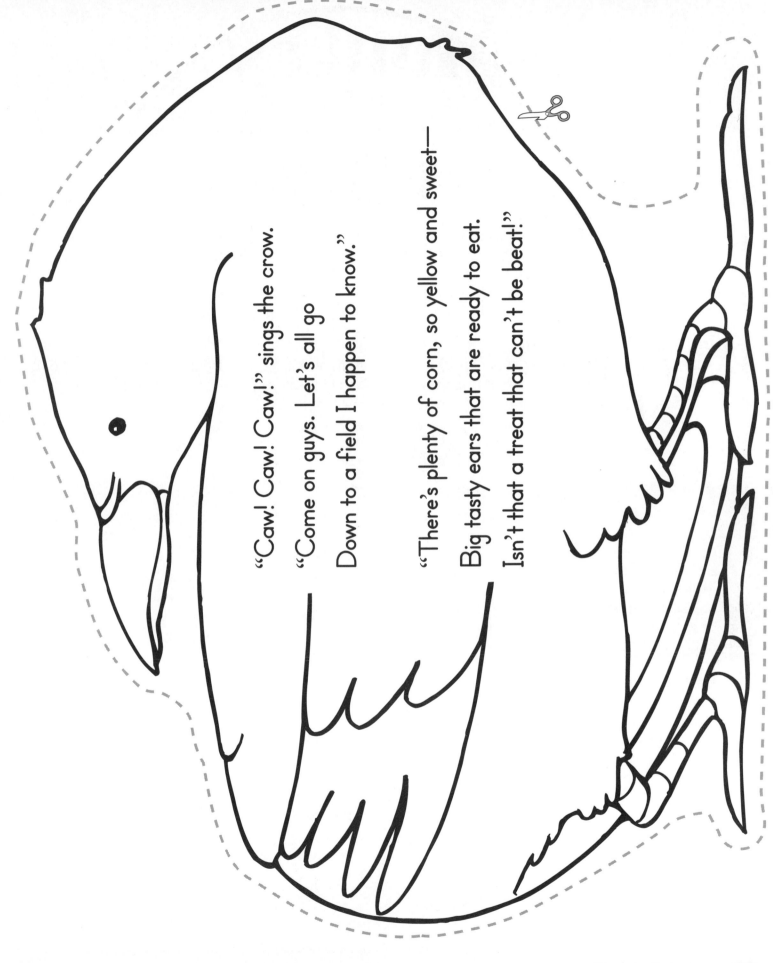

"Caw! Caw! Caw!" sings the crow.

"Come on guys. Let's all go
Down to a field I happen to know."

"There's plenty of corn, so yellow and sweet—
Big tasty ears that are ready to eat.
Isn't that a treat that can't be beat!"

Back Cover

Monkey

Literature Connections

Caps for Sale by Esphyr Slobodkina; HarperCollins Children's Books, 1988.
Five Little Monkeys Jumping on the Bed by Eileen Christelow; Houghton Mifflin Company, 1998.
Good Night, Gorilla by Peggy Rathmann; Putnam, 1996.
The Original Curious George by H.A. Rey; Houghton Mifflin Company, 1998.
So Say the Little Monkeys by Nancy Van Laan; Atheneum, 1998.

Concrete Experiences

Take students to the playground or gym. Have them swing on the jungle gym or horizontal bars. Can they hang by one arm? By their knees? When you return to the classroom, brainstorm words that describe how it felt to be swinging from a bar.

Let the Writing Begin

Emergent Writers

- **Six Little Monkeys**
Students draw a series of pictures beginning with a picture of six monkeys jumping on a bed. Each subsequent picture shows one monkey falling off and the other monkeys continuing to jump. When only one monkey is left, the last monkey goes to sleep. Chant the story of the six monkeys using the traditional chant "Ten Little Monkeys Jumping on the Bed" for a pattern.

- **Where Is the Monkey?**
Students think of places a monkey could hide in their houses. They draw pictures to illustrate their ideas. Then they tell about where the monkeys are.

Beginning Writers

- **Monkey See, Monkey Do**
Students draw themselves doing something. They draw monkeys copying the action. Then they copy and complete the sentences.

  I can _____.
  Monkey sees me _____.
  Monkey can _____, too.

- **If I Had a Tail Like a Monkey**
Students draw a picture to show what they would do if they had a monkey's tail. Then they copy and complete the sentence.

  If I had a tail like a monkey, _____.

Independent Writers

- **_____ for Sale**
In the style of *Caps for Sale*, students write about a tired salesperson and a monkey who steals the salesperson's wares.

- **Swinging in the Trees**
What would it feel like to swing in the trees? Students write about an imagined day swinging in the trees with a monkey.

©2002 by Evan-Moor Corp • The Ultimate Shape Book • EMC 6000

Front Cover   101

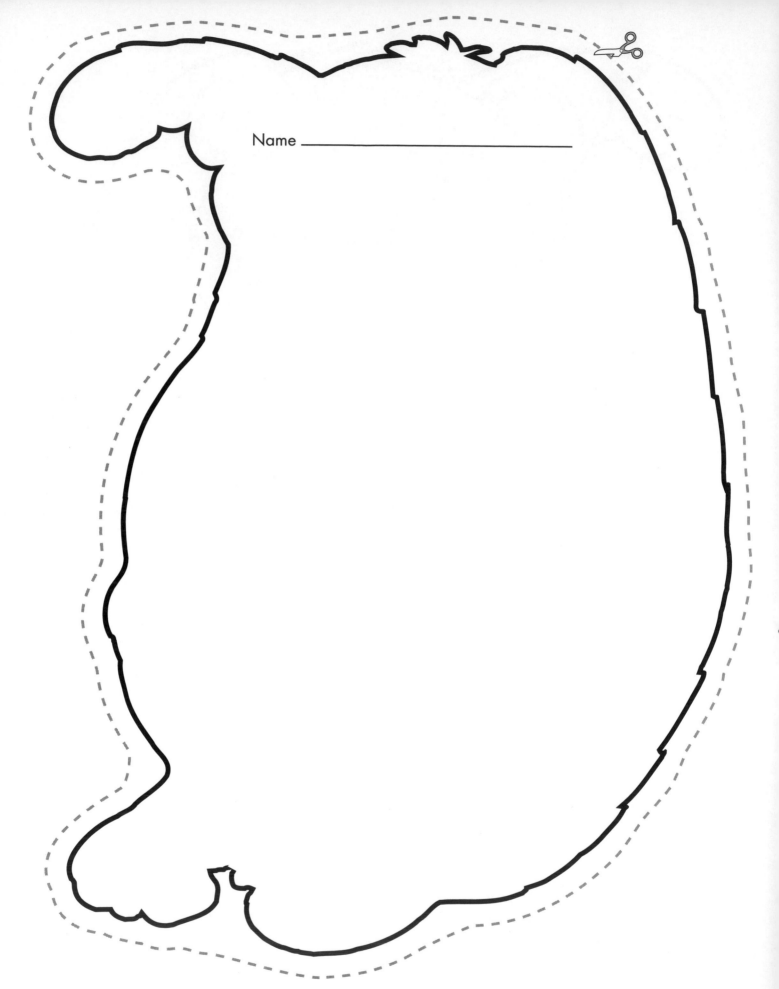

Name _____

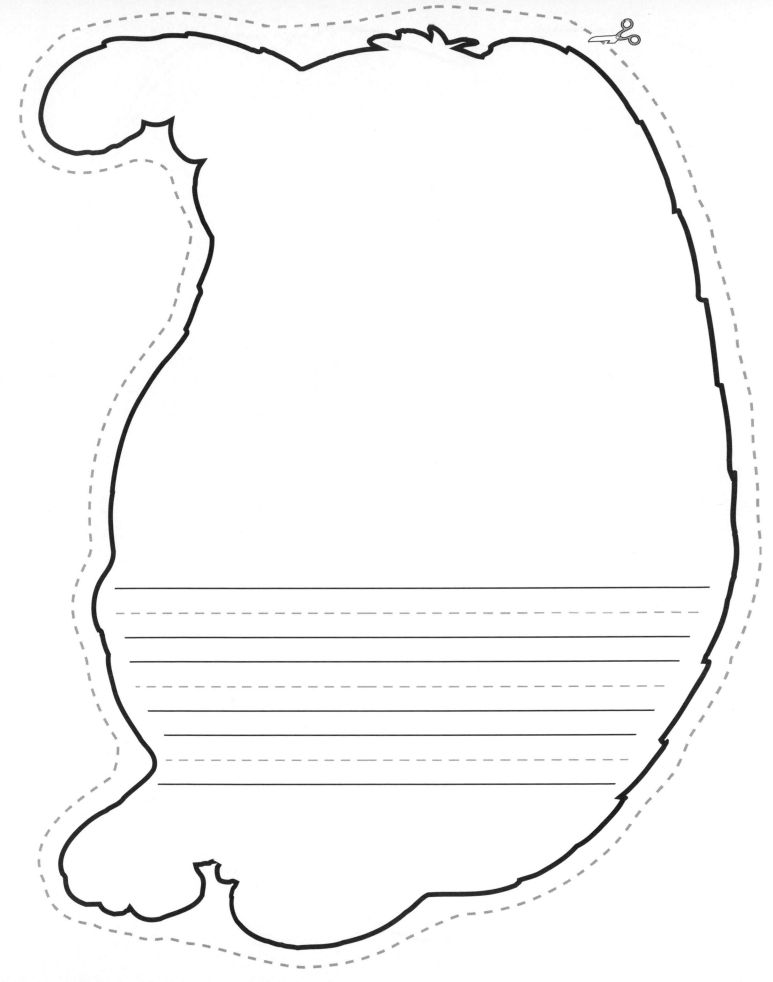

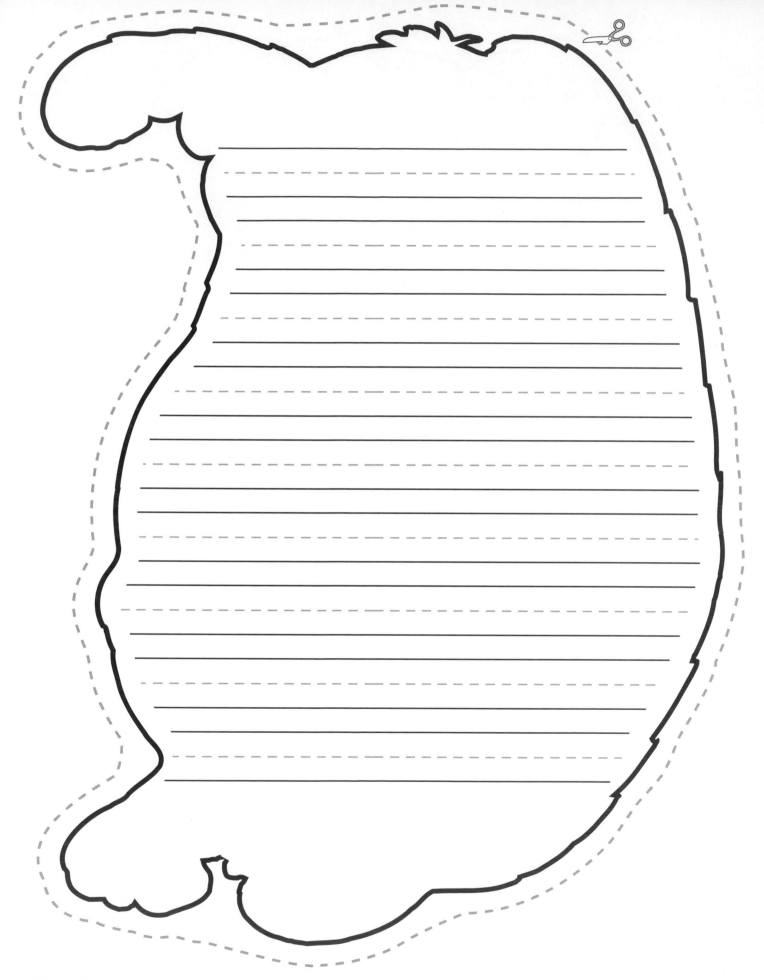

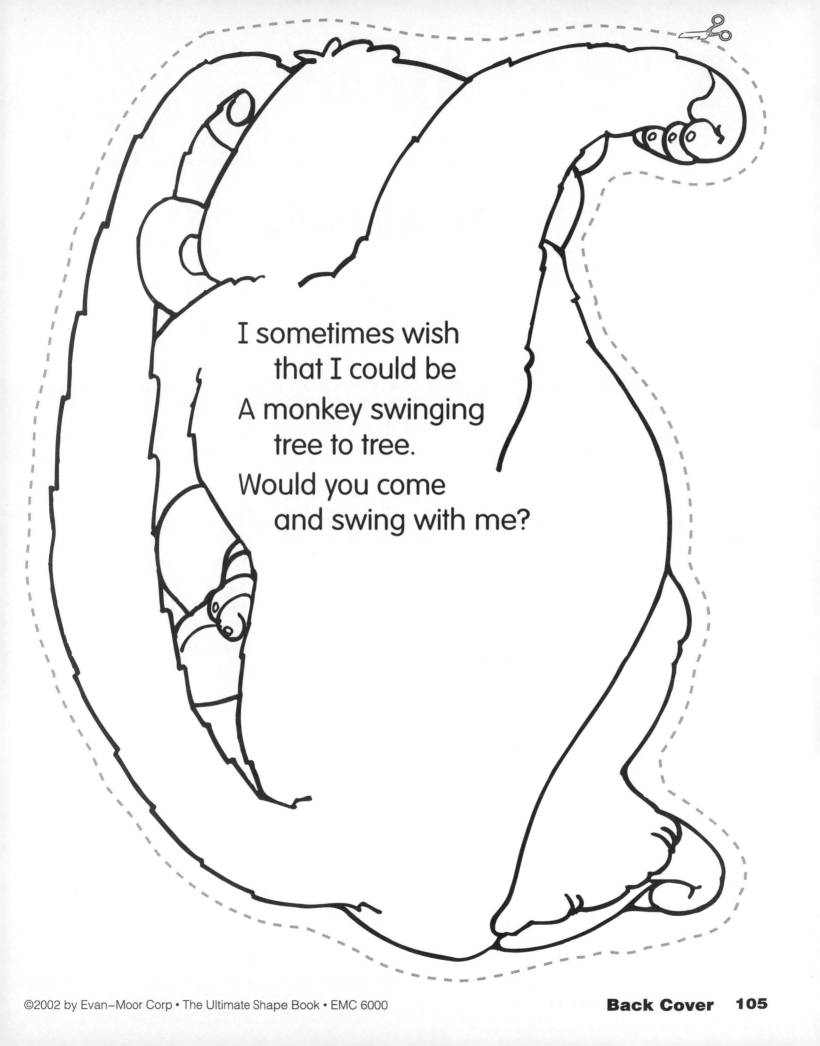

I sometimes wish
that I could be
A monkey swinging
tree to tree.
Would you come
and swing with me?

Bear

Literature Connections

Blueberries for Sal by Robert McCloskey; Viking Press, 1987.
Brown Bear, Brown Bear, What Do You See? by Bill Martin Jr.; Henry Holt, 1996.
Happy Birthday, Moon by Frank Asch; Aladdin Paperbacks, 1999.
Henry Hikes to Fitchburg by Donald B. Johnson; Houghton Mifflin Company, 2000.
Jamberry by Bruce Degen; HarperCollins Children's Books, 1995.
Time to Sleep by Denise Fleming; Henry Holt, 1997.
Tops and Bottoms by Janet Stevens; Harcourt Brace & Co., 1995.
We're Going on a Bear Hunt by Michael Rosen; Margaret McElderry, 1989.

Concrete Experiences

Have students bring their teddy bears to class. Introduce the bears and list words that describe how students feel about the bears.

Let the Writing Begin

Emergent Writers

- **Teddy and I**
  Students draw a picture of something that they do with their teddy bears. They tell about their pictures.

- **All Dressed Up!**
  Students draw a teddy bear in an outfit. They describe what the bear will do while wearing these clothes.

Beginning Writers

- **My Bear Can…**
  Students list things their bears can do. They illustrate several possibilities, and then for each picture, they copy and complete the sentence.

  My bear can _____.

- **Whispers**
  Students imagine what their teddy bears might whisper. They draw themselves and their bears. They copy and complete the sentences.

  It was late at night and all was quiet.
  Then Teddy whispered in my ear _____.

Independent Writers

- **Teddy's Trip**
  Students write about a trip that they take with their teddy bears.

- **The Lost Teddy Bear**
  Students write about what happens when Teddy is lost.

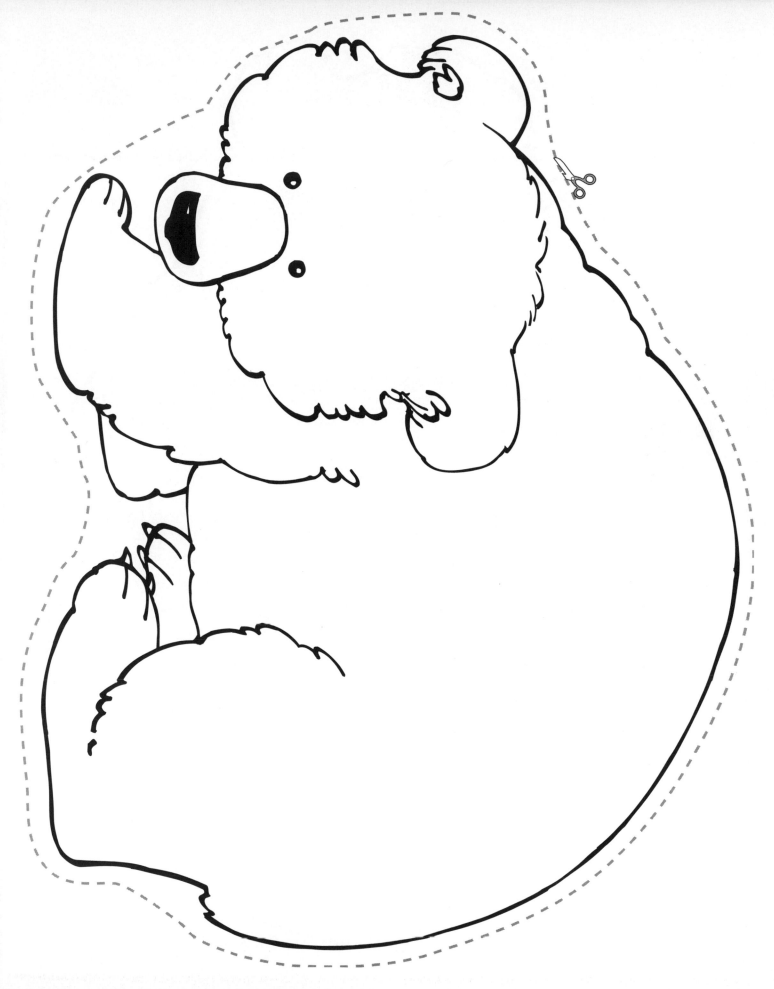

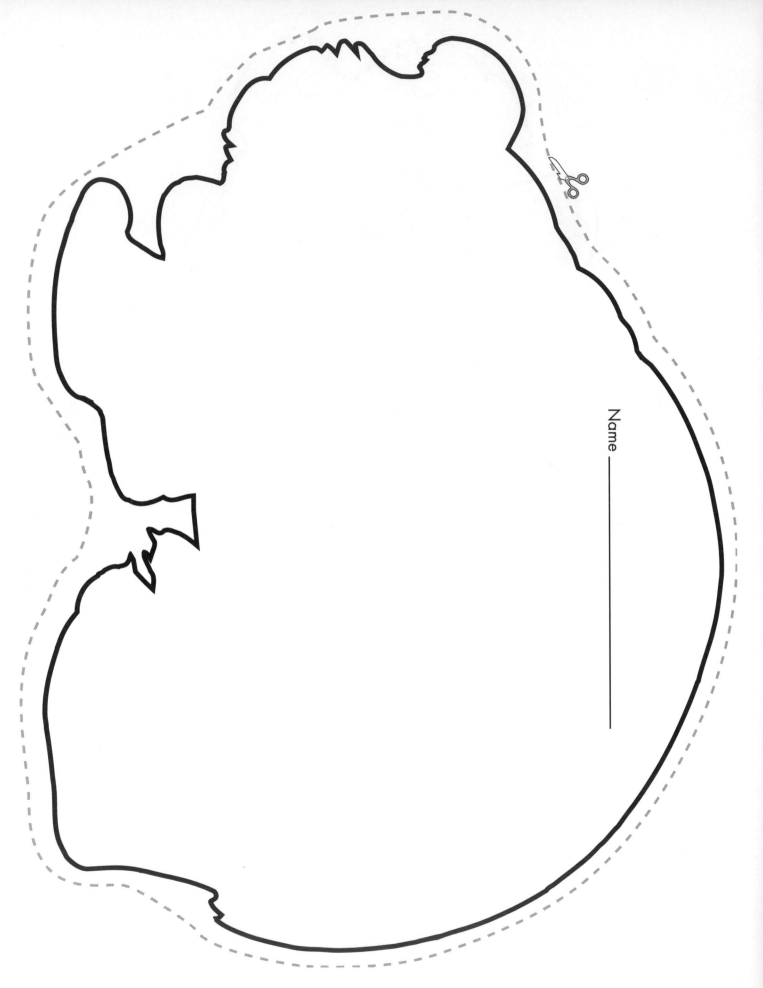

Name _____

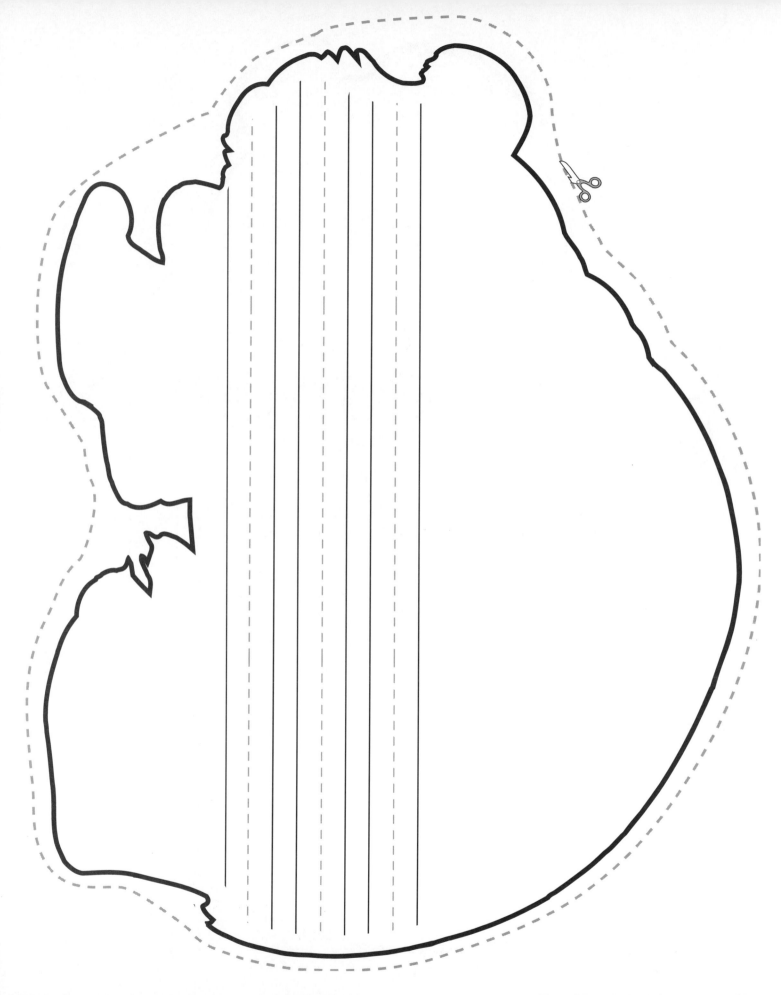

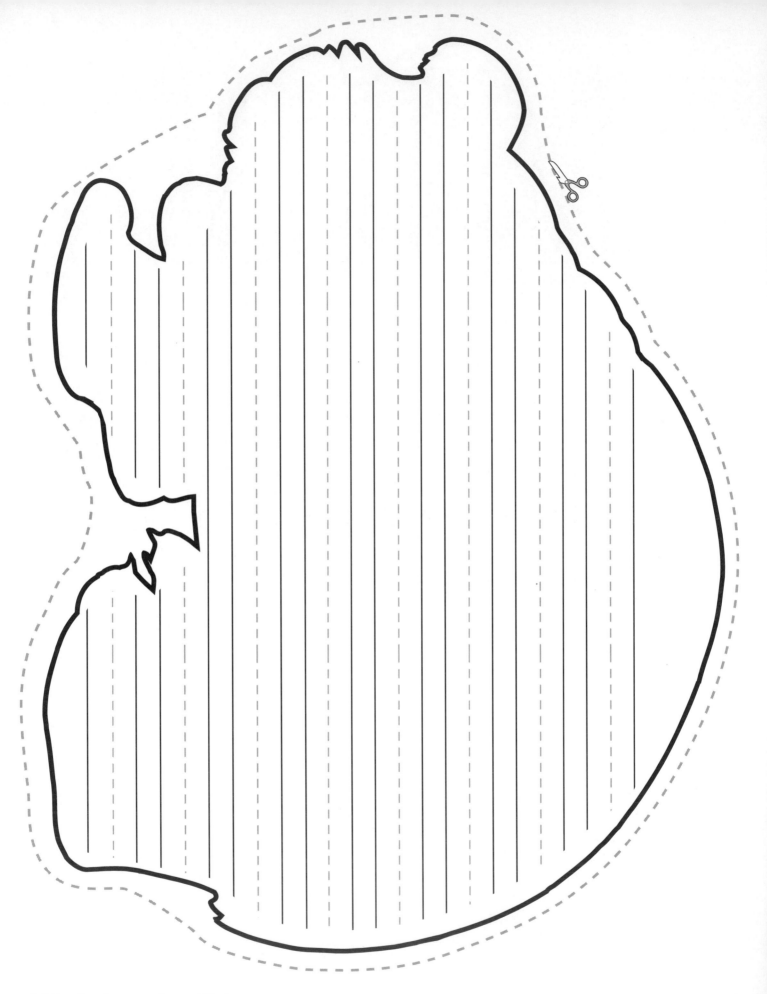

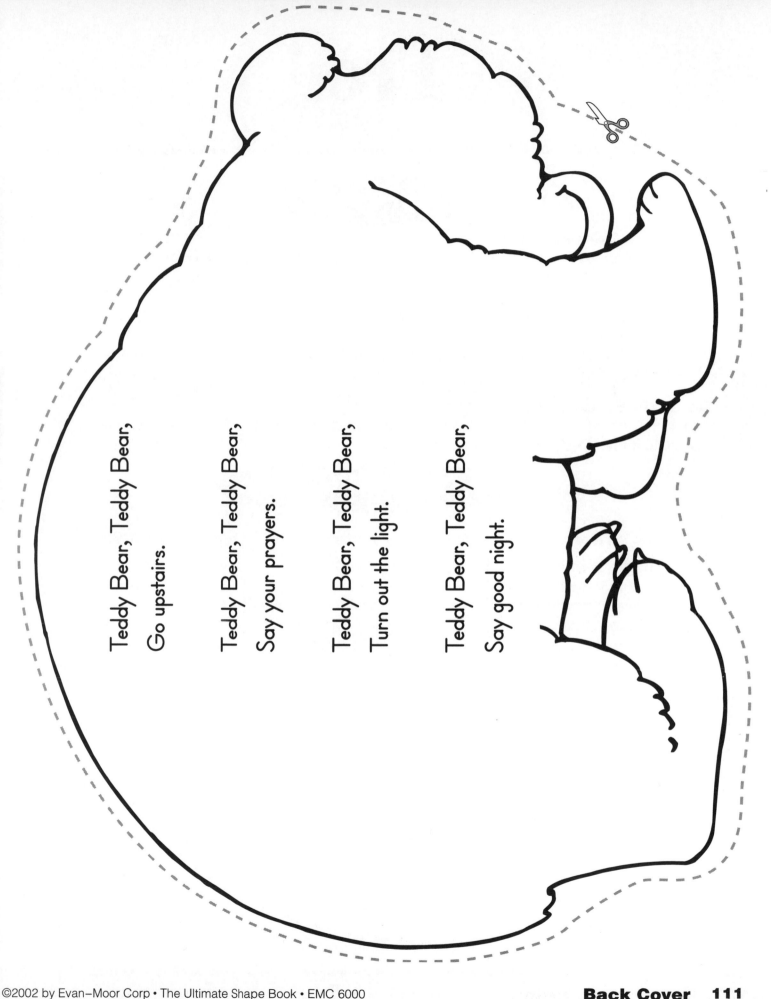

Teddy Bear, Teddy Bear,
Go upstairs.

Teddy Bear, Teddy Bear,
Say your prayers.

Teddy Bear, Teddy Bear,
Turn out the light.

Teddy Bear, Teddy Bear,
Say good night.

Frog

Literature Connections

Frog and Toad Are Friends by Arnold Lobel; HarperCollins Children's Books, 1970.
Froggy Plays Soccer by Jonathan London; Viking Children's Books, 1999.
Grandpa Toad's Secrets by Keiko Kasza; Paper Star, 1998.
It's a Frog's Life!: My Story of Life in a Pond by Steve Parker; Reader's Digest, 1999.
Tuesday by David Wiesner; Clarion Books, 1991.
The Wide-Mouthed Frog: A Pop-Up Book by Keith Faulkner; Dial Books for Young Readers, 1996.

Concrete Experiences

Have students jump. Ask, "Are there different ways of jumping?" Brainstorm synonyms for *jump*. List the words on a chart for reference.

Let the Writing Begin

Emergent Writers

- **A Frog in the Bathtub**
  Students imagine what it would be like to have a frog in the bathtub. They draw pictures to illustrate their ideas. Then they tell about their pictures.

- **Hop and Stop**
  Students draw frogs hopping and then show the frogs stopping. They say words that might go along with their picture. "Hop. Hop. Hop. Stop!"

Beginning Writers

- **How Many Flies?**
  Students draw a frog catching flies with its tongue. They copy and complete the question and answer.

  How many flies can you catch?
  I caught _____ flies.

- **Frog Is Jumping**
  Students draw a picture of a frog jumping. They copy and complete this poem.

  Frog jumps high.
  Frog jumps low.
  Frog _____.
  See it go.

Independent Writers

- **How to Catch a Fly**
  Students write step-by-step directions for catching a fly from a frog's viewpoint.

- **Welcome to My Pad!**
  Students imagine a frog's home on the lily pad. They describe the "pad" as if they were writing a magazine article.

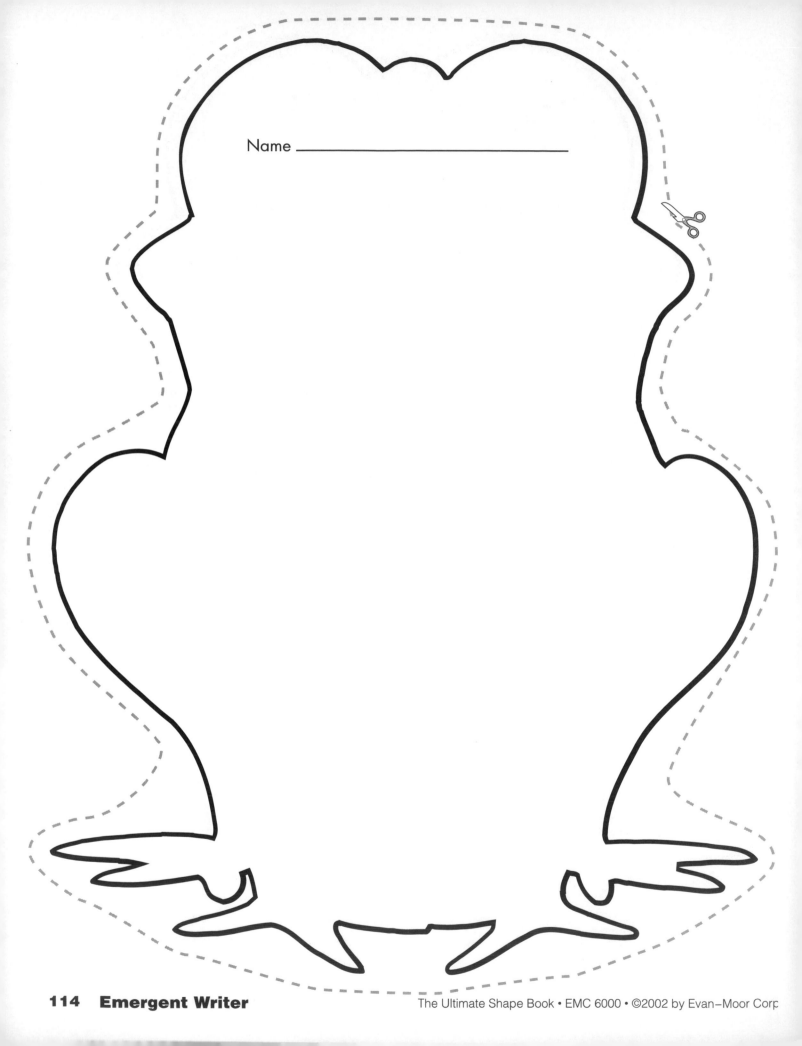

Name _____

The Ultimate Shape Book • EMC 6000 • ©2002 by Evan-Moor Corp

Frogs leaping away with smooth, shiny skin.

Toads hopping along are frog's "bumpy" kin.

Elephant

Literature Connections

Eyewitness: Elephant by Ian Redmond; Dorling Kindersley Publishing Inc., 2000.
Five Minutes' Peace by Jill Murphy; Paper Star, 1999.
Hide-and-Seek Elmer by David McKee; Lothrop, Lee & Shepard Books, 1998.
Horton Hears a Who by Dr. Seuss; Random House, 1954.
17 Kings and 42 Elephants by Margaret Mahy; E.P. Dutton, 1987.
Seven Blind Mice by Ed Young; Philomel Books, 1992.

Concrete Experiences

Have students move about as if they were elephants. Ask them, "How is the elephant's walk different than yours? What words describe the heavy, plodding walk?"

Let the Writing Begin

Emergent Writers

- **Big as an Elephant**
  Students draw several big things. They describe the things by comparing them to an elephant.

- **The Elephant's Trick**
  Students draw an elephant doing a trick. They tell about the trick.

Beginning Writers

- **Special Delivery**
  Students draw a picture to show an elephant making a special delivery. Then they copy and complete the question and answer.

  What did the elephant bring?
  It brought a _____.

- **Elephant Facts**
  Students draw an elephant. They copy and complete the sentences.

  Elephants have big _____.
  Elephants have little _____.

Independent Writers

- **The Day the Elephant Chewed Bubble Gum**
  Students imagine what would happen if an elephant found a package of bubble gum and chewed it.

- **An Enormous Problem**
  Students think of a problem that an elephant's owner might have, and write a story about the problem and how it was solved.

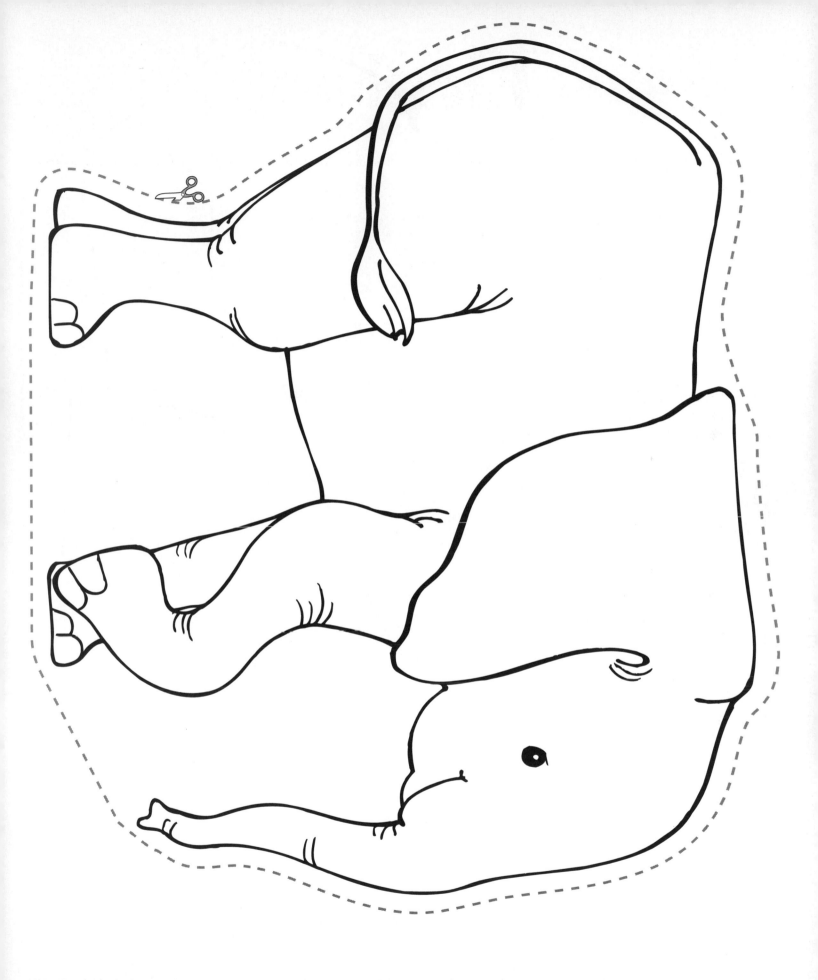

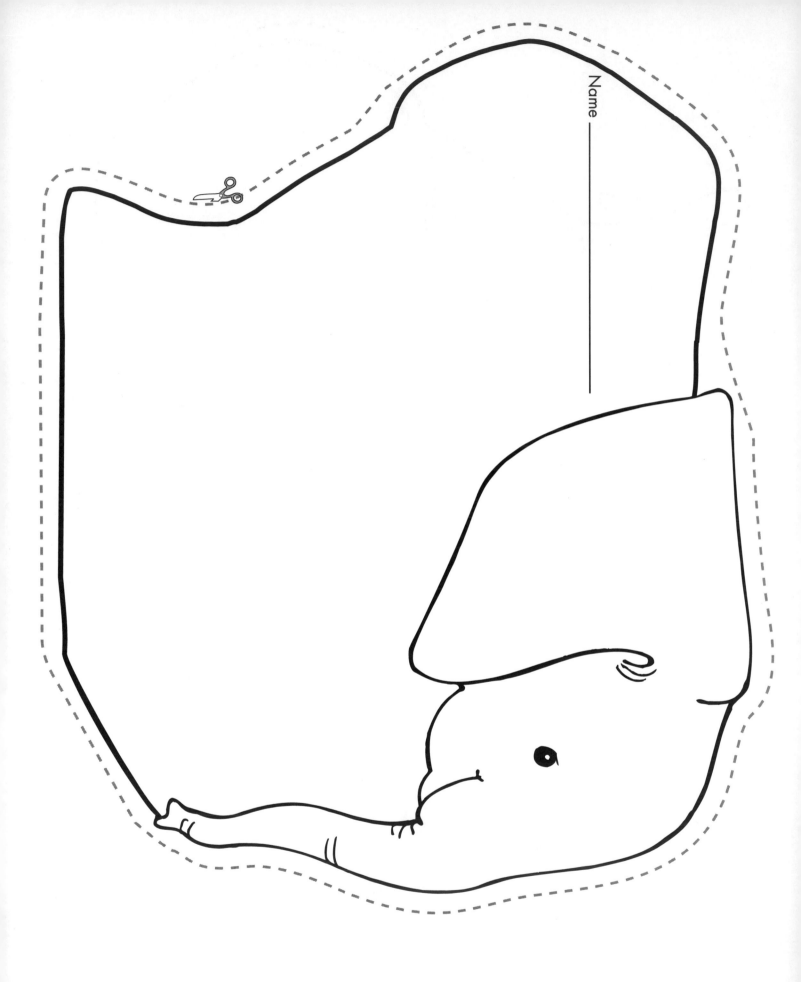

Name _____

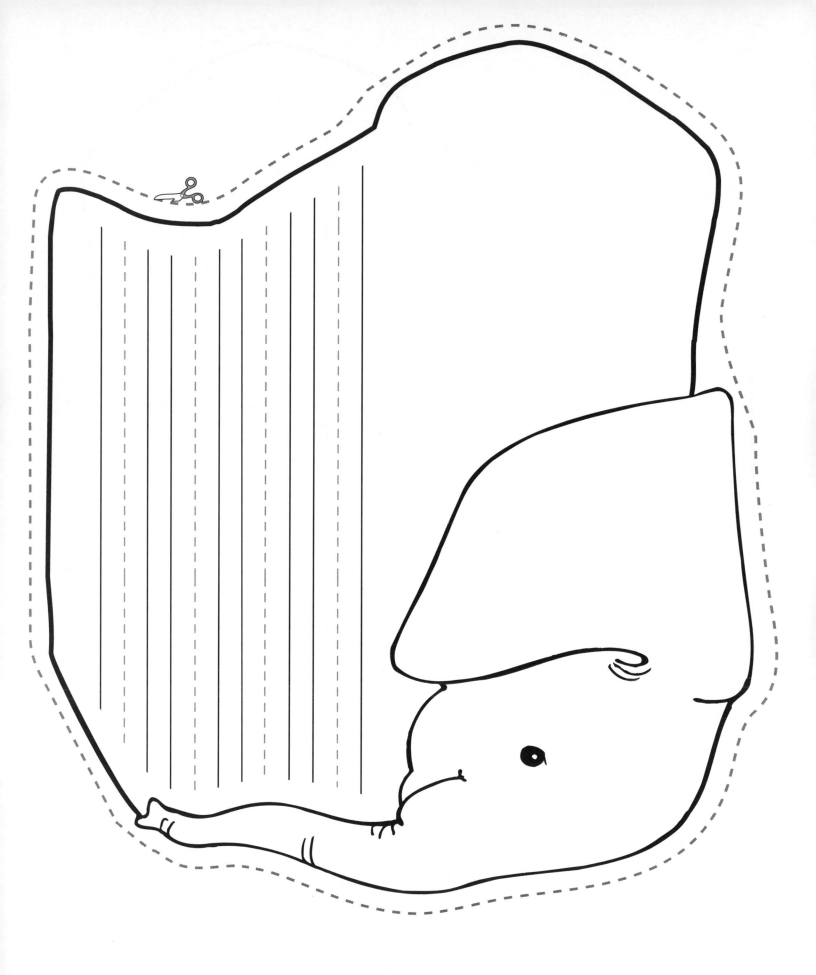

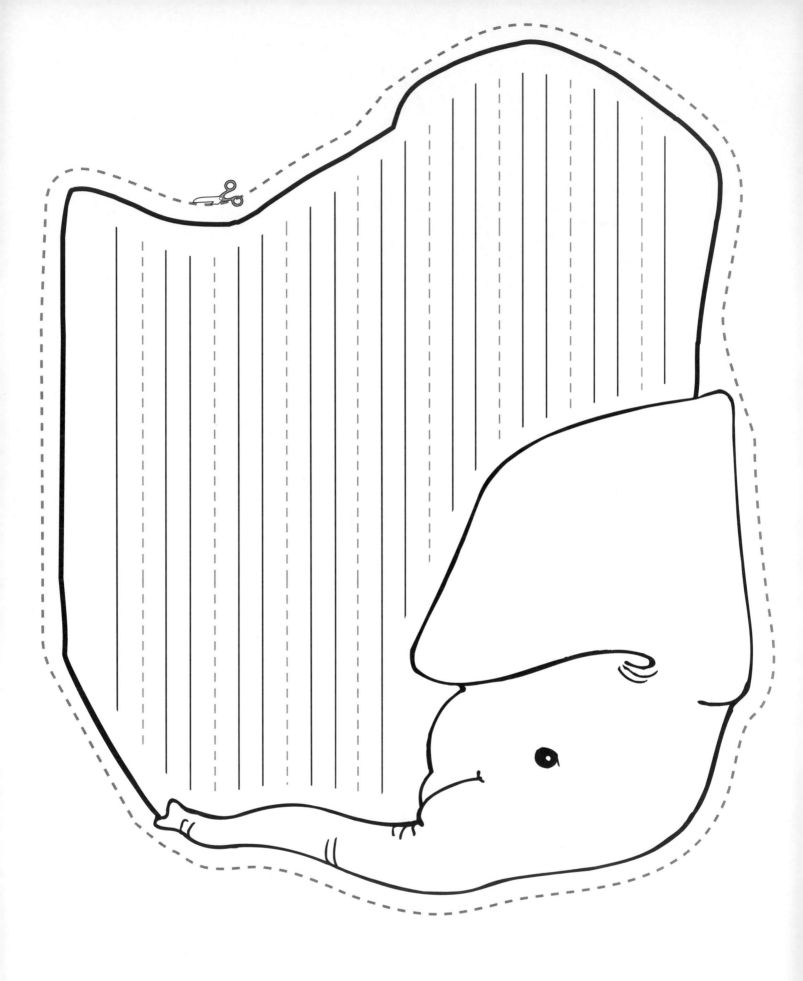

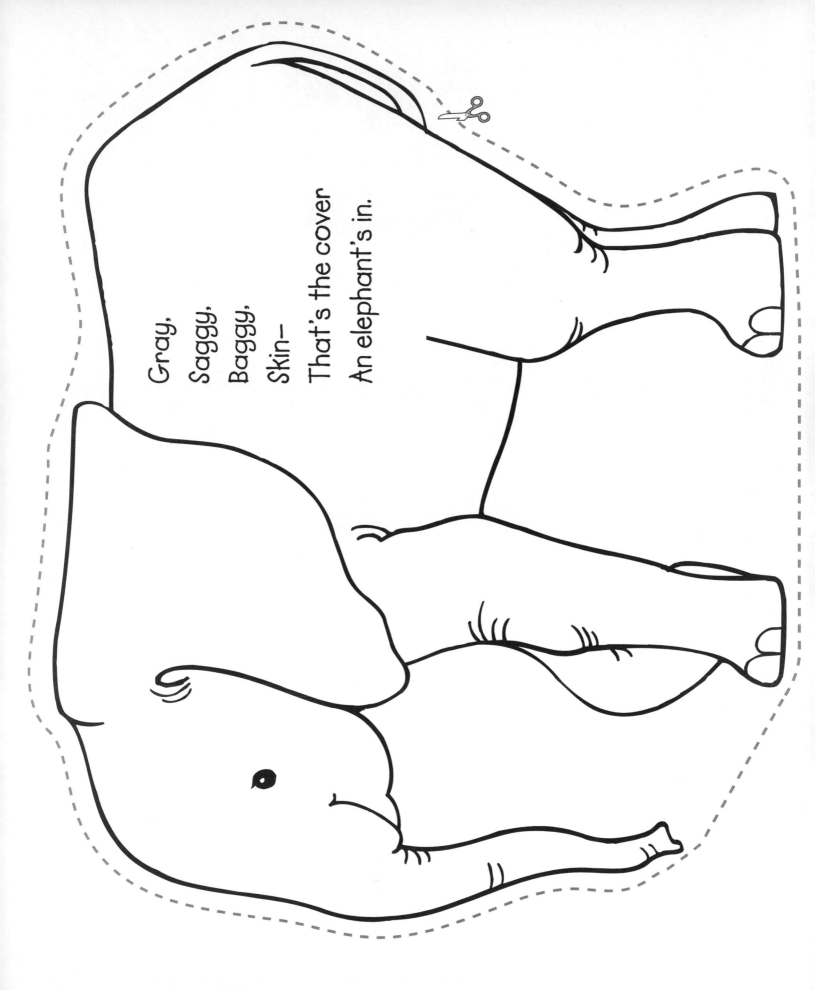

Gray,
Saggy,
Baggy,
Skin—
That's the cover
An elephant's in.

Apple

Literature Connections

Apple Picking Time by Michele Benoit Slawson; Dragonfly, 1998.
The Apple Pie Tree by Zoe Hall; Scholastic Trade, 1996.
How Do Apples Grow? (Let's Read-and-Find Out Book) by Betsy C. Maestro; HarperTrophy, 1993.
How to Make an Apple Pie and See the World by Marjorie Priceman; Dragonfly, 1996.
The Life and Times of the Apple by Charles Micucci; Orchard Books, 1995.
The Seasons of Arnold's Apple Tree by Gail Gibbons; Harcourt Brace & Co., 1988.
Ten Apples up on Top! by Dr. Seuss; Random House, 1998.

Concrete Experiences

Taste several varieties of apples and brainstorm words or phrases that describe how the apple looks, smells, tastes, feels, and sounds.

Let the Writing Begin

Emergent Writers

- **What Can You Do with an Apple?**
  Students draw a picture showing one use for apples. They describe how the apple is used.

- **Apples of All Colors**
  Students draw four apples and color them different colors. Then they tell about the colors of their apples.

Beginning Writers

- **My Home**
  Students draw a worm living in an apple. Then they copy and complete the sentences.

  My name is _____.
  I live in this _____ apple.
  I like my tasty home.

- **My Favorite Apple**
  Students draw their favorite apples and copy and complete the sentences to tell what makes the apples special.

  My favorite apple is _____.
  It is special because _____.

Independent Writers

- **Dear Johnny**
  Students write a letter to Johnny Appleseed thanking him for planting apple trees.

- **The Lonely Apple**
  Students write a lament from the point of view of the last apple left on the tree.

©2002 by Evan–Moor Corp • The Ultimate Shape Book • EMC 6000   **Front Cover   125**

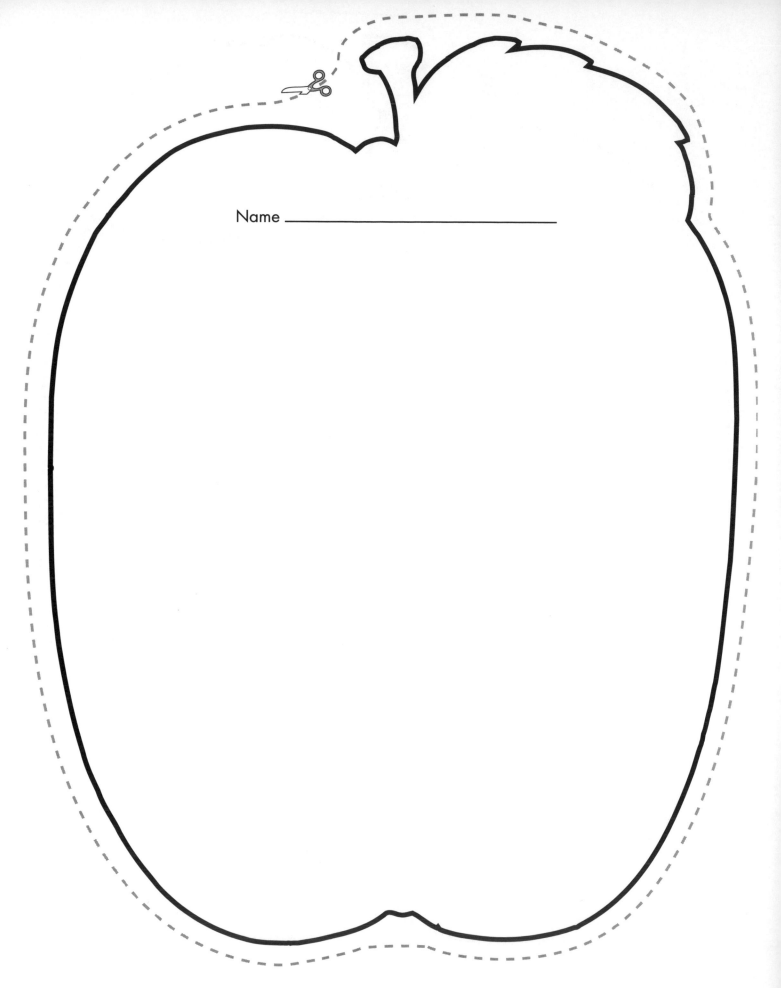

Name _____

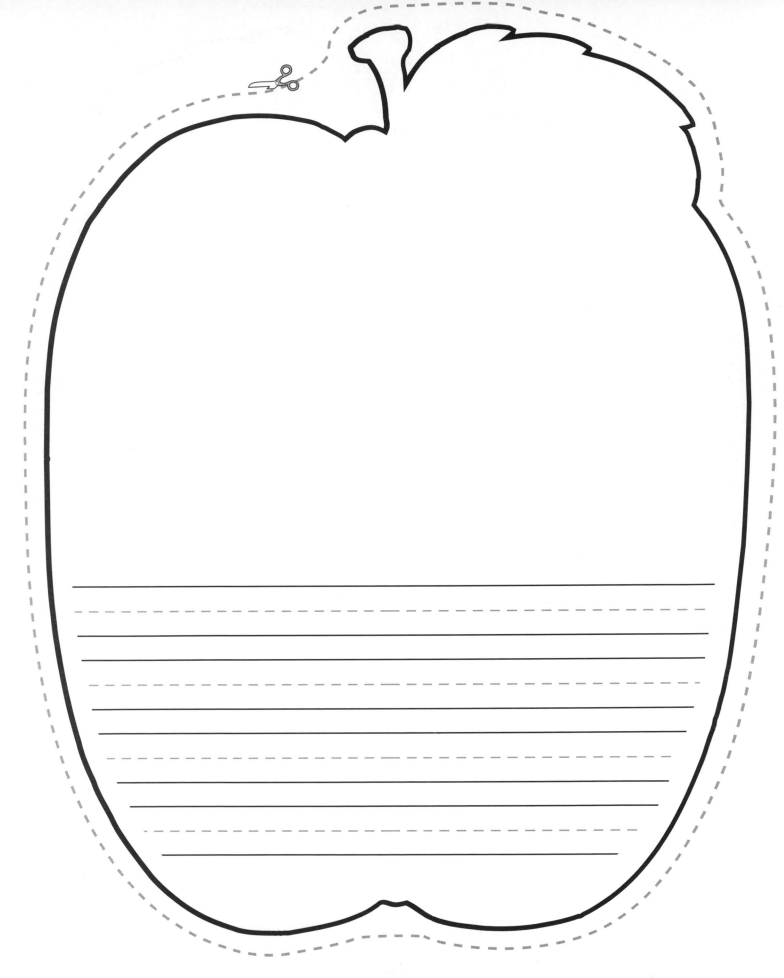

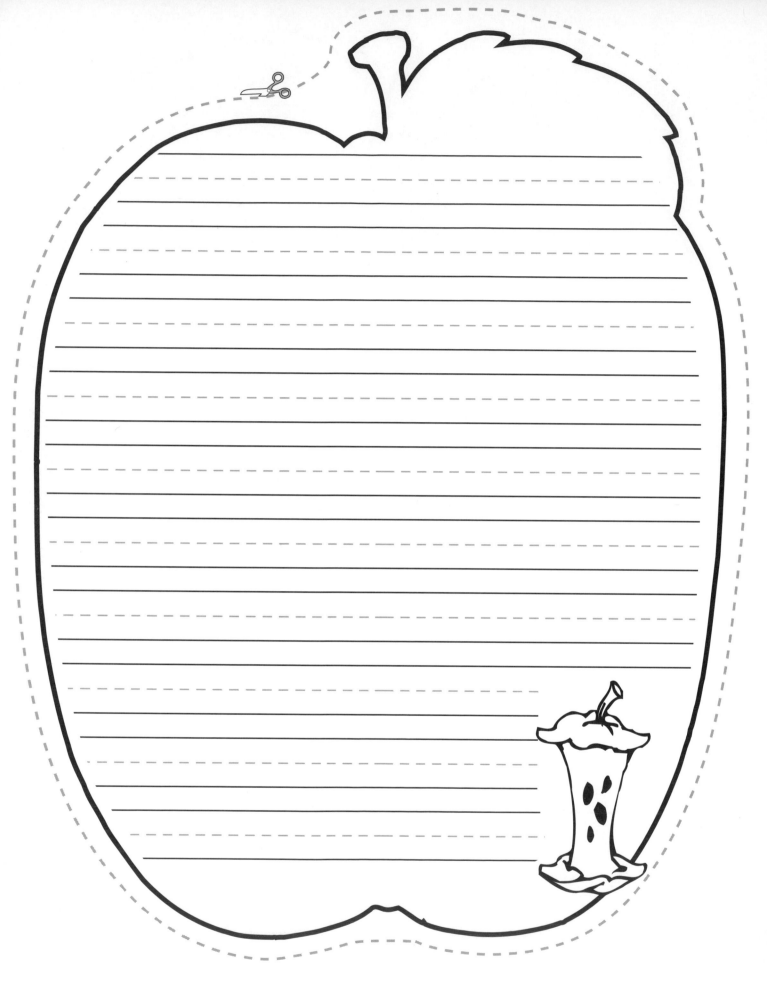

The Ultimate Shape Book • EMC 6000 • ©2002 by Evan-Moor Corp

Red, green, and yellow apple skin
Hide the yummy taste that's within.
No matter what color the skin may be,
A fresh, juicy bite is waiting for me.

House

Literature Connections

Building a House by Byron Barton; Mulberry Books, 1990.
Goodbye House by Frank Asch; Aladdin Paperbacks, 1989.
Housebuilding for Children by Lester R. Walker; Overlook Press, 1988.
Houses and Homes (Around the World Series) by Ann Morris; Mulberry Books, 1995.
The Little House by Virginia Lee Burton; Houghton Mifflin Company, 1978.
The Napping House by Audry Wood; Harcourt Brace & Co., 1984.
Old MacDonald Had an Apartment House by Judi Barrett; Atheneum, 1998.
We Were Tired of Living in a House by Liesel Moak Skorpen; Putnam, 1999.

Concrete Experiences

Take a "house walk" through the neighborhood beside your school. When you return to the classroom, list and discuss the different houses that you saw.

Let the Writing Begin

Emergent Writers

- **My Family**
  Students draw their families inside the house and describe them orally.

- **A Mouse in the House**
  Students draw a cute mouse hiding inside the house, and describe where the mouse is hiding and what it is doing.

Beginning Writers

- **When I Look Outside**
  Students draw themselves looking out the window, and copy and complete the following sentence.

  When I look outside the window, I see _____.

- **What Makes It Different?**
  Students draw a unique feature of their real or imagined house, and copy and complete this question and answer.

  What makes this house different?
  It has a _____.

Independent Writers

- **How to Build a House**
  Students write a simple how-to guide for building a house.

- **The Three Bears' House**
  Students describe the three bears' house, backing up their description with facts from the story.

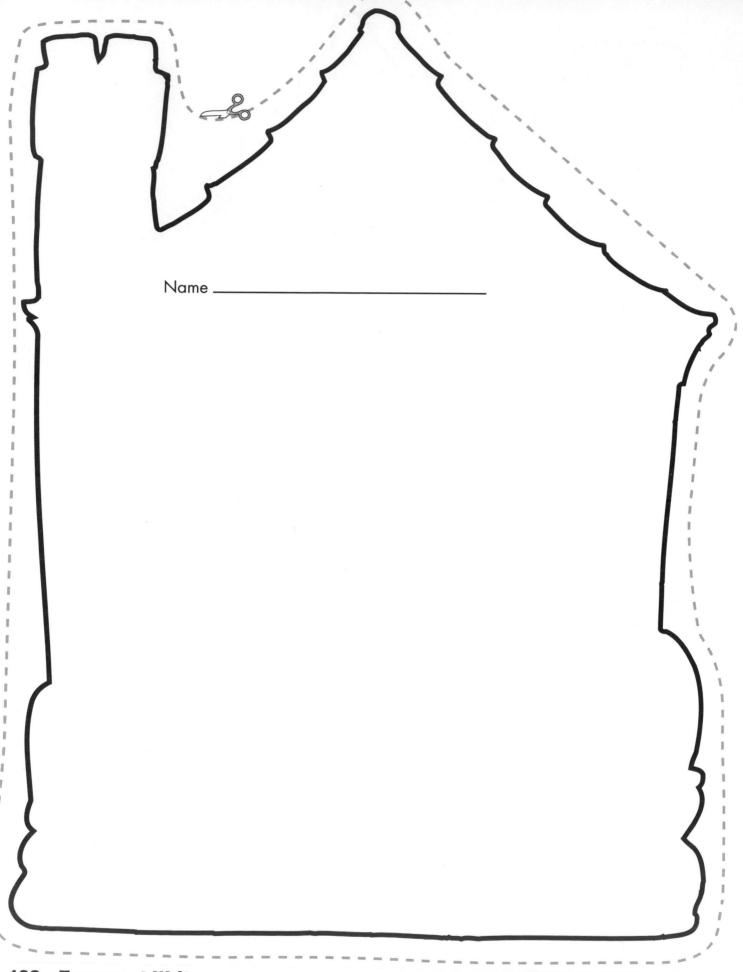

Name _____

A fish lives in a brook.
A bird lives in a tree.
But a house is the best
For a person like me.

Dog

Literature Connections

Charlie's Checklist by Rory S. Lerman; Orchard Books, 2000.
Clifford: The Big Red Dog by Norman Bridwell; Scholastic Trade, 1997.
Dog Breath!: The Horrible Trouble with Hally Tosis by Dave Pilkey; Scholastic Trade, 1994.
Dog Heaven by Cynthia Rylant; Scholastic Trade, 1995.
Go, Dog, Go! by Philip D. Eastman; Random House, 1961.
How to Talk to Your Dog by Jean Craighead George; HarperCollins Children's Books, 2000.
Open Me...I'm a Dog by Art Spiegelman; HarperCollins Children's Books, 1997.
The Other Dog by Madeleine L'Engle; SeaStar Publishing Co., 2001.
The Stray Dog: From a True Story by Reiko Sassa; HarperCollins Children's Books, 2001.
Tallyho, Pinkerton! by Steven Kellogg; Dial Books for Young Readers, 2001.

Concrete Experiences

Invite a representative from the SPCA or a dog trainer to visit your classroom. Discuss dog care. List terms and words used on a chart for easy reference.

Let the Writing Begin

Emergent Writers

- **That Dog Can…**
  Students draw a dog doing something and then tell about the dog's accomplishment.

- **Run, Dog, Run**
  Students draw a picture of a dog running and tell about what is happening in the picture.

Beginning Writers

- **Where's the Bone?**
  Students draw a place where a dog might hide a bone. Then they copy and complete the sentences.

  The dog hid the bone.
  The bone is _____.

- **The Chase**
  Students draw a series of animals running and then write sentences to describe the chase.

  The girl ran from the mouse.
  The mouse ran from the cat.
  The cat ran from the dog.
  The dog ran from the boy.
  What a chase!

Independent Writers

- **Training a Puppy**
  Students describe the process of training a puppy in one behavior.

- **The Dirty Pup**
  Students describe how a pup gets dirty and then what happens as a result of the dirt.

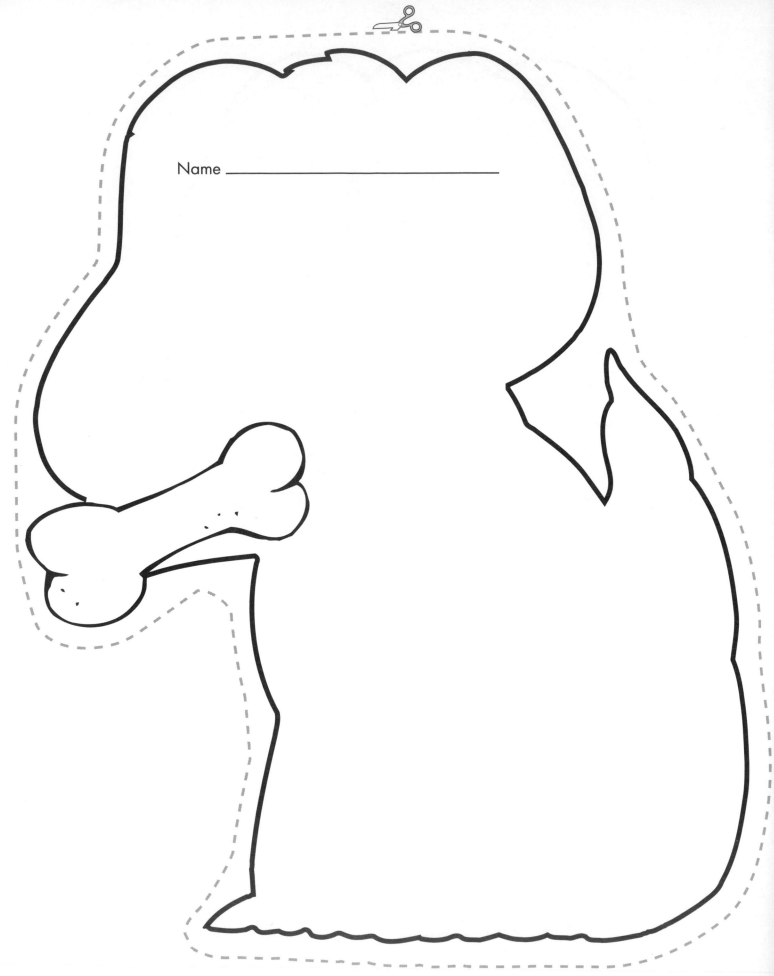

Name _____

The Ultimate Shape Book • EMC 6000 • ©2002 by Evan–Moor Corp

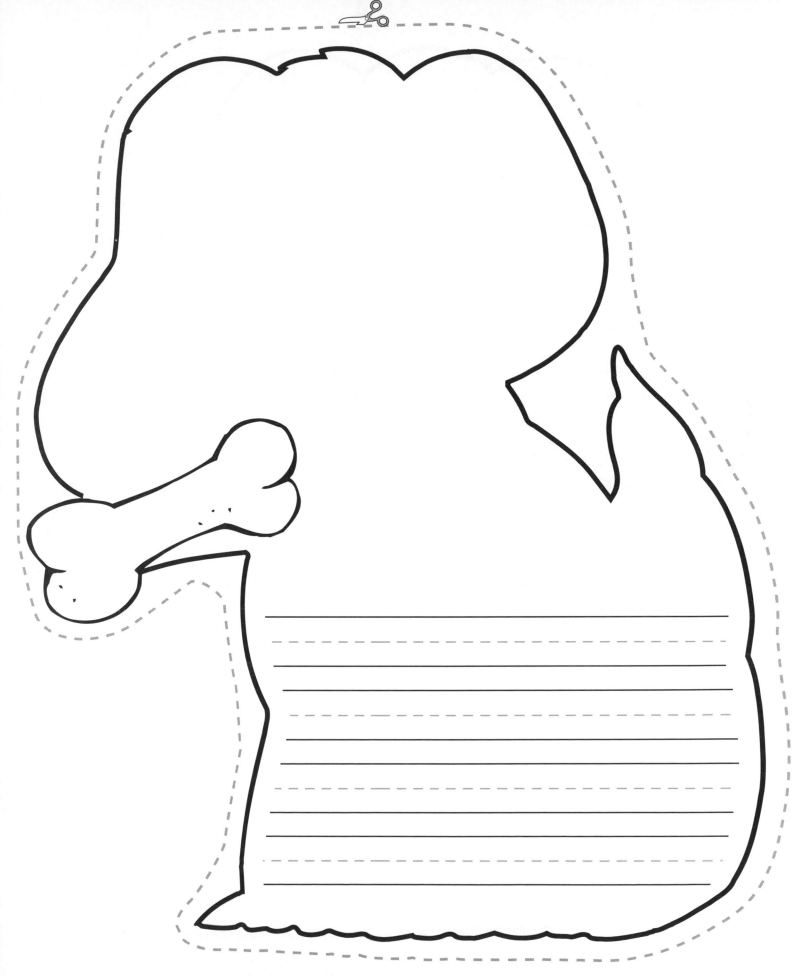

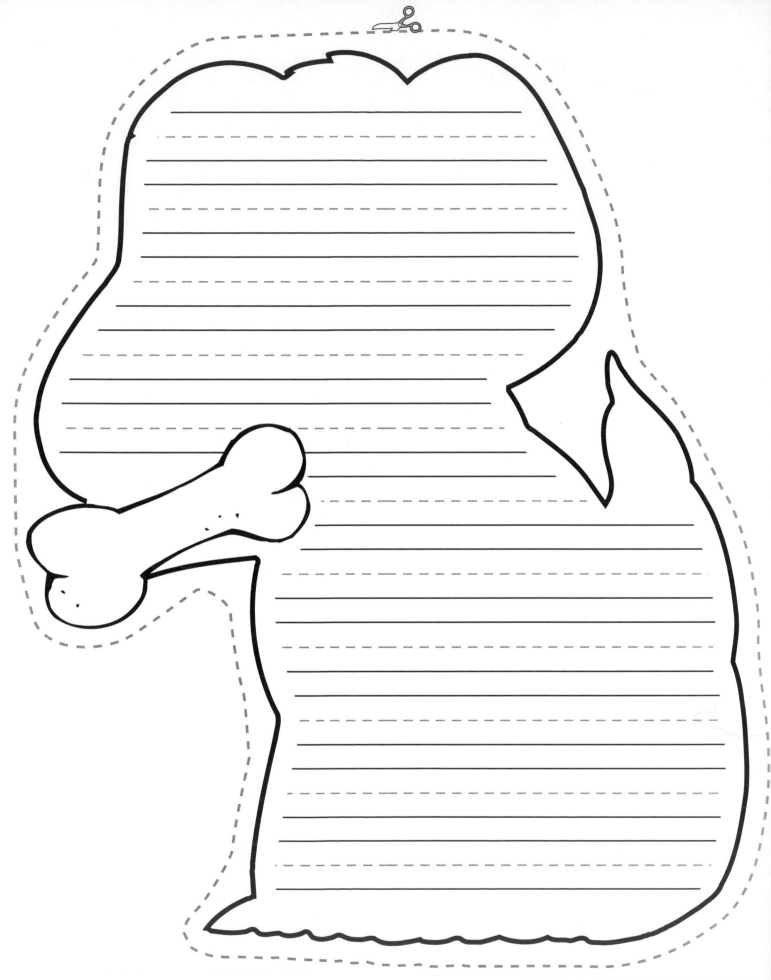

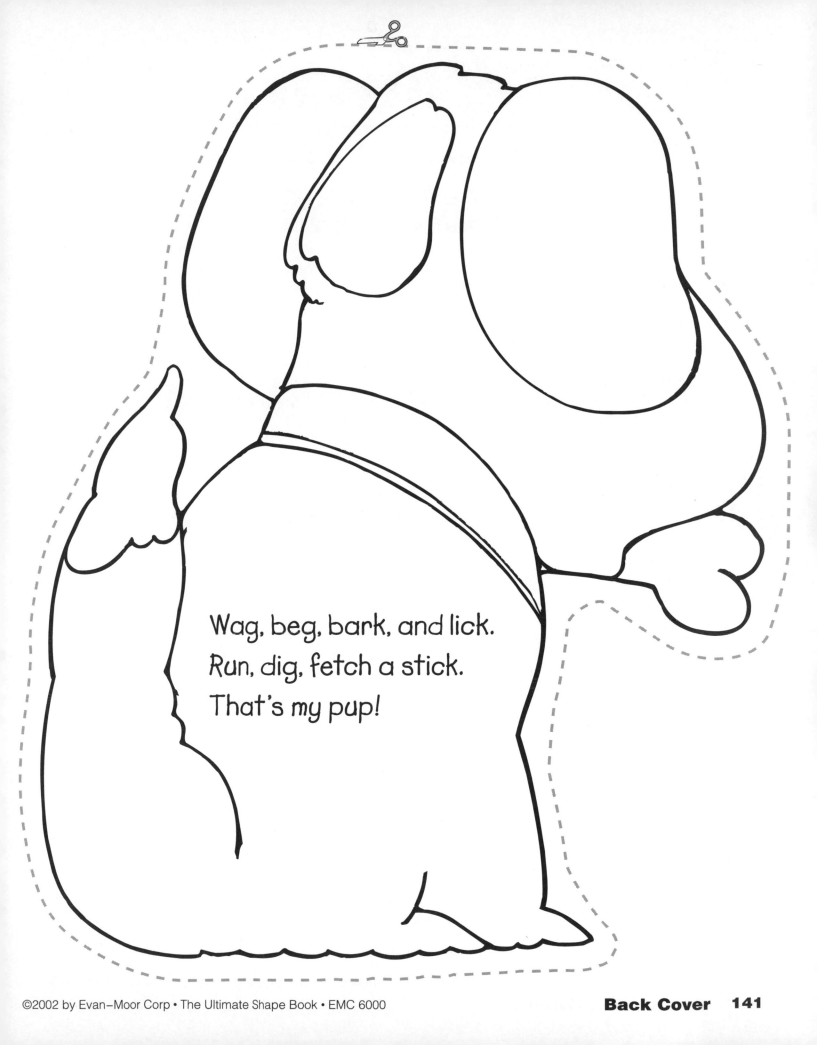

Wag, beg, bark, and lick.
Run, dig, fetch a stick.
That's *my* pup!

Clown

Literature Connections

Be a Clown: Techniques from a Real Clown by Ron Burgess; Williamson Publishing, 2001.

Bravo, Zan Angelo!: A Comedia Dell'Arte Tale with Story & Pictures by Niki Daly; Farrar, Straus & Giroux Inc., 1998.

Clown by Quentin Blake; Henry Holt, 1996.

Mister Tubby's Lemonade Stand by Linda J. B. Williford; Lemondrop Press, 2000.

The Most Excellent Book of How to Be a Clown by Catherine Perkins; Copper Beech Books, 1996.

Rodeo Clown: Laughs and Danger in the Ring by Keith Elliot Greenberg; Blackbirch Press Inc., 1995.

Concrete Experiences

View a video or filmstrip that has a clown. List words that describe the clown's movements and appearance.

Let the Writing Begin

Emergent Writers

• _____ the Clown
Students draw and name a clown. They describe the appearance of the clown.

• The Clown's Shoe
Students draw a shoe that a clown would wear. They explain why the shoe would be good for a clown.

Beginning Writers

• The Sad Clown
Students draw a sad clown, and then copy and complete the sentence to tell why the clown is sad.

The clown is sad because _____.

• Clowning Around
Students draw themselves dressed up as clowns. Then they copy and complete the poem.

Look at me.
I am a clown.
See me _____.
See me fall down.

Independent Writers

• Why I Want (or Don't Want) to Be a Clown
Students express their opinions about whether they would like to be clowns.

• The Clown Who Couldn't Make People Laugh
Students write about a clown with a problem and tell about how the problem is solved.

Name _____

Be a clown! Be a clown!

Jumping up, falling down.

Do some tricks. Tell some jokes

For the happy, smiling folks.

Run around here and there,

Bringing laughter everywhere.

Pig

Literature Connections

Chester, the Worldly Pig by Bill Peet; Houghton Mifflin Company, 1978.
If You Give a Pig a Pancake by Laura Joffe Numeroff; HarperCollins Children's Books, 1998.
In Wibbly's Garden: A Lift the Flap Book by Mick Inkpen; Viking Children's Books, 2000.
Pig and Crow by Kay Chorao; Henry Holt, 2000.
Pigs from A to Z by Arthur Geisert; Houghton Mifflin Company, 1996.
Poppleton Everyday by Cynthia Rylant; Scholastic Trade, 1998.
The Three Little Cajun Pigs by Berthe Amoss; MTC Press, 1999.
The Three Little Wolves and the Big Bad Pig by Eugene Trivizas; Margaret McElderry, 1993.

Concrete Experiences

Pigs love mud. Mix dirt and water to make mud. Enjoy squishing the mud between your hands and fingers. List words that describe how the mud feels.

Let the Writing Begin

Emergent Writers

- **P is for Pig**
  Students draw several things that begin with the letter *p*. They name the things they have drawn.

- **The Pig with a _____ Tail**
  Students draw a pig with an unusual tail. Have students describe the tail to complete the title of the book given above.

Beginning Writers

- **Peek-a-boo Pig**
  Students draw a pig, add a flap of paper to cover the drawing, and then draw the place that the pig is hiding. Students copy and complete the sentences.

  Peek-a-boo, Pig.
  Where are you?
  Pig is hiding behind the
  _____.

- **Piggy's Picnic**
  Students draw a picnic for a pig. They copy the sentences and list the foods they have drawn.

  Piggy went on a picnic.
  She had _____.

Independent Writers

- **The Perfectly Polite Pig**
  Students write about a pig with impeccable manners.

- **To Market, To Market**
  Students describe Pig's trip to the market to buy food.

Front Cover 149

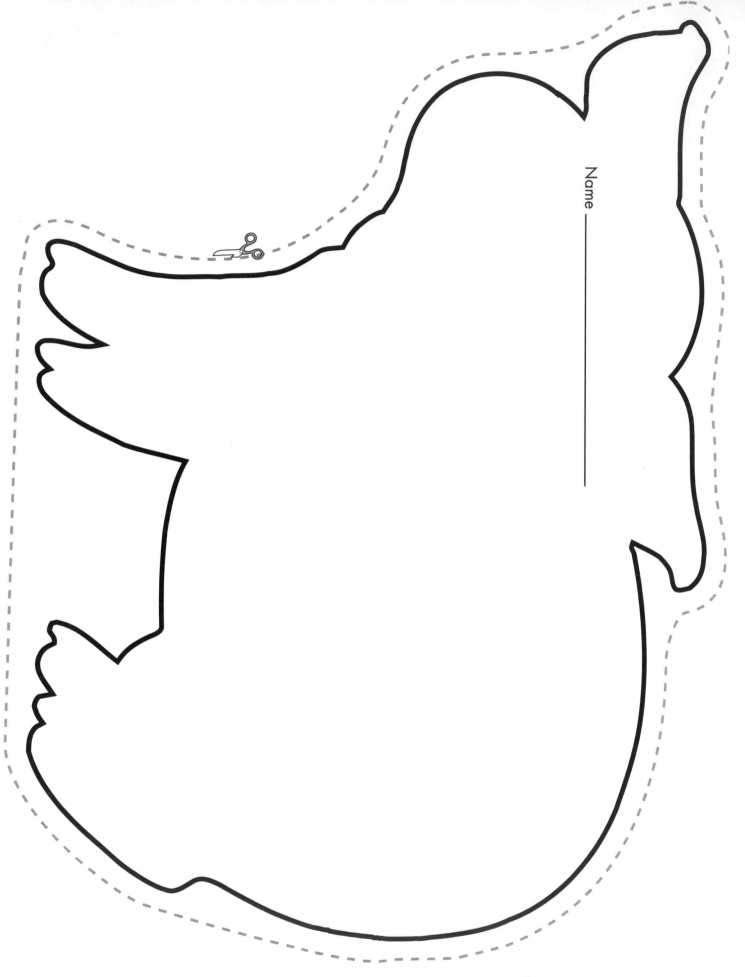

Name _____

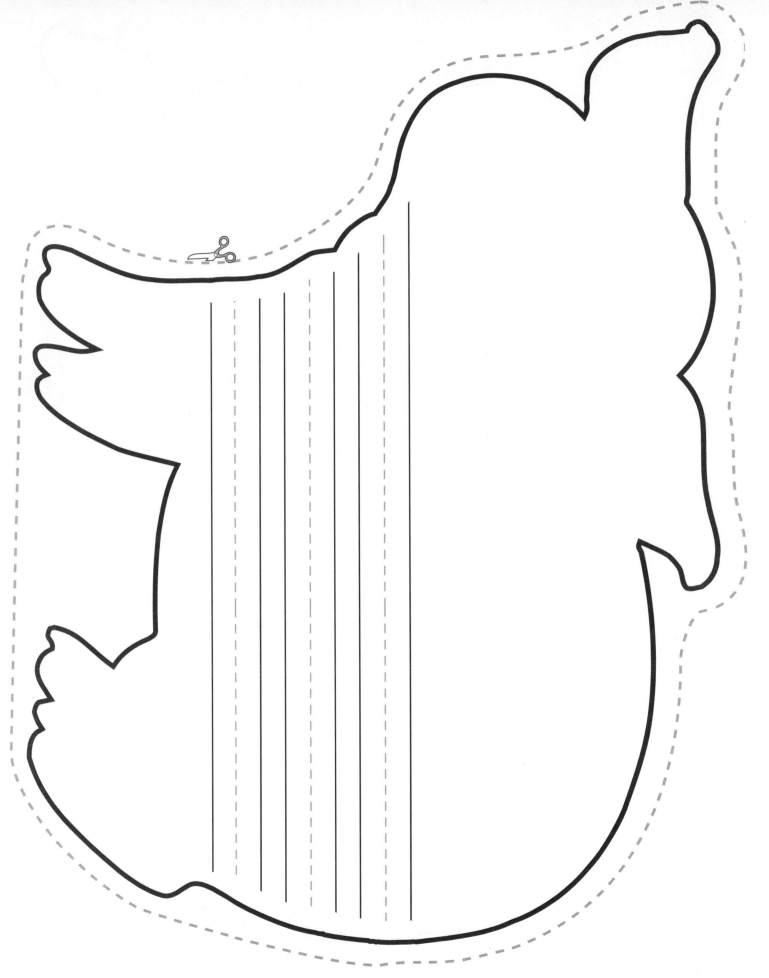

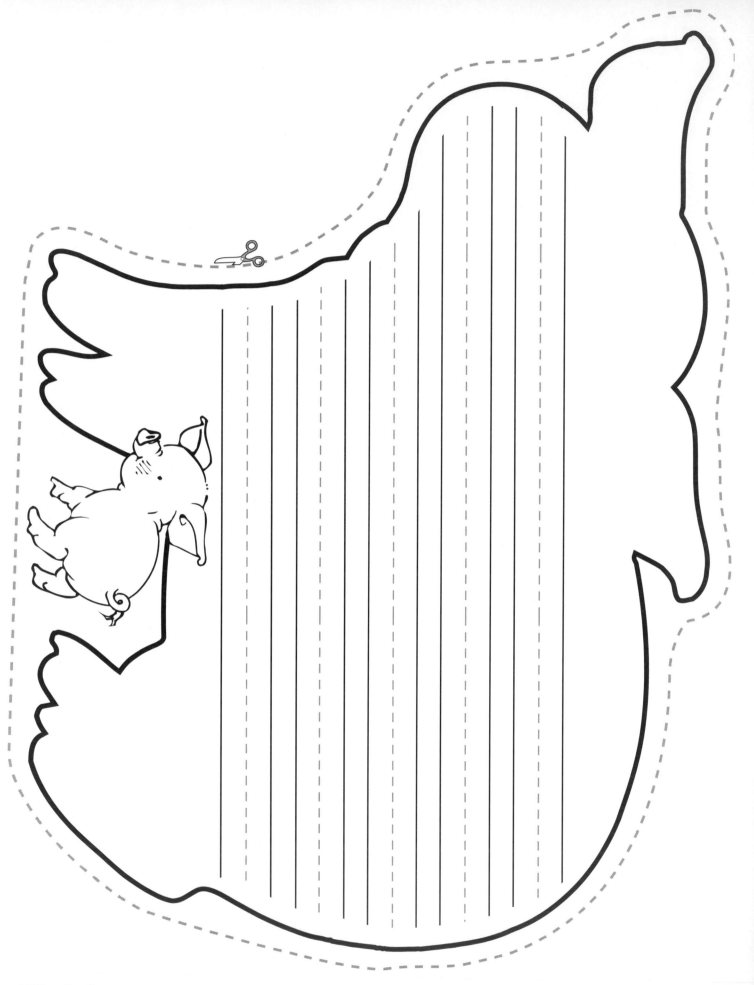

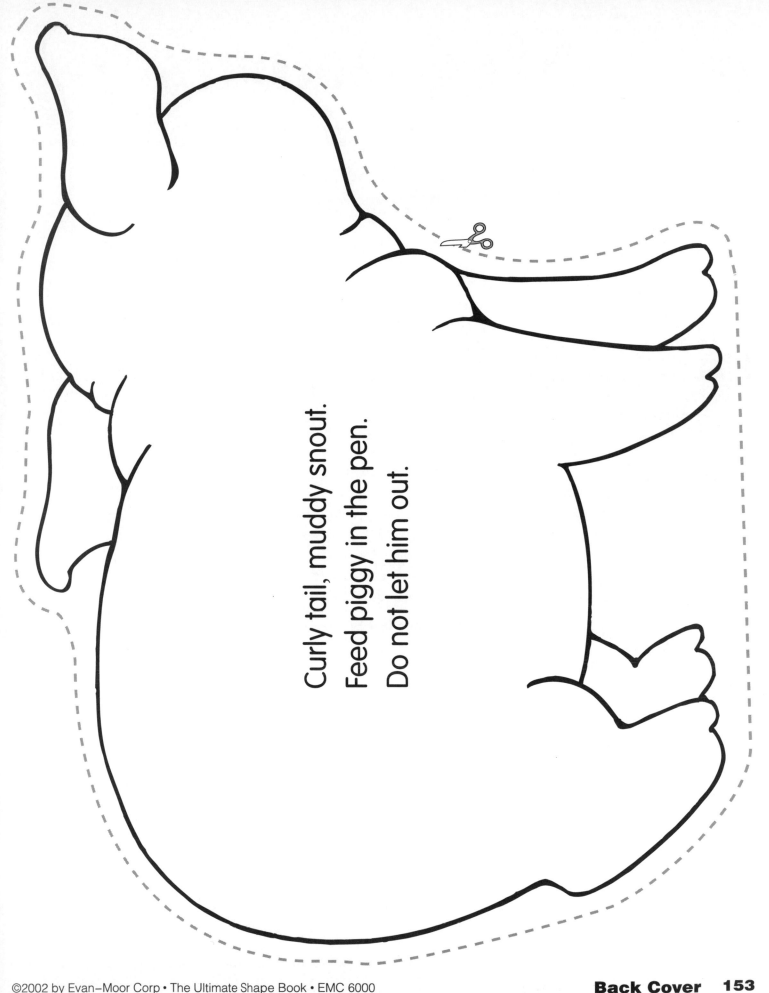

Curly tail, muddy snout.
Feed piggy in the pen.
Do not let him out.

Stegosaurus

Literature Connections

Can I Have a Stegosaurus, Mom? Can I? Please!? by Lois G. Grambling; BridgeWater
   Books, 1995.
How Do Dinosaurs Say Good Night? by Jane Yolen; Scholastic Trade, 2000.
Stegosaurus by Harry N. Abrams; Harry N. Abrams, 2000.
Stegosaurus (A True Book) by Elaine Landau; Children's Press, 1999.
Ultimate Dinosaur Book by David Lambert; Dorling Kindersley Publishing Inc., 1993.

Concrete Experiences

Present some facts about the stegosaurus.
- Stegosaurus had 17 bony plates embedded in its back.
- The stegosaurus had tail spikes at the end of its flexible tail. The spikes were up to
  4 feet (1.2 m) long.
- Stegosaurus was about 30 feet long (9 m) and about 9 feet tall (2.75 m). It weighed
  about 6,800 pounds (3,100 kg).

Compare a big animal your students are familiar with to the stegosaurus.

Let the Writing Begin

Emergent Writers

- **Standing with Stegosaurus**
  Students draw themselves beside a stegosaurus. They dictate a statement comparing their size to the stegosaurus's size.

- **D is for Dinosaur**
  Students draw a stegosaurus. Inside the plates on the dinosaur's back, they draw other things that start with the sound of *d*.

Beginning Writers

- **Dinosaur Facts**
  Students draw a stegosaurus. Then they copy and complete these sentences.

  *Stegosaurus is a dinosaur.
  Stegosaurus can _____.*

- **If I Met a Dinosaur**
  Students draw an illustration to show what would happen if they met a dinosaur, and then copy and complete the sentence.

  If I met a dinosaur, I would _____.

Independent Writers

- **My Dinosaur Tale**
  Encourage students to use what they know about a stegosaurus to give their dinosaur stories a hint of realism.

- **Why Am I Extinct?**
  Students propose an explanation for the extinction of dinosaurs.

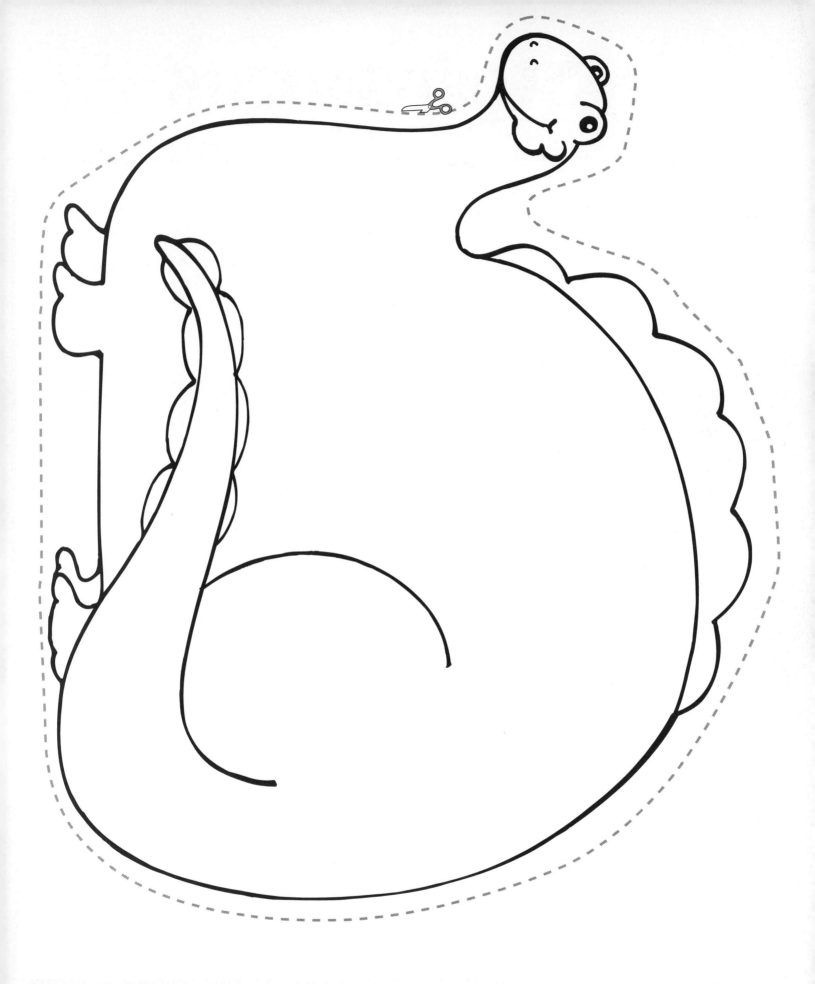

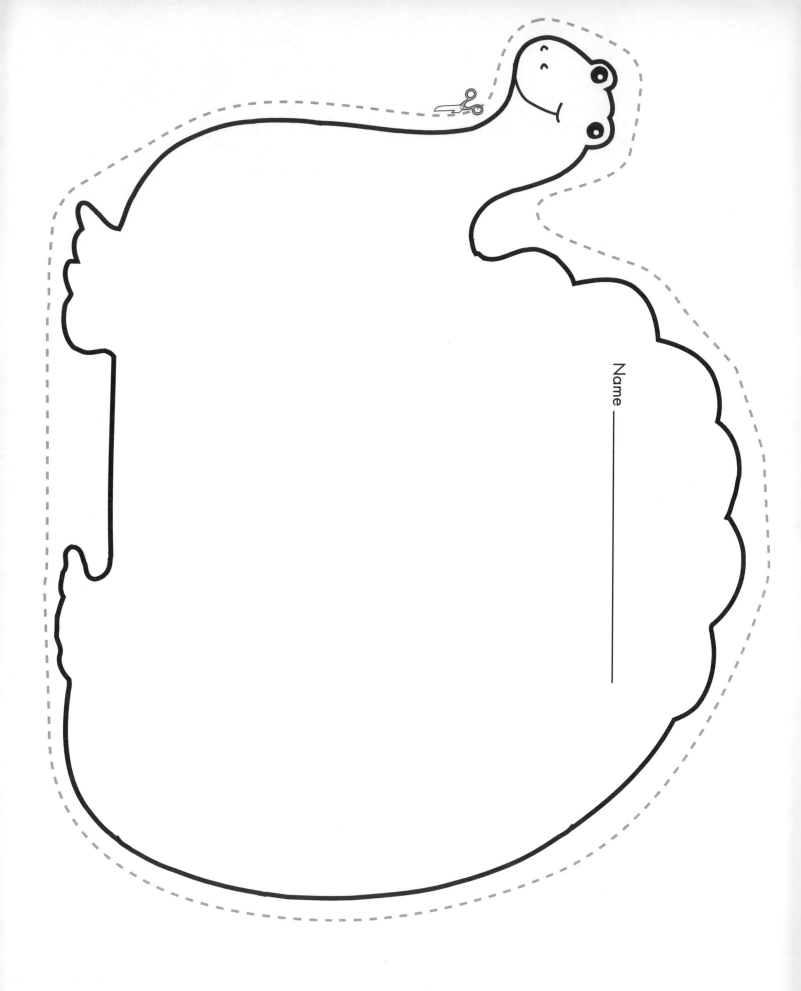

Name _____

The Ultimate Shape Book • EMC 6000 • ©2002 by Evan-Moor Corp.

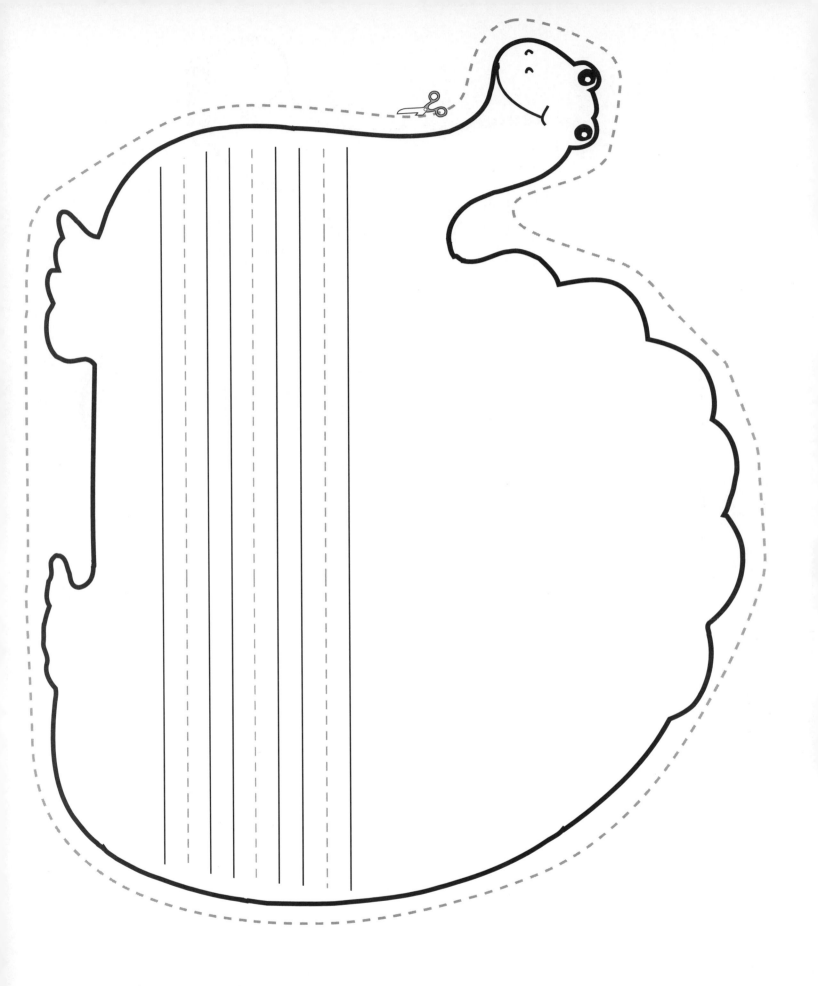

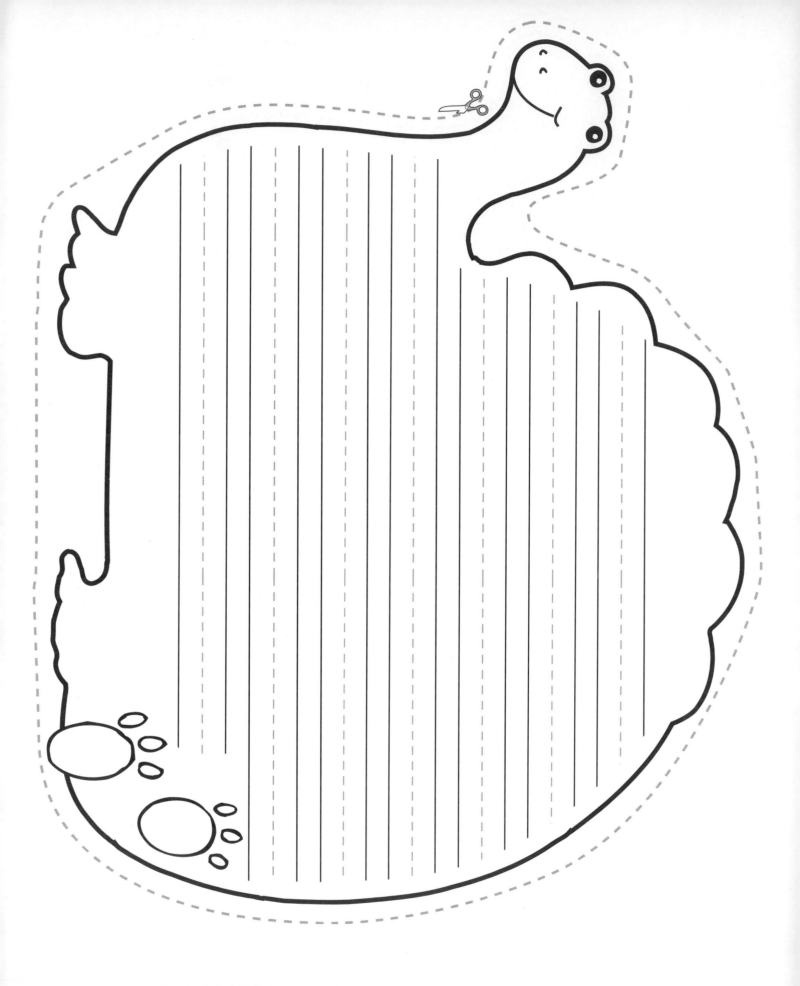

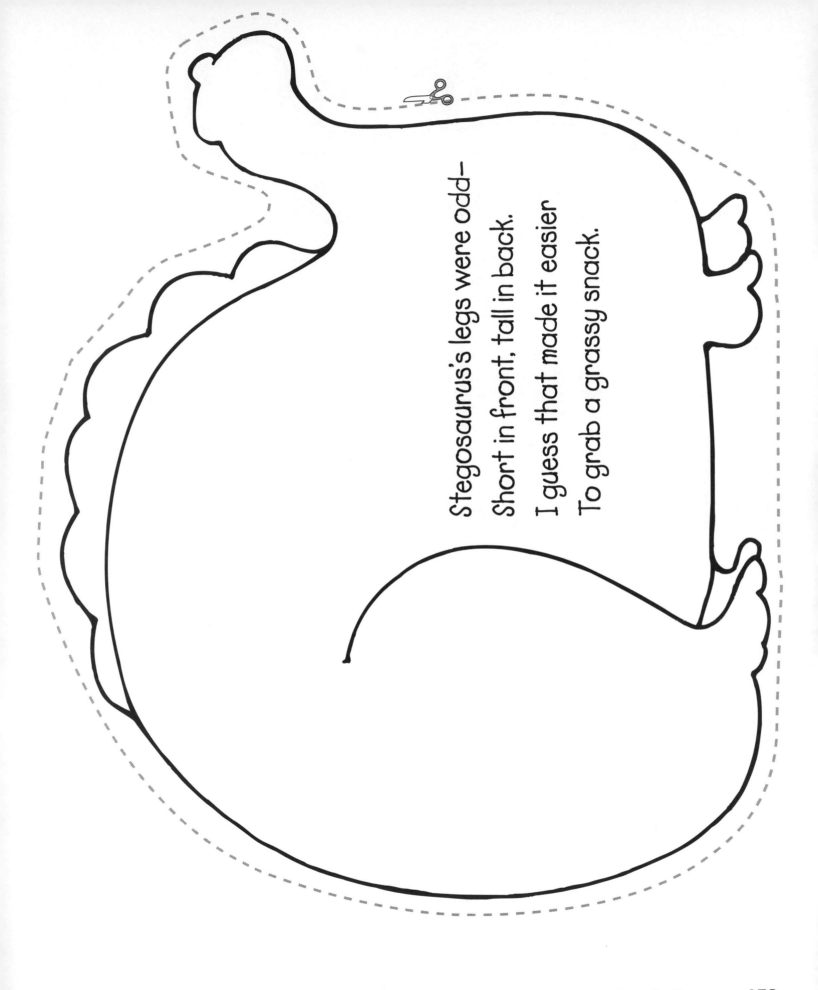

Stegosaurus's legs were odd—
Short in front, tall in back.
I guess that made it easier
To grab a grassy snack.

Basket

Literature Connections

Basket Moon by Mary Lyn Ray; Little, Brown and Company Inc., 1999.
Baskets by Meryl Doney; Franklin Watts Inc., 1998.
Basket Weaver and Catches Many Mice by Janet Gill; Alfred A. Knopf Inc., 1999.
A Birthday Basket for Tia by Pat Mora; Simon & Schuster, 1992.
Grandmother's Five Baskets by Lisa Larrabee; Roberts Rinehart Publishing, 1993.
A Sweet, Sweet Basket by Margie Willis Clary; Sandlapper Publishing Co., 1995.
The Shopping Basket by John Burningham; Candlewick Press, 1996.
Weaving a California Tradition: A Native American Basketmaker by Linda Yamane; Lerner Publications Co., 1996.

Concrete Experiences

Take a basket walk. See how many baskets you can find in your classroom, in the office, in the library, etc. List the different ways the baskets are used.

Let the Writing Begin

Emergent Writers

- **My Picnic Basket**
  Students draw a picture of the items they will take on a picnic. Then they tell about the picnic.

- **Who Is in the Basket?**
  Students draw an animal in their baskets. Then they tell who the animal is and why it is in the basket.

Beginning Writers

- **A Secret in My Basket**
  Students imagine a secret thing they might carry in a basket and draw it. Then they copy and complete the following sentences.

  I have a secret in my basket. It's a _____.

- **Off to Grandma's House**
  Students recall Red Riding Hood's basket of goodies and draw the things they would take to their grandmother's house. Then they copy and complete the sentence.

  I packed _____ for Grandmother.

Independent Writers

- **The Bottomless Basket**
  Students write a tale about a bottomless basket of bread and its owner. What happens when the basket's owner distributes the bread to hungry people?

- **A Picnic for _____**
  Students choose a storybook character and create a picnic for that character. Their story should describe what happens on the picnic.

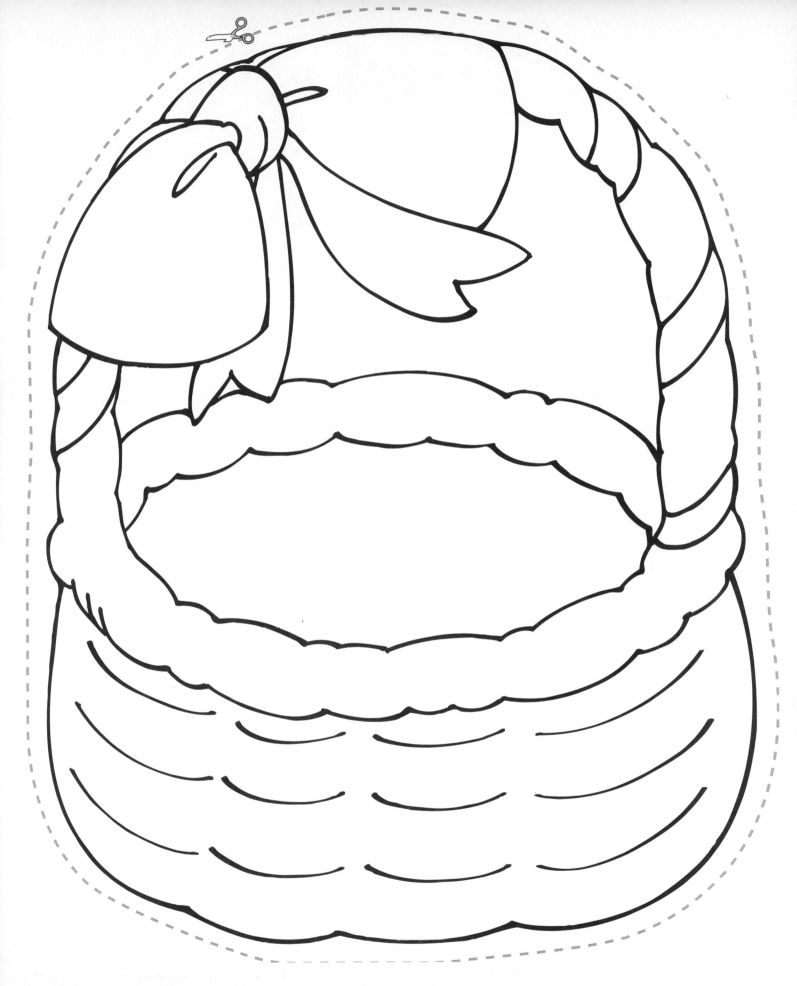

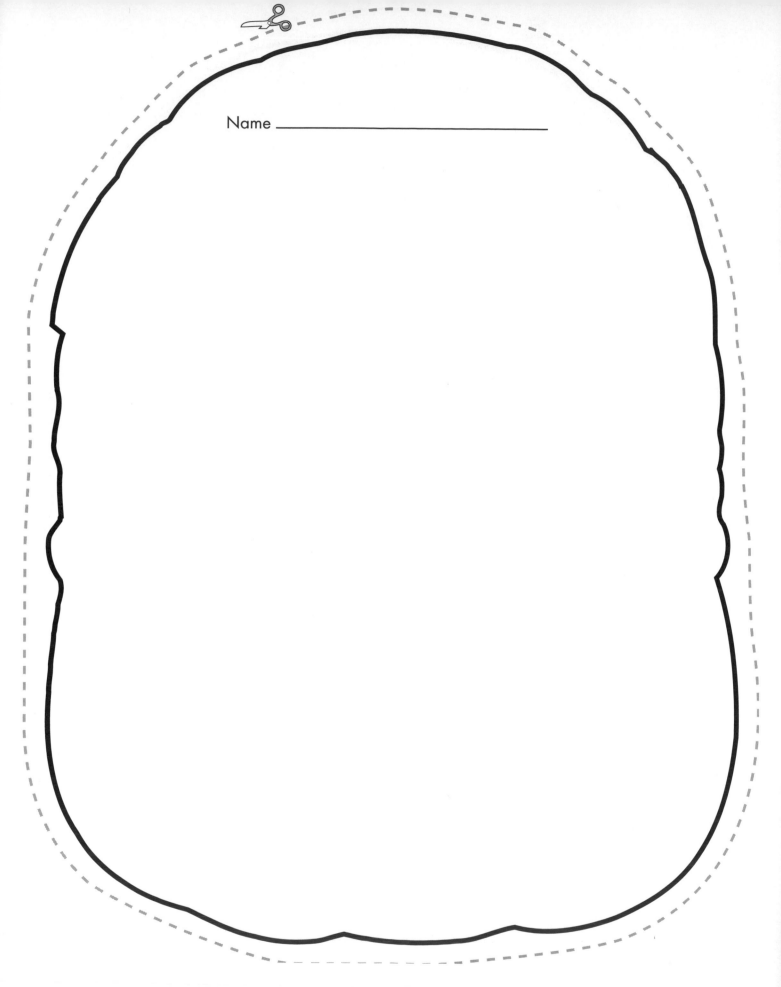

Name _____

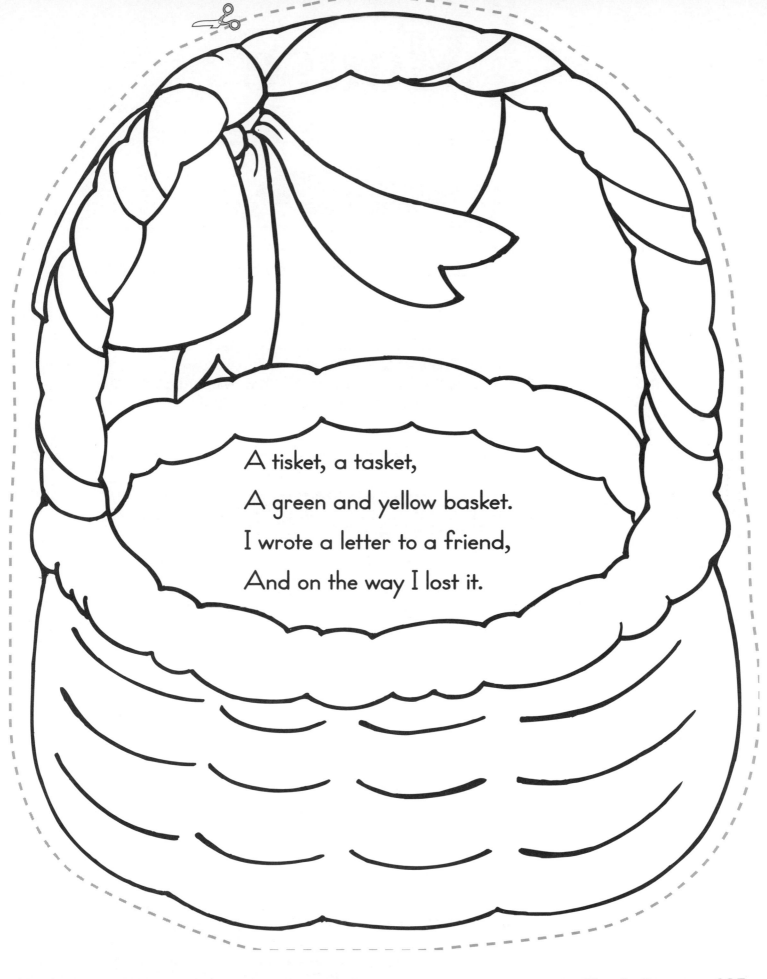

A tisket, a tasket,

A green and yellow basket.

I wrote a letter to a friend,

And on the way I lost it.

Mouse

Literature Connections

It's a Mouse! by D.M. Souza; Carolrhoda Books, Inc., 1998.

The Little Mouse, the Red Ripe Strawberry, and the Big Hungry Bear by Audrey Wood; Child's Play, 2001.

Mice by Kevin J. Holmes; Bridgestone Books, 1998.

Mouse Mess by Linnea Asplind Riley; Scholastic Trade, 1997.

Mouse Tales by Arnold Lobel; HarperCollins Children's Books, 1972.

Seven Blind Mice by Ed Young; Philomel Books, 1992.

The Story of Jumping Mouse by John Steptoe; Lothrop, Lee & Shepard Books, 1985.

Whose Mouse Are You? by Robert Kraus; Aladdin Paperbacks, 1986.

Concrete Experiences

List adjectives that describe mice—the way they look and the way they move. Read "Mice" by Rose Fyleman as a starting point.

Let the Writing Begin

Emergent Writers

- **Marching Mice**
  Students draw a line of mice marching. They should think of a place that starts with the *m* sound that the mice might march—in the mud? at the mall?

- **Nibble, Nibble, Little Mouse**
  Students draw a mouse snack and tell about what the mouse is nibbling.

Beginning Writers

- **The Country Mouse and the City Mouse**
  Students draw a mouse in the country and a mouse in the city. They copy and complete the following sentences.

  Country Mouse likes _____.
  City Mouse likes _____.
  But they both like _____.

- **I Like (or Don't Like) Mice!**
  Students draw a picture showing an experience they have had with mice and write a reason why they do or do not like mice.

Independent Writers

- **How to Get Away from a Cat**
  Students write a how-to manual for escaping from a cat, from a mouse's point of view.

- **Mice, Mice, Mice**
  In the style of Ruth Krauss's "Bears, Bears, Bears," students write a rhyming list of things mice might do.

  Mice, Mice, Mice
  chewing on ice,
  chop–sticking rice,
  checking a price,
  playing with dice,
  measuring a slice,
  adding the spice,
  Mice, Mice, Mice

Front Cover   167

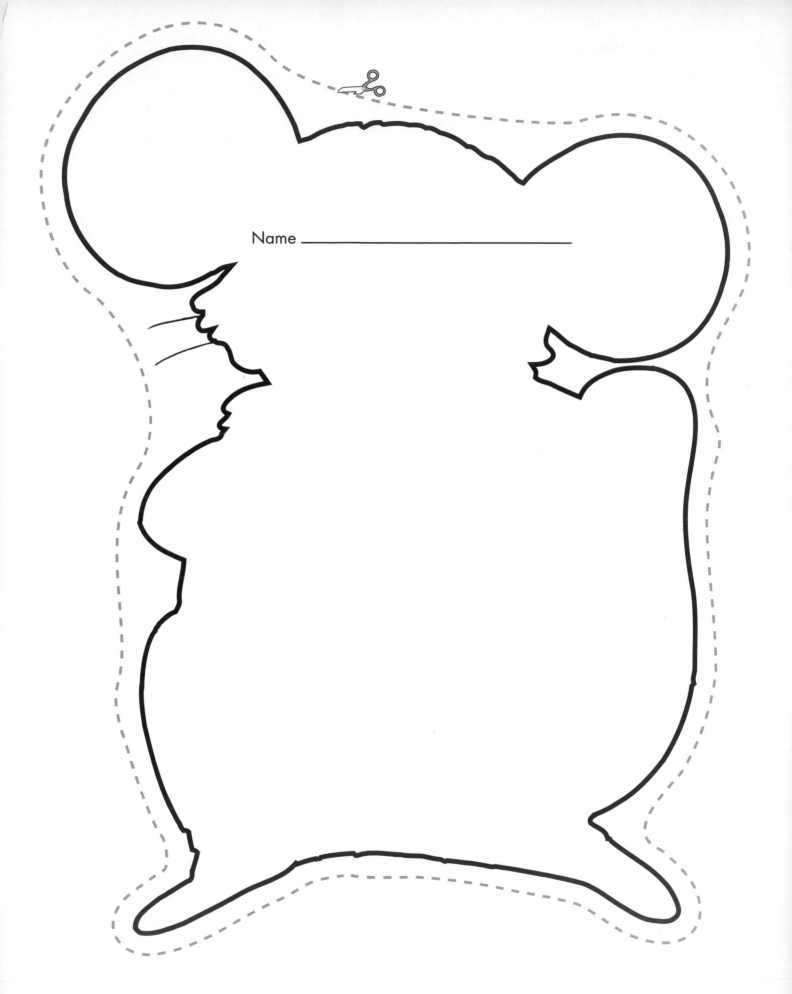

Name _____

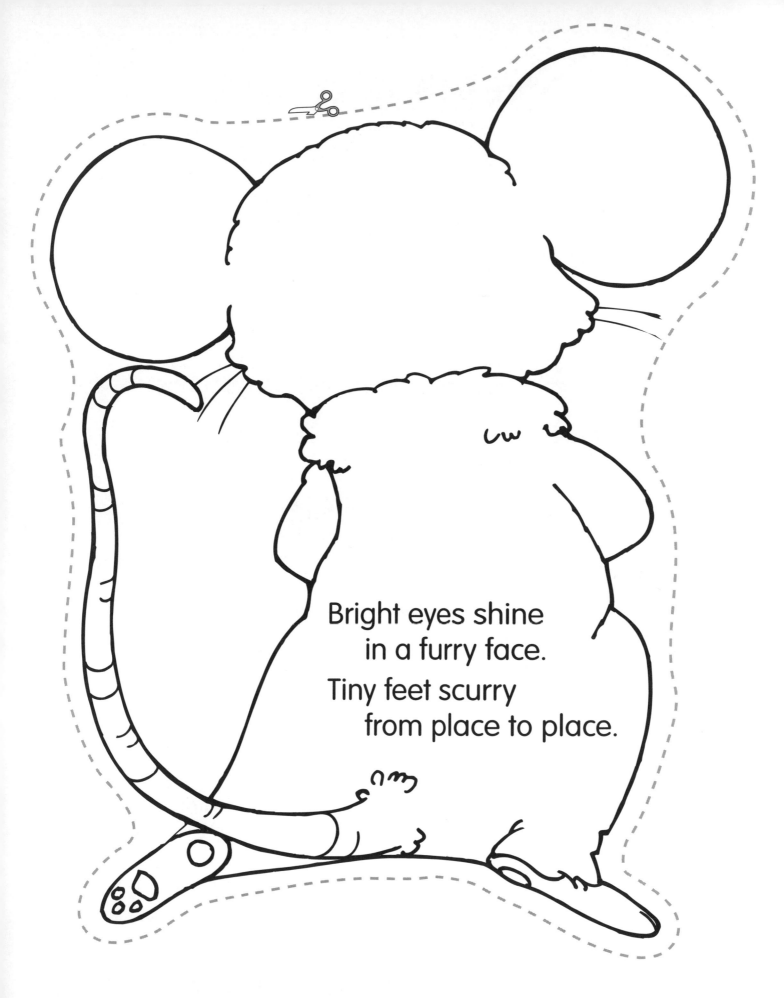

Bright eyes shine
in a furry face.
Tiny feet scurry
from place to place.

Snowman

Literature Connections

The Biggest, Best Snowman by Margery Cuyler; Scholastic, 1998.
The Black Snowman by Phil Mendez; Scholastic, 1989.
Snowballs by Lois Ehlert; Voyager Books, 1999.
Snowmen: Snow Creatures, Crafts, and Other Winter Projects by Peter Cole; Chronicle Books, 1999.
Spring Snowman by Jill Barnes; Garrett Educational Corp., 1990.
Stranger in the Woods: A Photographic Fantasy by Carl R. Sams; Carl Sams II Photography, 2000.

Concrete Experiences

If you are in an area where snow is available, bring a bucket of snow into the classroom and talk about how it looks and how it feels. Discuss what happens to snow in the sun.

Let the Writing Begin

Emerging Writers

• **A Hat for Snowman**
Snowman needs a hat. Have students draw hats for the snowman and then tell where Snowman got his hat.

• **Snowman's Friend**
Students draw a friend for Snowman and tell about what the two friends do together.

Beginning Writers

• **Snowman's Treat**
Have students draw a treat for the snowman and copy and complete the following couplet.

What does a snowman like to eat?
_____ *is his favorite treat.*

• **What a _____ Snowman!**
Students draw a series of pictures, adding one detail each time, and then write a list describing their additions.

Give the snowman a long carrot nose.
Give the snowman two tennis ball eyes. (and so on)

Independent Writers

• **The Sun Scare**
Students describe problems occurring when the sun comes out, from a snowman's point of view.

• **The Most Unusual Snowman**
Students write a newspaper report featuring a description of the most unusual snowman in the local snowman contest.

Front Cover   173

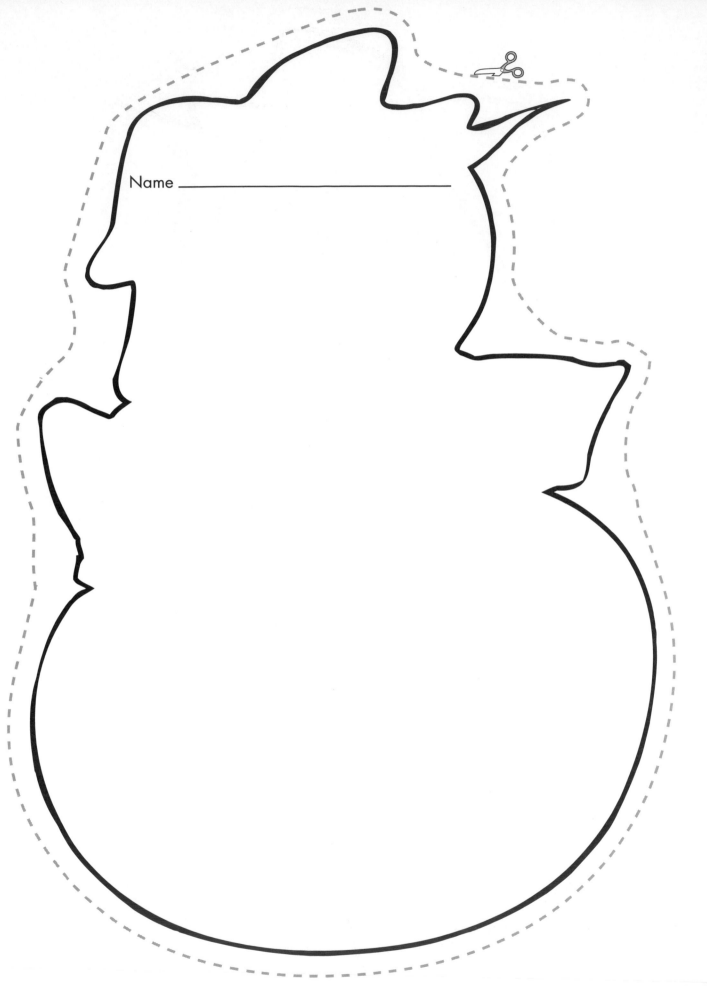

Name _____

Snowman gives an icy grin.
His hand is raised in greeting.
Why don't you invite him in?
He's definitely worth meeting.
You can share a cookie
And hot chocolate in a cup.
Then he'll have to hurry out
Before his temperature goes up.

Turtle

Literature Connections

Box Turtle at Long Pond by William T. George; Greenwillow, 1989.

How Turtle's Back Was Cracked: A Traditional Cherokee Tale retold by Gayle Ross; Dial Books for Young Readers, 1995.

Into the Sea by Brenda Z. Guiberson; Henry Holt, 2000.

Splash! by Ann Jonas; Greenwillow, 1995.

Turtle Dreams by Marion Dane Bauer; Holiday House, 1997.

What Newt Could Do for Turtle by Jonathan London; Candlewick Press, 1998.

Concrete Experiences

"Invite" a turtle to visit your classroom. Have students describe the way the turtle moves and eats.

Let the Writing Begin

Emergent Writers

• **Where Is Turtle?**
  Students draw a turtle and its surroundings. Then they tell where the turtle is. Pay close attention to position words.

• **Just Look at That Shell!**
  Students draw a turtle with an unusual shell and then describe the shell.

Beginning Writers

• **If I Were a Turtle**
  Students draw a picture showing something they would do if they were turtles, and copy and complete the sentence.

  If I were a turtle, I would _____.

• **Slow as a Turtle**
  Students think of something they do slowly. They draw themselves and turtles. Then they copy and complete the following sentences.

  I _____ slowly.
  I am as slow as a turtle.

Independent Writers

• **The Trouble with My Shell**
  Students imagine a problem a turtle might have with its shell and tell about that problem from the turtle's point of view.

• **Turtle Facts**
  Students report interesting information about turtles in a nonfiction report.

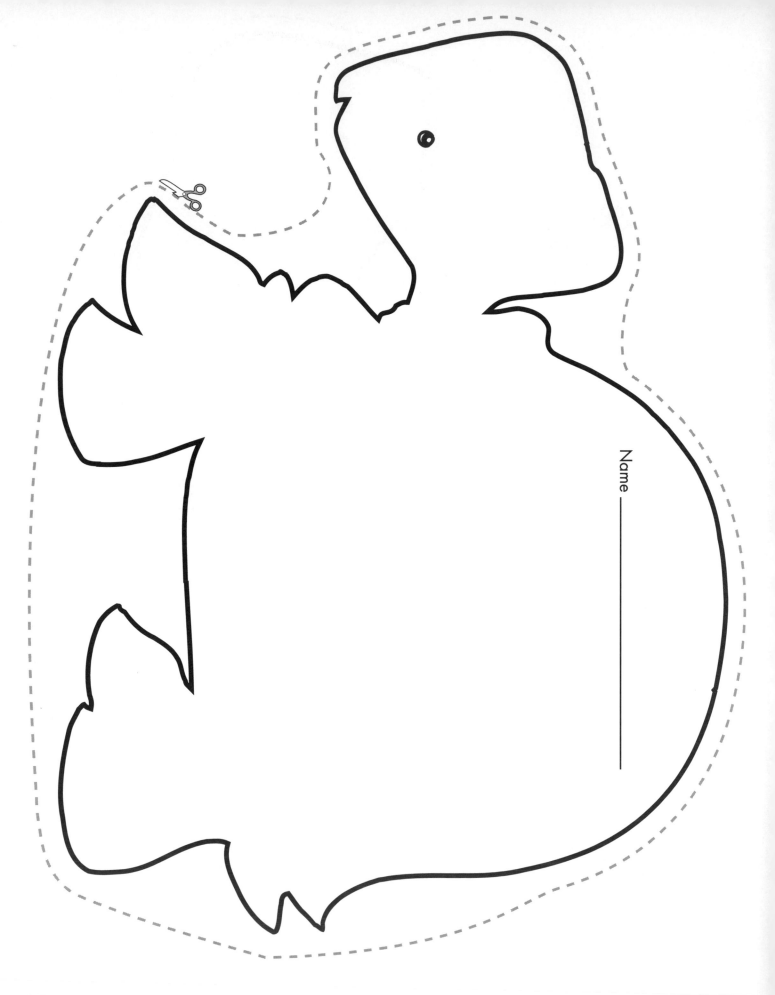

Name _____

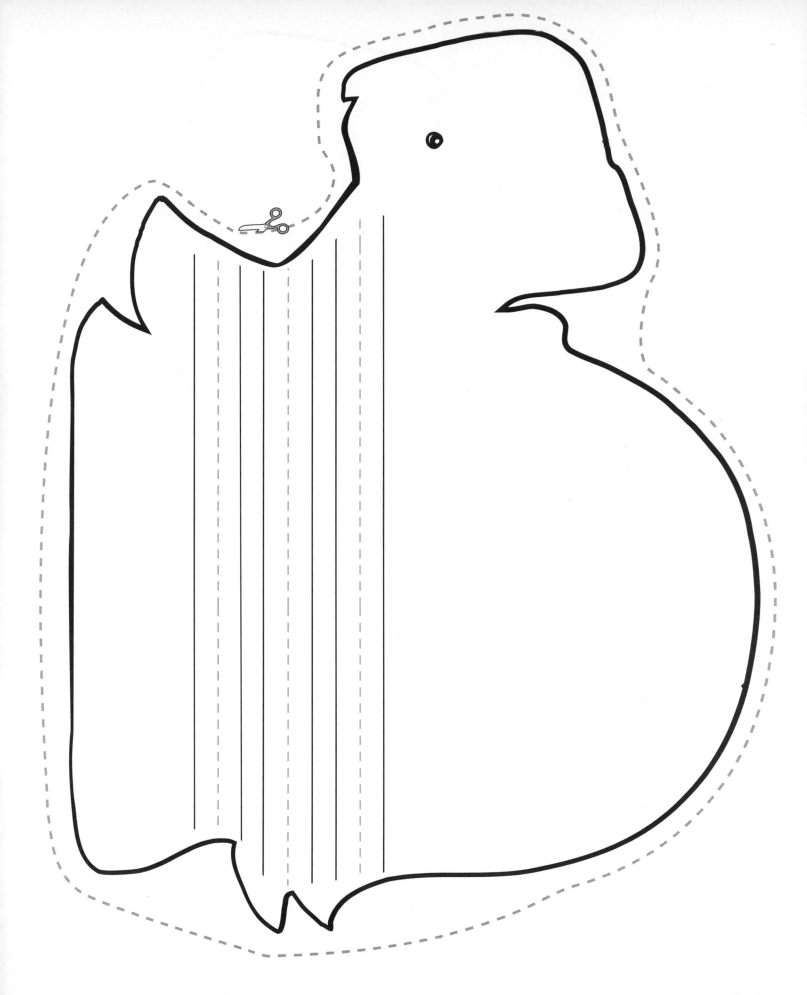

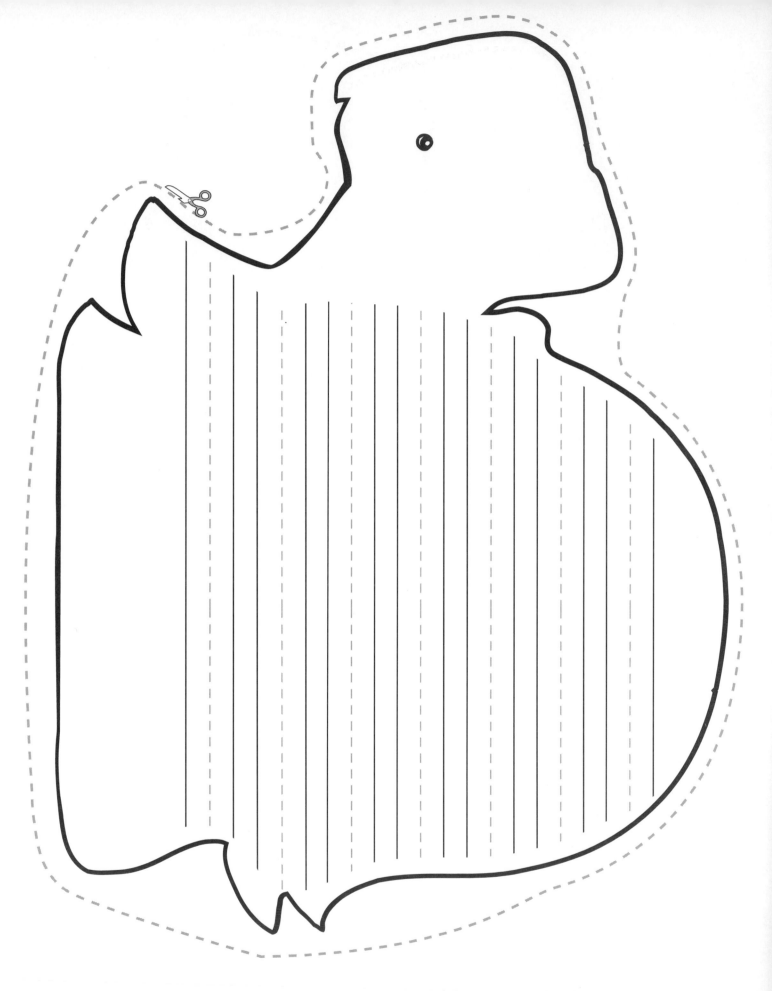

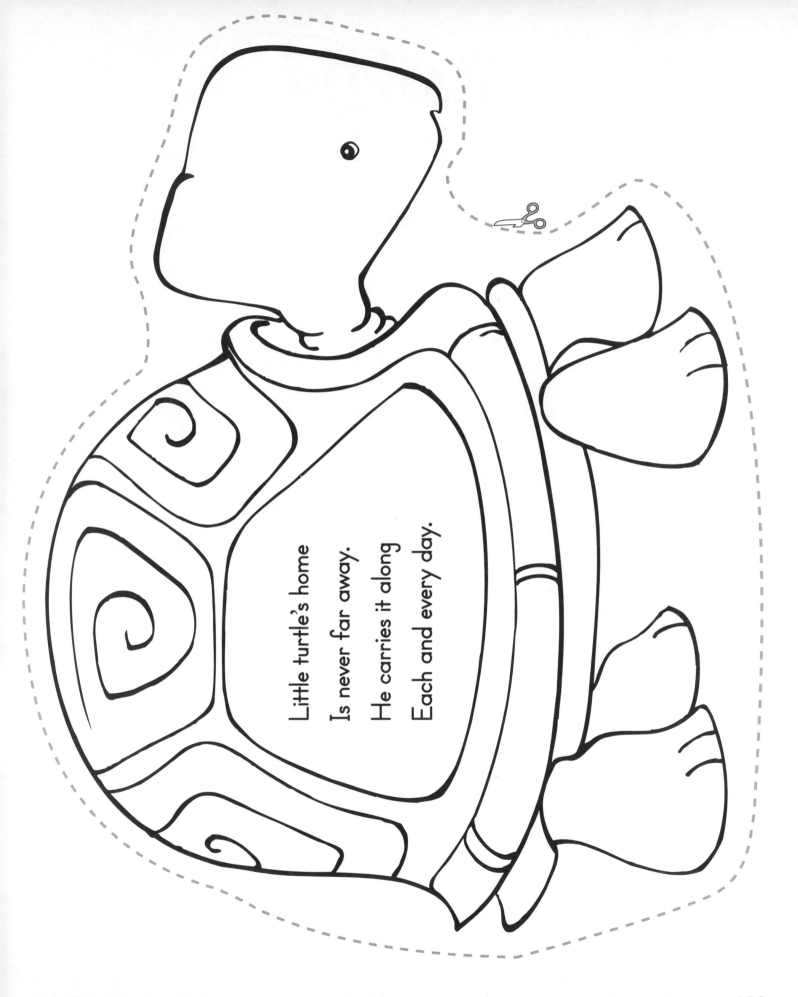

Little turtle's home
Is never far away.
He carries it along
Each and every day.

Knight

Prewriting

Literature Connections

Good Knight by Linda Rymill; Henry Holt, 1998.

In the Time of Knights: The Real-Life Story of History's Greatest Knight by Shelley Tanaka; Hyperion Books for Children, 2000.

The Knight and the Dragon by Tomie dePaola; Putnam, 1980.

Knights in Shining Armor by Gail Gibbons; Little, Brown and Company Inc., 1995.

William the Curious: Knight of the Water Lilies by Charles Santore; Random House, 1997.

Concrete Experiences

Show a picture of a suit of armor. Have students describe the armor and how it would feel to move wearing it. What are the advantages of wearing armor during a battle? What are the disadvantages?

Let the Writing Begin

Emergent Writers

• **Who's Inside?**
Students draw a picture to show who is wearing the suit of armor.

• **The Brave Knight**
Students draw pictures to show the brave deeds that knights do, and they describe those deeds.

Beginning Writers

• **Meeting a Dragon**
Students draw a picture to show what happens when the knight meets the dragon, and then copy and complete this sentence.

When the knight met the dragon _____.

• **Outside or Inside**
Students imagine how a knight looks from the outside and how it might feel inside the armor. Then they draw the inside version, and copy and complete the following sentences.

On the outside, the knight looks _____.
On the inside, the knight feels _____.

Independent Writers

• **What a Knight Needs to Know**
Students write five important things that a knight needs to know and explain why it is important to know each thing.

• **Stuck!**
Describe the problems a knight has when he becomes stuck in his suit of armor.

Front Cover   185

Name _____

The Ultimate Shape Book • EMC 6000 • ©2002 by Evan-Moor Corp

Independent Writer

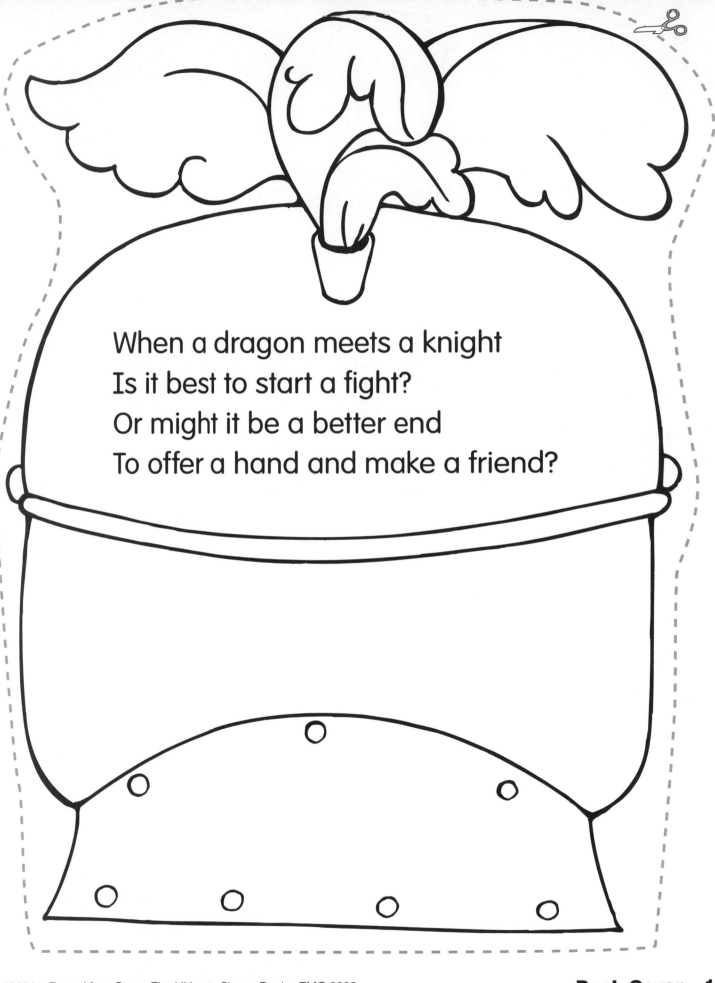

When a dragon meets a knight
Is it best to start a fight?
Or might it be a better end
To offer a hand and make a friend?

Bunny

Literature Connections

Blue Rabbit and Friends by Christopher Wormell; Phyllis Fogelman Books, 2000.
Bunny Money by Rosemary Wells; Puffin, 2000.
Foolish Rabbit's Big Mistake by Rafe Martin; Putnam, 1985.
Just Enough Carrots by Stuart J. Murphy; HarperCollins Publishers, 1997.
Rabbit Food by Susanna Gretz; Candlewick Press, 1999.
Who's in Rabbit's House?: A Masai Tale retold by Verna Aardema; Dial Books for Young Readers, 1979.

Concrete Experiences

A stuffed bunny will help students list special attributes of a bunny. Create a word bank of bunny words.

Let the Writing Begin

Emergent Writers

- **Hopping Down the Bunny Trail**
  Where did Bunny hop? Have students draw a destination and then tell about their drawings.

- **Bunny's Bouquet**
  Students draw Bunny with a bouquet of flowers, and tell where Bunny picked the flowers and what she will do with them.

Beginning Writers

- **Carrot Chef**
  Students draw Bunny cooking in a kitchen filled with carrots. Then they copy and complete this poem.

  Bunny baked a carrot pie.
  It was very sweet.
  Then he baked a carrot

  _____

  For all his friends to eat!

- **If I Had Bunny Ears...**
  Students draw themselves with bunny ears. Then they copy and complete the following sentence.

  If I had bunny ears, I would
  _____.

Independent Writers

- **100 Carrots!**
  Students write a story to tell how Bunny got 100 carrots and what he would do with them.

- **How Bunny Got a Fluffy Tail**
  Students write a tale explaining how Bunny got a fluffy tail.

Name _____

Bunny twitches its nose.
Bunny flicks its long ears.
Bunny sees a carrot.
The carrot disappears!

Squirrel

Literature Connections

Flying Squirrels by Lynn M. Stone; Rourke Corp., 1993.
Heart to Heart by George Shannon; Houghton Mifflin Company, 1995.
How Chipmunk Got His Stripes: A Tale of Bragging and Teasing as told by Joseph Bruchac & James Bruchac; Dial Books for Young Readers, 2001.
Maple Moon by Connie Brummel Crook; Stoddart Kids, 1998.
Nuts to You! by Lois Ehlert; Harcourt Brace & Co., 1993.
Squirrels and Chipmunks by Allan Fowler; Children's Press, 1997.

Concrete Experiences

Compare a squirrel to other tree-living animals. Read books to gather information about squirrels. If you live in an area where squirrels are common, try to observe a real squirrel.

Let the Writing Begin

Emergent Writers

- **Squirrel's Home**
  Students draw a home for a squirrel and then tell about it.

- **Nuts and Berries**
  Students draw a set of nuts and a set of berries that Squirrel might have gathered. They write a number sentence that describes the sets. Then they tell about the sets.

Beginning Writers

- **Stop, Thief**
  Students draw a picture of a squirrel escaping up a tree with a stolen item. Then they copy and complete the couplet.

  Little squirrel ran up the tree
  To hide a _____ he took
  from me.

- **Tales of Tails**
  Students draw animals with special tails. Then they copy and complete the sentences.

  A squirrel has a big, fluffy tail.
  A _____ has a _____ tail.
  (for each animal)

Independent Writers

- **Escape from the Hawk**
  Students write an adventure for a squirrel trying to escape from a hungry hawk.

- **"Preparing for Winter" by S. Squirrel**
  Students write a guide for preparing for winter from a squirrel's viewpoint.

Front Cover 197

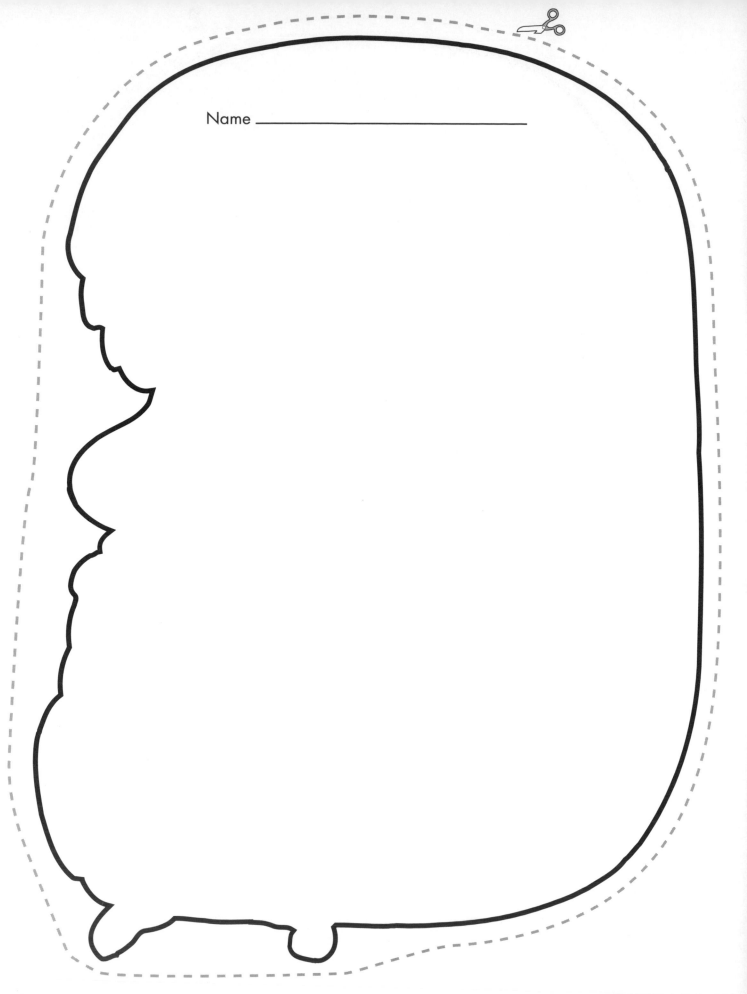

Name _____

The Ultimate Shape Book • EMC 6000 • ©2002 by Evan-Moor Corp.

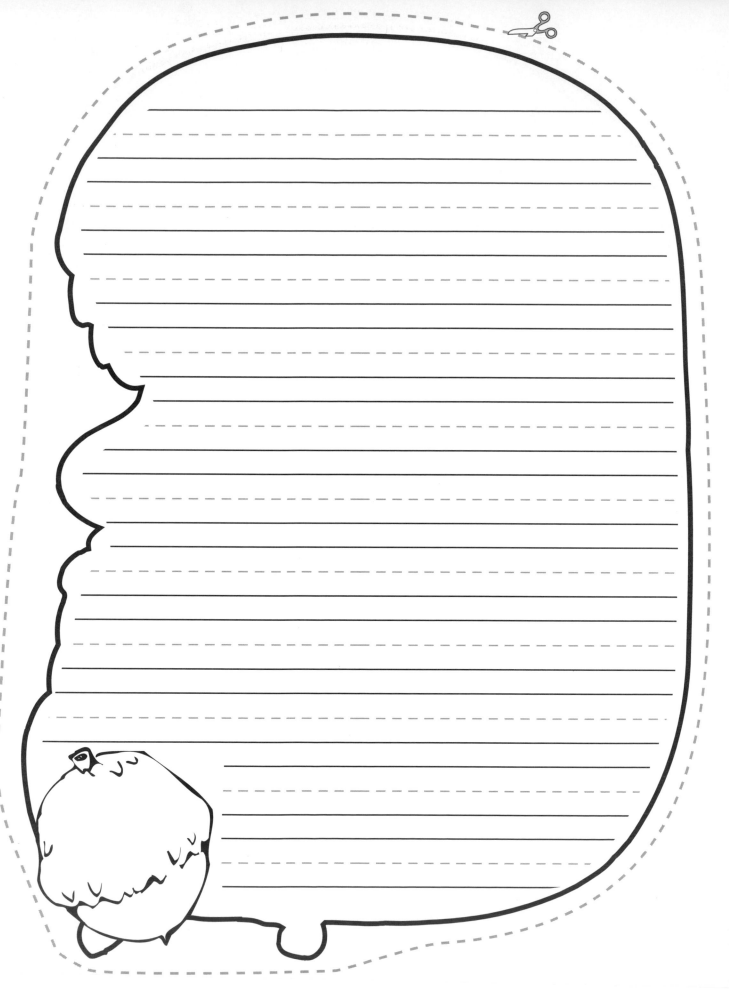

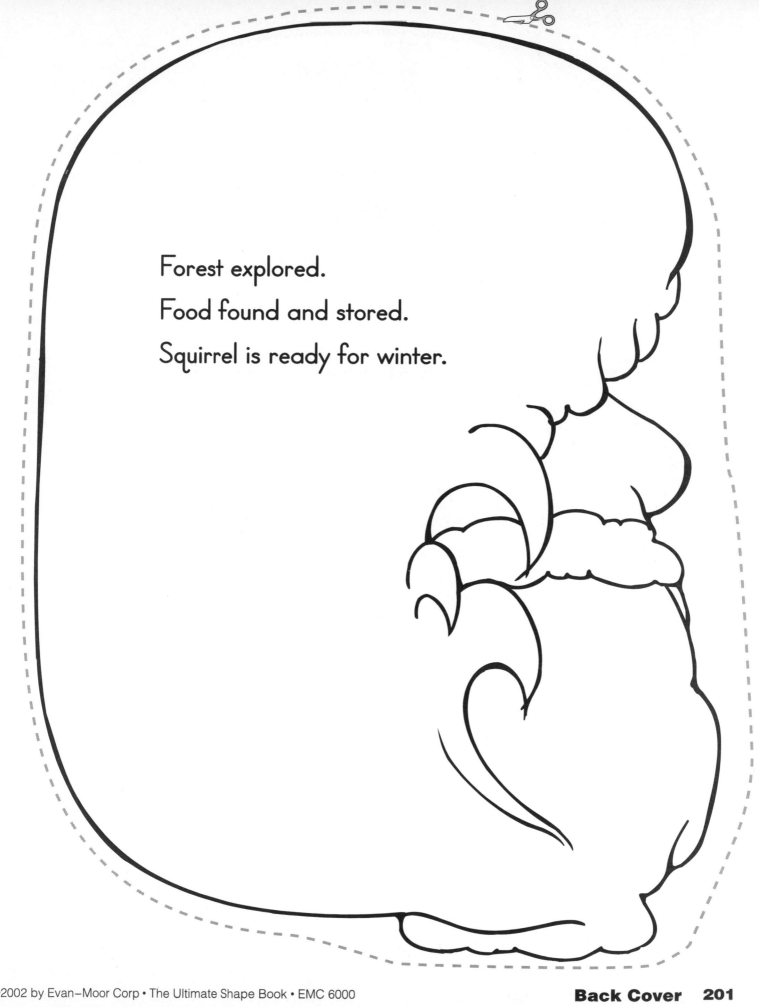

Forest explored.

Food found and stored.

Squirrel is ready for winter.

Tree

Prewriting

Literature Connections

Animals in Trees by Moira Butterfield; Raintree/Steck-Vaughn, 2000.

The Ghost-Eye Tree by Bill Martin, Jr. and John Archambault; Henry Holt, 1985.

The Magic Tree: A Folktale from Nigeria by T. Obinkaram Echewa; Morrow Junior Books, 1999.

Night Tree by Eve Bunting; Harcourt Brace & Co., 1991.

Someday a Tree by Eve Bunting; Clarion Books, 1993.

A Tree for Me by Nancy Van Laan; Knopf, 2000.

Concrete Experiences

Observe a tree near your classroom over a period of several weeks. How does the tree change? How does the tree stay the same? Have students draw the tree each time they make an observation.

Let the Writing Begin

Emergent Writers

- **My Home in a Tree**
  Students draw something that lives in a tree and then tell about the thing.

- **Gifts from a Tree**
  Students draw things that they get from trees and explain how they use each thing. (fruit, wood, paper, shade, etc.)

Beginning Writers

- **An _____ Tree**
  Students draw something growing in a tree. (The items may be something that would actually grow on a tree or something fanciful.) Then they copy and complete the couplet.

  Take a look and you will see _____ growing on my tree.

- **The Seasons of an Apple Tree**
  Students draw an apple tree in spring, summer, fall, and winter. They copy and complete a sentence for each tree.

  In the _____ the apple tree _____.

Independent Writers

- **Woodsman, Spare That Tree**
  Students write a persuasive argument for preserving a tree.

- **My View**
  Students write an observation from a tree's viewpoint about everyday events on the ground below.

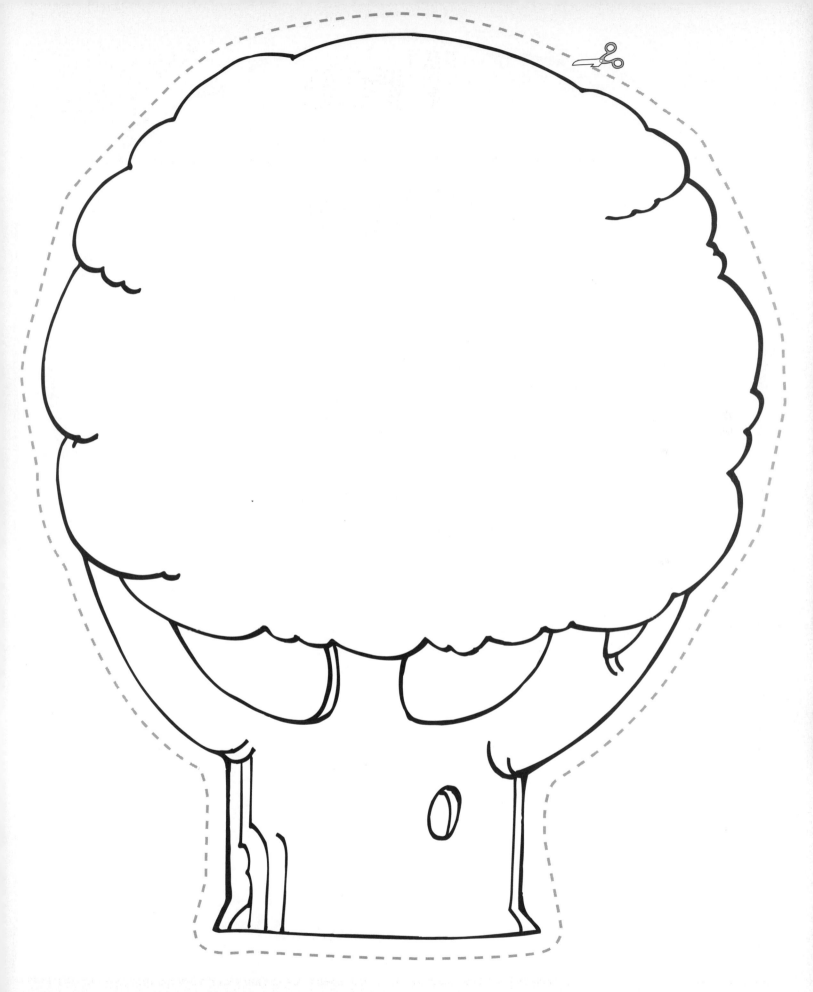

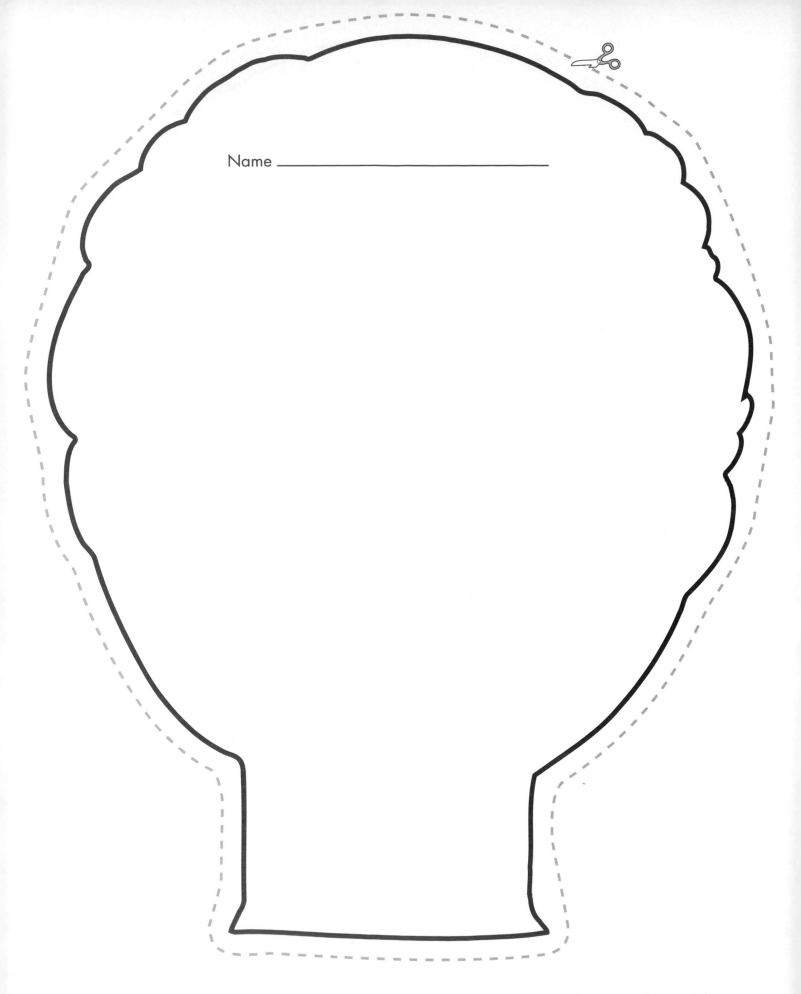

Name _____

The Ultimate Shape Book • EMC 6000 • ©2002 by Evan-Moor Corp

In the wind I bend and sway,
Whispering secrets all the day.

Ship

Literature Connections

Clipper Ship by Thomas P. Lewis; HarperTrophy, 1992.

The Lady with the Ship on Her Head by Deborah Nourse Lattimore; Harcourt Brace & Co., 1990.

Loud Emily by Alexis O'Neill; Simon & Schuster, 1998.

The Mary Celeste: An Unsolved Mystery from History by Jane Yolen et al.; Simon & Schuster, 1999.

On the Mayflower: Voyage of the Ship's Apprentice and a Passenger Girl by Kate Waters; Scholastic, 1996.

Trapped by the Ice!: Shackleton's Amazing Antarctic Adventure by Michael McCurdy; Walker and Co., 1997.

Concrete Experiences

Imagine an ocean voyage aboard a small ship like the one on the cover of this book. Whether you are studying Columbus, one of the pilgrims, or an explorer searching for new lands, your understanding of the dangers will increase as you think about the size of the ship in relationship to the vast ocean.

Let the Writing Begin

Emergent Writers

• **What I Would Take**
Explain how limited space on the small ship was, and that only the most important items could be taken. Students draw one possession that they would have taken on their journey. Provide time for them to share the pictures and explain why the item was chosen.

• **A Sailing Ship**
Students draw themselves aboard the ship and tell about a journey they take.

Beginning Writers

• **Across the Sea**
Students draw a picture of the ship's destination. Then they copy and complete the poem.

My sailing ship went across the sea.
It carried _____, and it carried me.

• **_____'s Journey**
Students imagine they are sailing to a faraway land. They draw a picture of the voyage and list three things that happened on the trip.

Independent Writers

• **A Stowaway**
Students write a story about a stowaway on a historic voyage. They relate facts about the voyage through the stowaway's observations.

• **Storm at Sea**
Students describe a storm at sea from the viewpoint of a ship's captain.

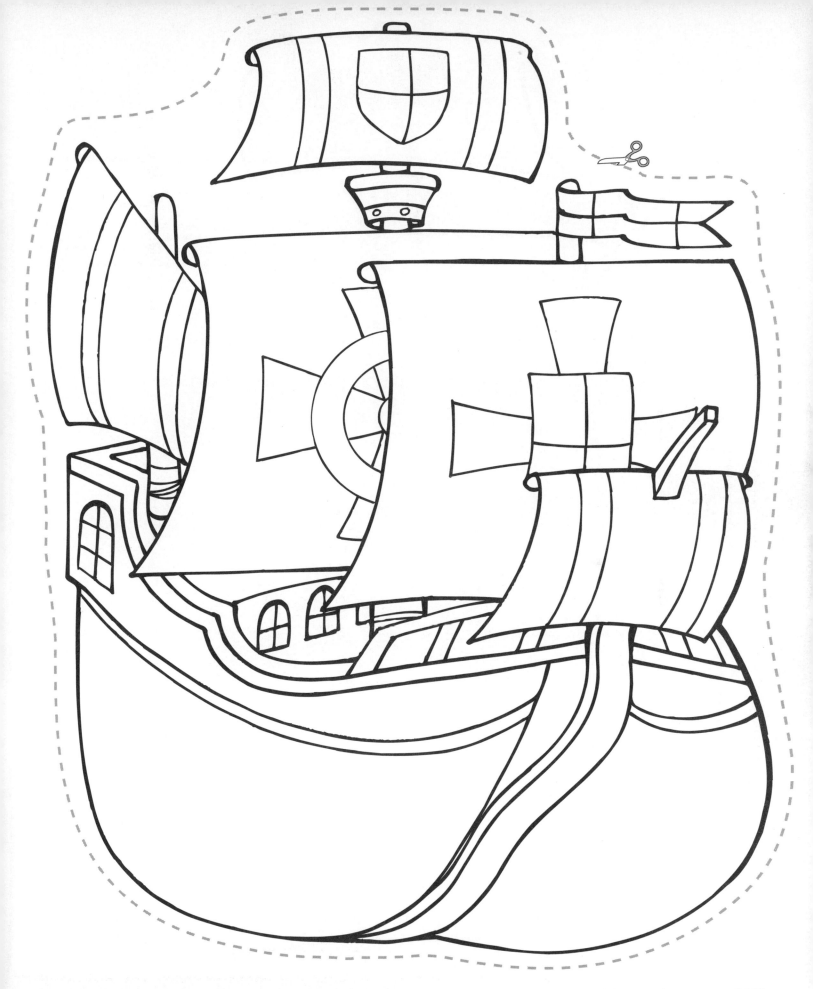

Front Cover 209

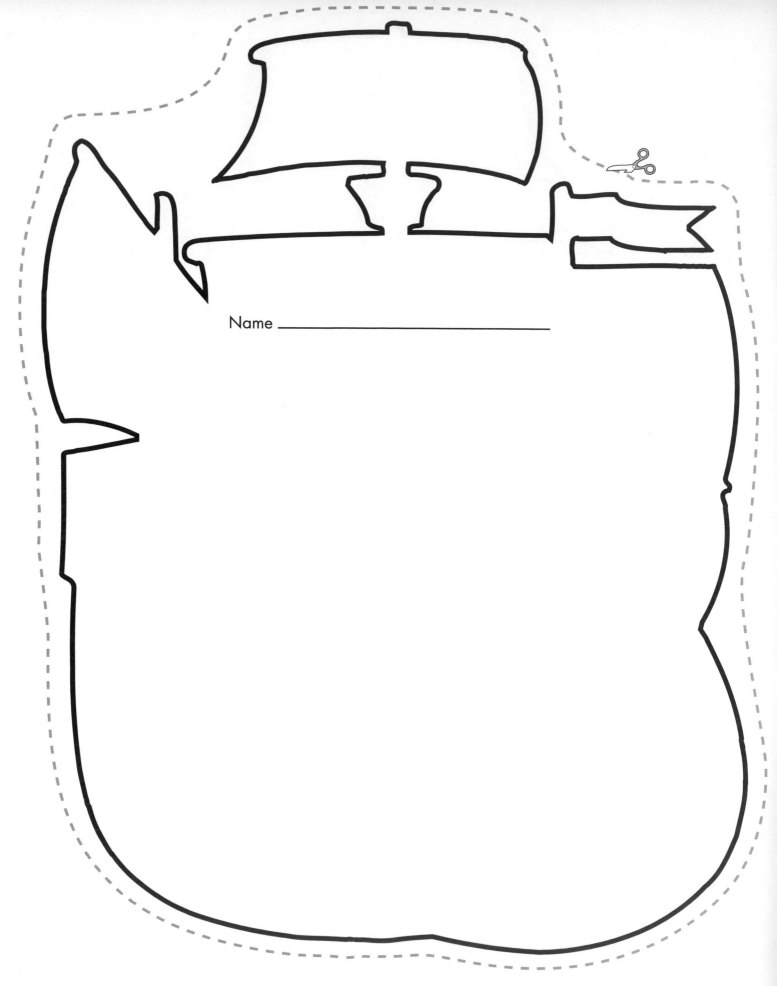

Name _____

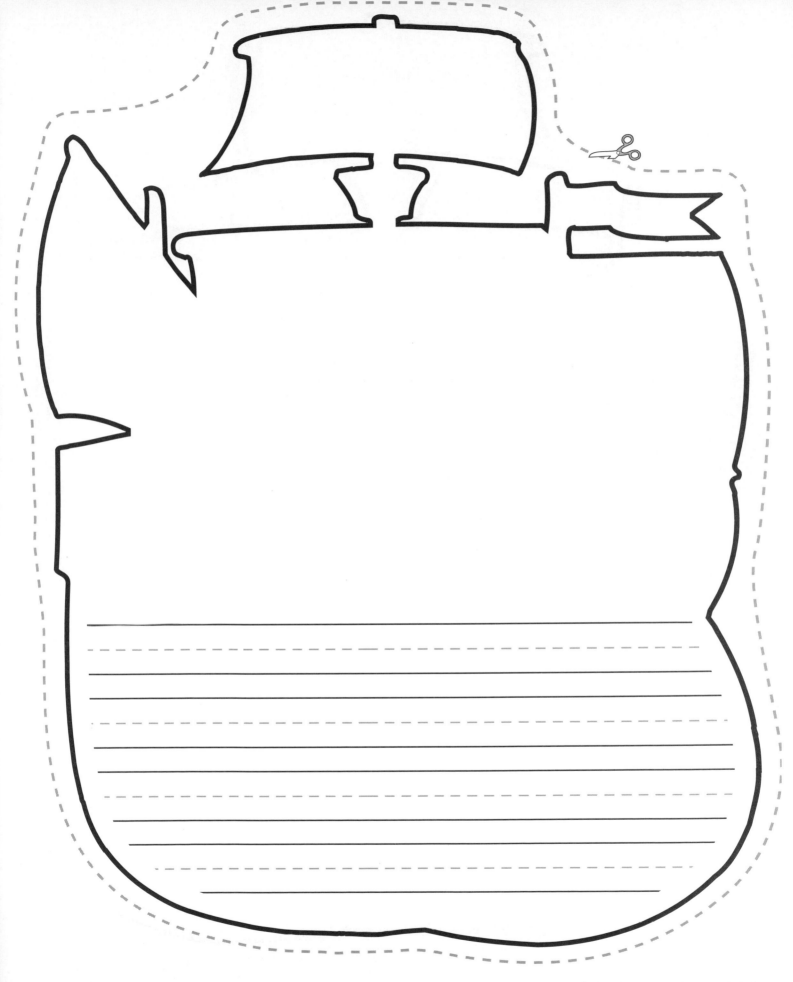

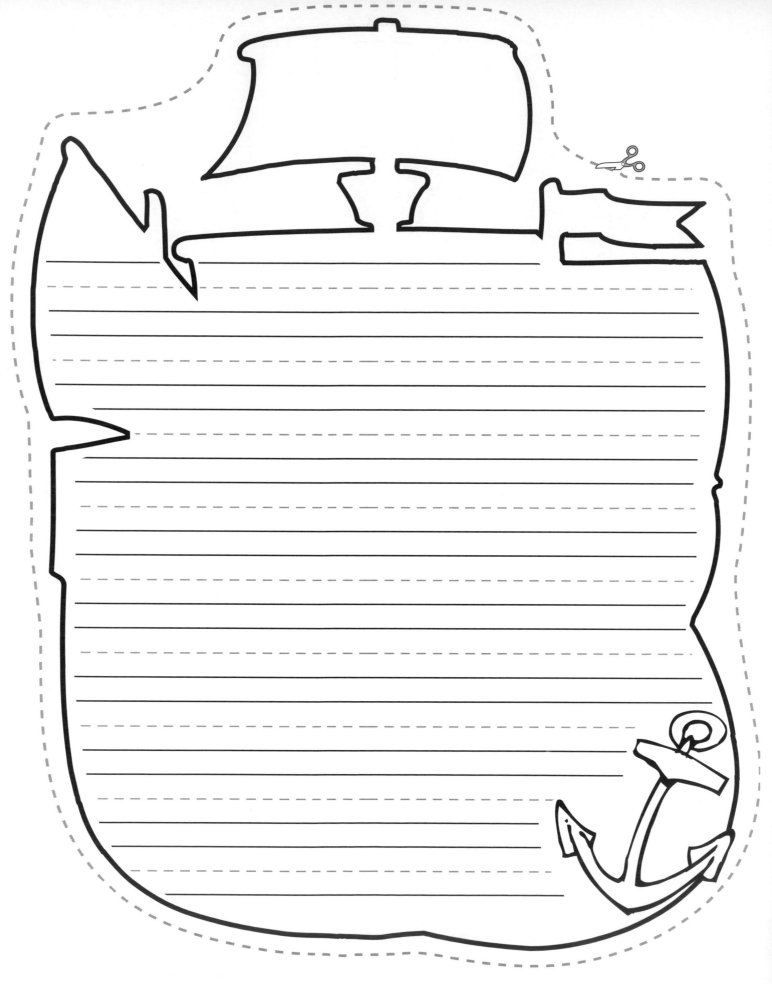

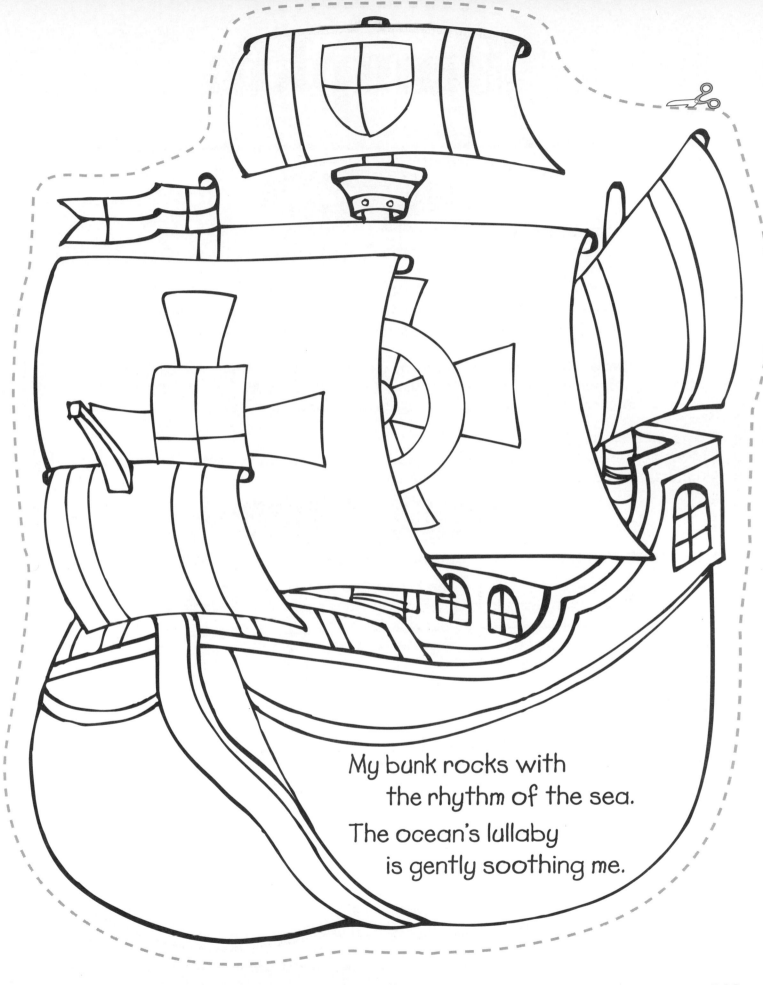

My bunk rocks with
the rhythm of the sea.
The ocean's lullaby
is gently soothing me.

Pumpkin

Literature Connections

Albert's Halloween: The Case of the Stolen Pumpkins by Leslie Tryon; Atheneum Books for Young Readers, 1998.

The Biggest Pumpkin Ever by Steven Kroll; Scholastic, 1984.

Jeb Scarecrow's Pumpkin Patch by Jana Dillon; Houghton Mifflin Company, 1992.

Kid's Pumpkin Projects: Planting and Harvest Fun by Deanna F. Cook; Williamson Publishing Co., 1998.

Pumpkin Circle: The Story of a Garden by George Levenson; Tricycle Press, 1999.

Pumpkin, Pumpkin by Jeanne Titherington; Greenwillow, 1986.

Pumpkin Soup by Helen Cooper; Farrar, Straus & Giroux Inc., 1999.

Concrete Experiences

Measure and weigh a real pumpkin. Count the seeds as you hollow out the inside. Record numbers and words on a class chart for easy reference.

Let the Writing Begin

Emergent Writers

- **A Pumpkin Smile**
  Students draw a pumpkin face and add a smile by gluing real seeds in place. They tell what would make a pumpkin smile.

- **Five Little Pumpkins**
  Students draw and number five pumpkins. Then they recite "Five Little Pumpkins." (See back cover on page 219.)

Beginning Writers

- **The Magic Pumpkin**
  If you rub the magic pumpkin, your wish will come true. Students draw what they would wish for, and copy and complete the following sentences.

  I rubbed the magic pumpkin. It felt _____. Poof! _____. My wish came true.

- **The Best Pumpkin in the Patch**
  Students draw a picture of an ideal pumpkin and then write to describe the best pumpkin in the patch.

  My pumpkin is _____. It's the best pumpkin in the patch.

Independent Writers

- **How to Make a Jack-O'-Lantern**
  Students write simple and complete directions for making a jack-o'-lantern.

- **The Last Pumpkin**
  Students write a story about the last pumpkin left at the pumpkin patch from the pumpkin's point of view.

216

Front Cover   **215**

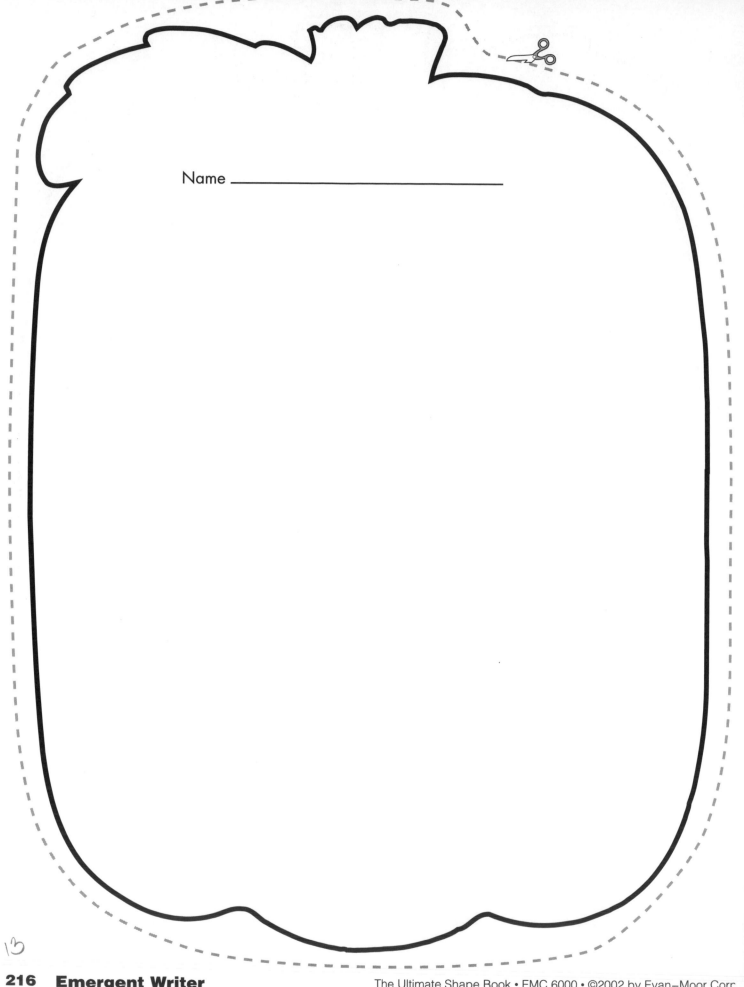

Name _____

13

Five little pumpkins sitting on a gate.

The first one said, "Oh my, it's getting late."

The second one said, "There are witches in the air."

The third one said, "Oh, I don't care."

The fourth one said, "Let's run and run and run."

The fifth one said, "Isn't Halloween fun!"

Then "ooooooo" went the wind, and out went the light,

And the five little pumpkins ran fast out of sight.

Cornucopia

Prewriting

Literature Connections

Albert's Thanksgiving by Leslie Tryon; Atheneum Books for Young Readers, 1994.

Alligator Arrived with Apples: A Potluck Alphabet Feast by Crescent Dragonwagon; Aladdin Paperbacks, 1987.

Gracias, The Thanksgiving Turkey by Joy Cowley; Scholastic, 1996.

A Pioneer Thanksgiving: A Story of Harvest Celebrations in 1841 by Barbara Greenwood; Kids Can Press, 1999.

A Strawbeater's Thanksgiving by Irene Smalls; Little, Brown and Company Inc., 1998.

Thanksgiving Day by Anne Rockwell; HarperCollins Publishers, 1999.

Concrete Experiences

Bring a cornucopia to class. Talk with students about where they have seen cornucopias and what was inside. Explain the symbolism associated with the cornucopia.

Let the Writing Begin

Emergent Writers

- **I'm Thankful**
  Students draw something they are thankful for. Provide time to share the drawings.

- **Harvest Time**
  Discuss the idea of harvest and have students draw vegetables and fruits that might be a part of a harvest.

Beginning Writers

- **A Good Harvest**
  Students draw sets of 1, 2, 3, 4, and 5 objects appropriate to a harvest. Then they copy and complete these sentences.

  In my cornucopia I have 1 _____, 2 _____, 3 _____, 4 _____, and 5 _____. What a good harvest!

- **I Give Thanks**
  Students draw two things they are thankful for. Then they copy and complete the sentence for each item.

  I give thanks for_____.

Independent Writers

- **A Thanksgiving Blessing**
  Students write a factual account of a positive thing that has happened to them for which they are grateful.

- **The Magical Cornucopia**
  Imagine a cornucopia that spills only goodness. Students write a tale about who owns such a cornucopia and what good deeds the owner is able to do.

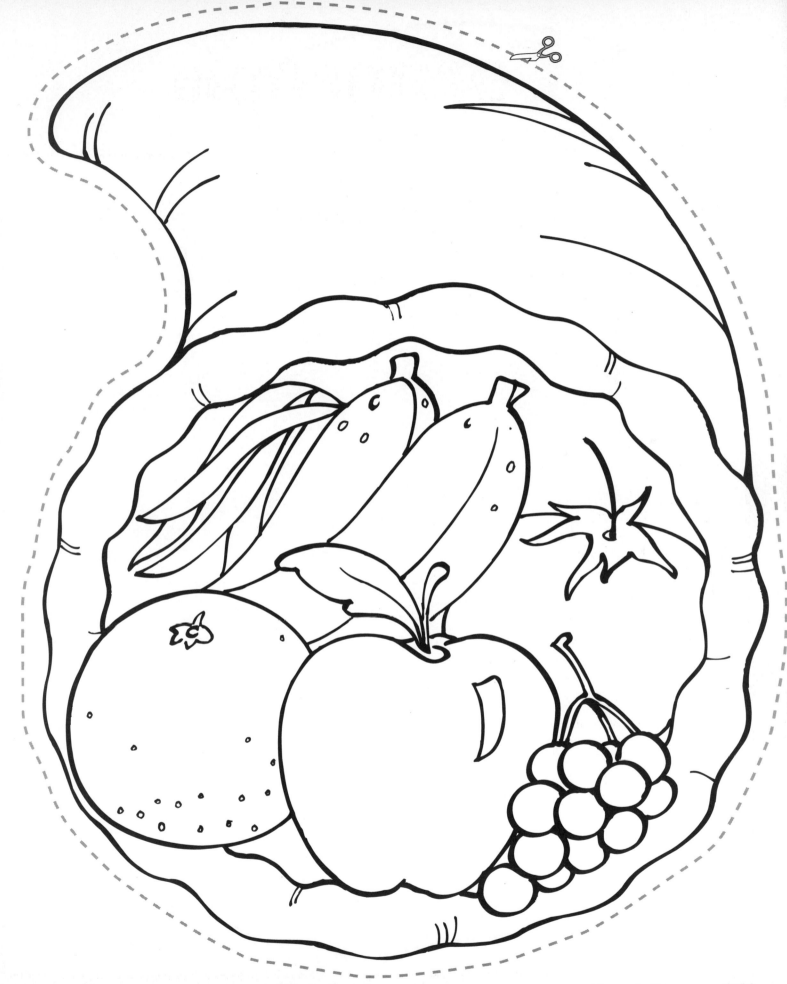

13

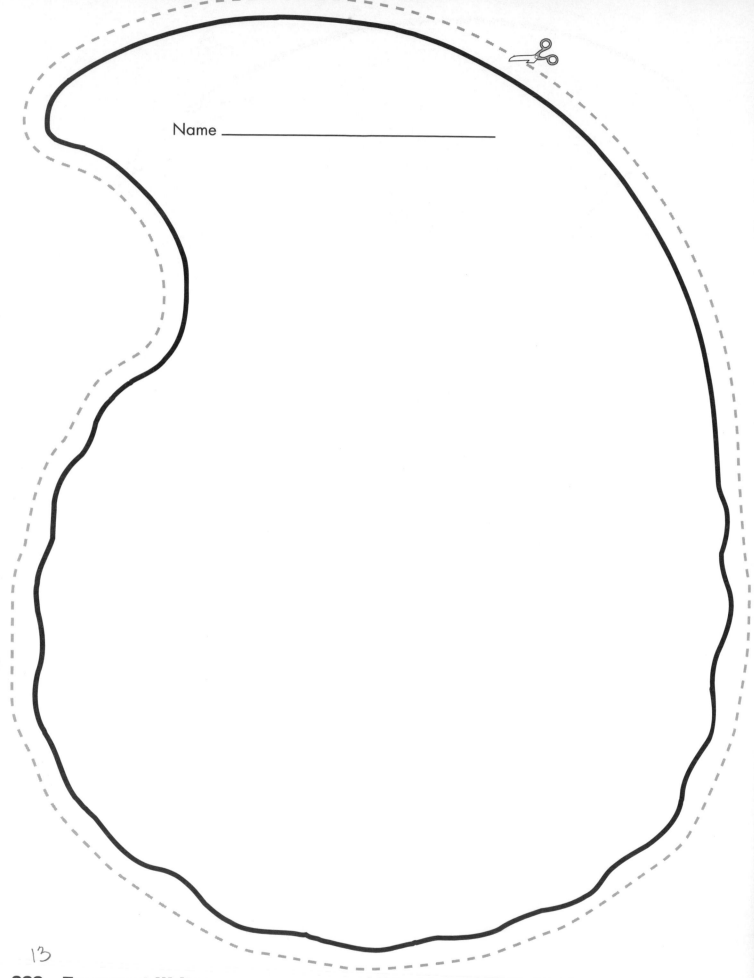

Name _____

13

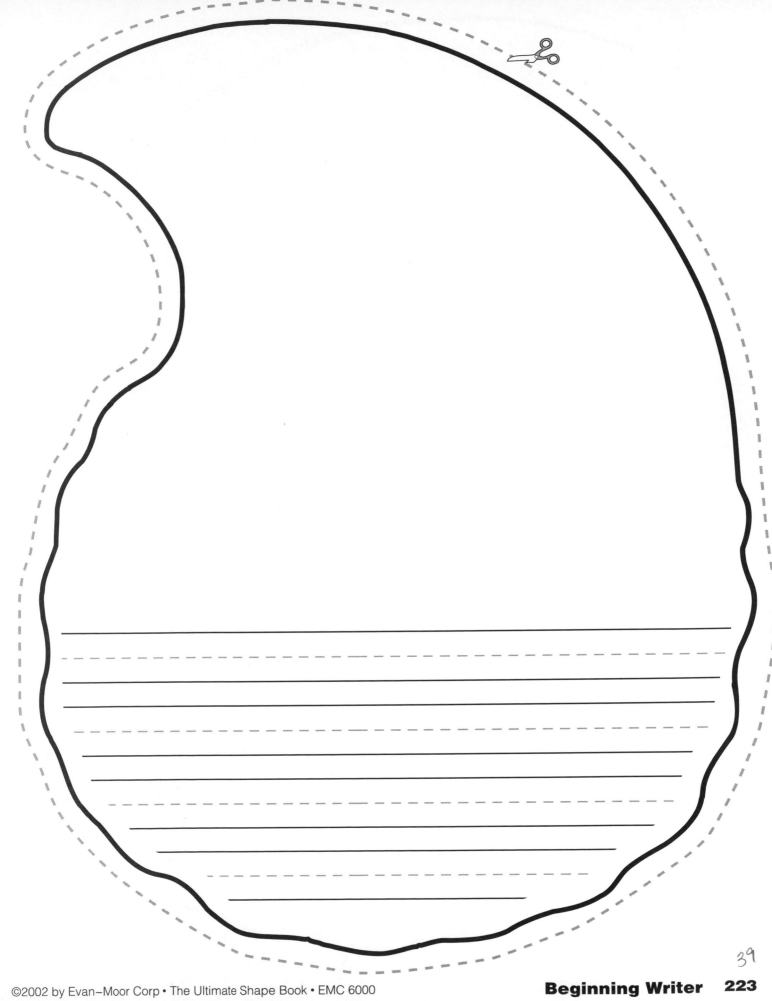

39

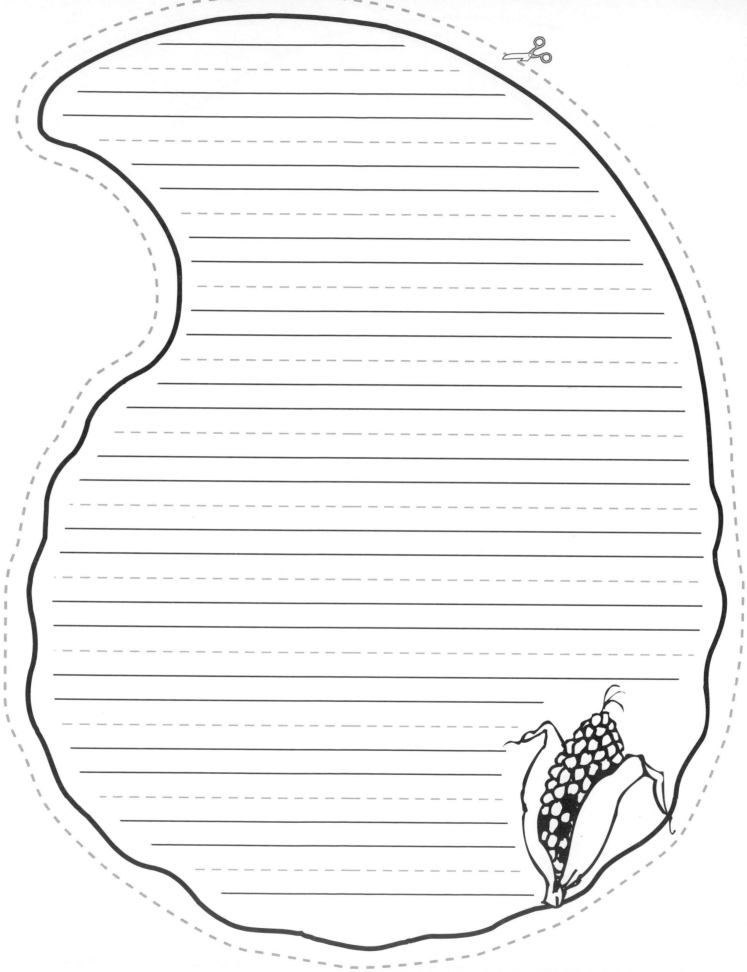

The basket on the table
Is shaped just like a horn.
It holds apples and walnuts.
It holds flowers, leaves, and corn.

It's called a horn of plenty.
That's easy to understand.
It represents the harvest
We have taken from the land.

13

Piñata

Prewriting

Literature Connections
Hispanic Holidays by Faith Winchester; Bridgestone Books, 1996.
Hooray! A Piñata! by Elisa Kleven; Dutton Children's Books, 1996.
Nine Days to Christmas by Marie Hall Ets and Aurora Labastida; Viking Press, 1959.

Concrete Experiences
If your students are not familiar with piñatas, bring one to class or make one with your students. Stuff the piñata with goodies and break it.

Let the Writing Begin

Emergent Writers

- **Inside the Piñata**
  Students draw what they think might be inside the piñata and tell about their drawings.

- **P is for Piñata**
  Students fill their piñatas with things that begin with the letter *p*. (Students may draw the things or cut them from magazines.) List the names of the things along the edge of the page.

Beginning Writers

- **What a Surprise!**
  Students imagine a surprise that might be put into a piñata and draw the surprise falling out. Then they copy and complete the sentence.

  Carumba, were we surprised when _____ fell out of the piñata!

- **A Piñata for My Party**
  Students draw a piñata for a party. Then they copy and complete the sentence.

  My piñata looks like a _____.

Independent Writers

- **Celebrating Christmas in Mexico**
  Students write a factual account of the nine days of Christmas traditionally celebrated in Mexico.

- **Swing the Stick**
  Students use descriptive language as they tell about swinging the stick and breaking the piñata.

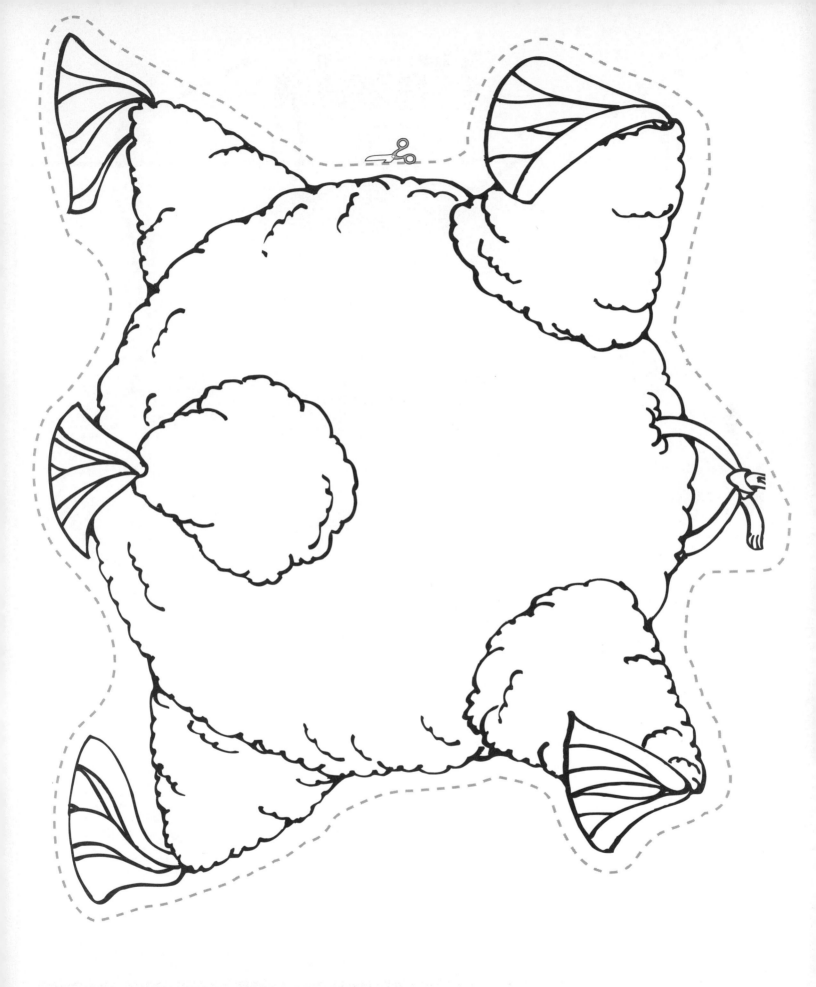

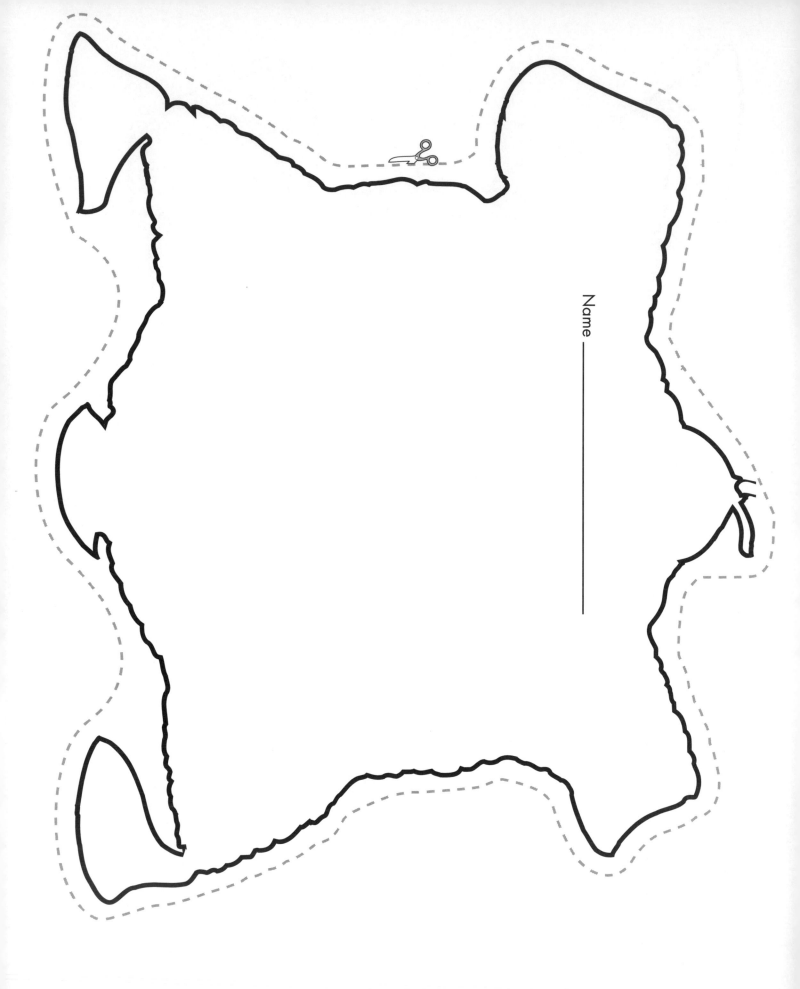

Name _____

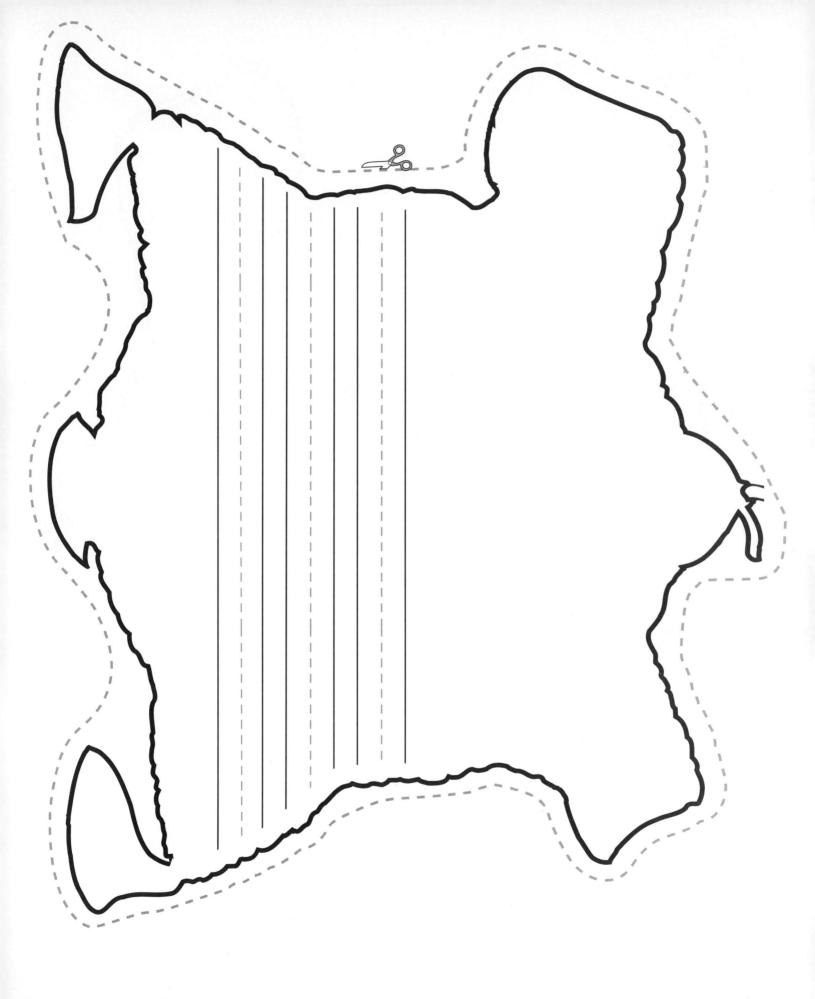

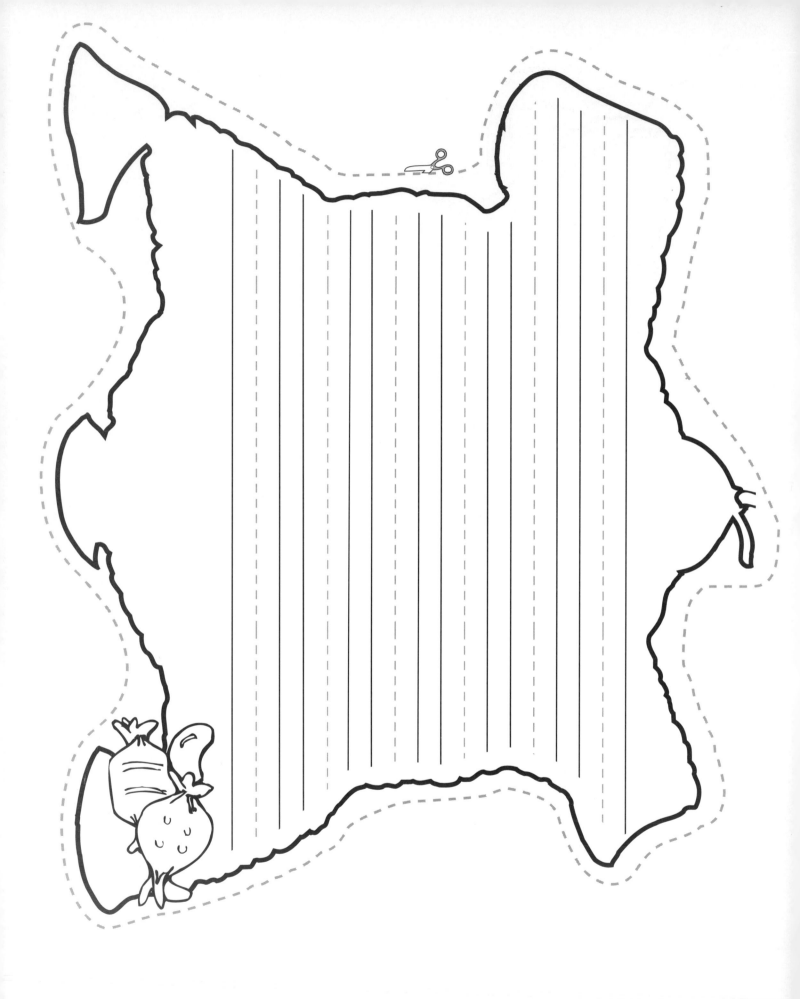

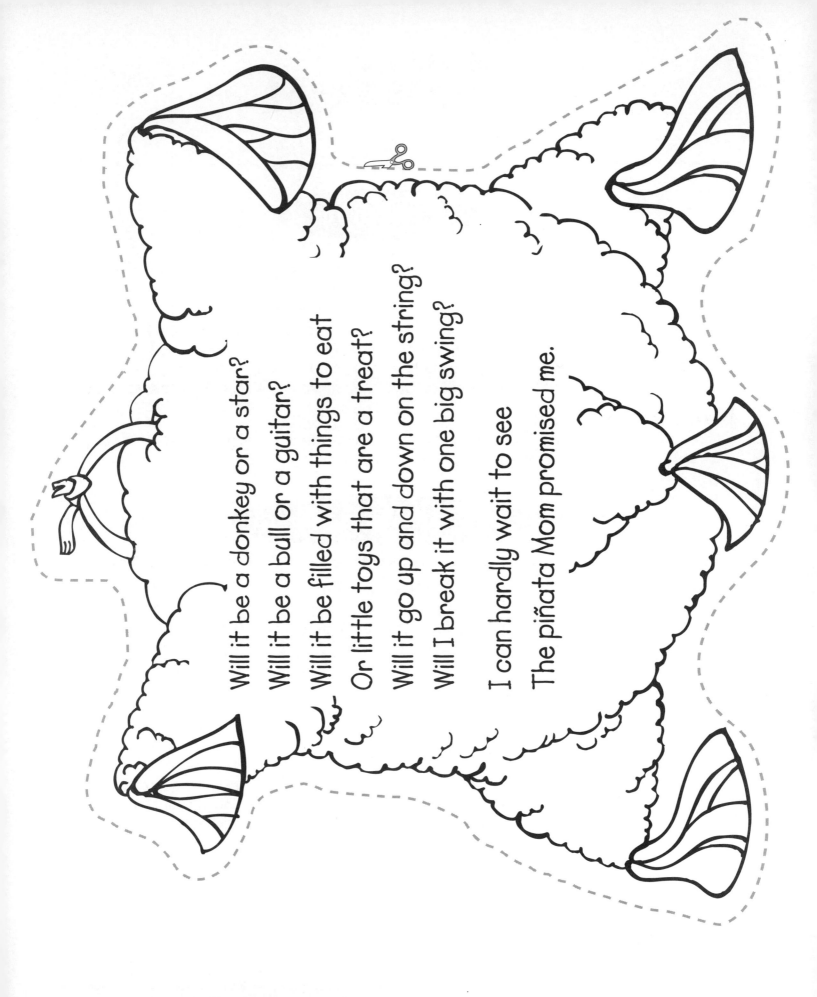

Will it be a donkey or a star?
Will it be a bull or a guitar?
Will it be filled with things to eat
Or little toys that are a treat?
Will it go up and down on the string?
Will I break it with one big swing?

I can hardly wait to see
The piñata Mom promised me.

Mitten

Prewriting

Literature Connections

Caps, Hats, Socks, and Mittens: A Book About the Four Seasons by Louise Borden; Scholastic, 1992.

A Hat for Minerva Louise by Janet Morgan Stoeke; Puffin, 1997.

The Missing Mitten Mystery by Steven Kellogg; Dial Books for Young Readers, 2000.

Missing Mittens by Stuart J. Murphy; HarperCollins Publishers, 2001.

The Mitten: A Ukrainian Folktale adapted by Jan Brett; Putnam, 1989.

Samuel Todd's Book of Great Inventions by E.L. Konigsburg; Aladdin Paperbacks, 1999.

Concrete Experiences

Have students bring a pair of mittens to class. Notice the different types of mittens, the way patterns are located on the mittens, and the way that some mittens are attached to each other.

Let the Writing Begin

Emergent Writers

- **Mitten Weather**
  Students draw a day when they would wear mittens. Have them describe the weather. You may want to sing or recite "The Mitten Song."

- **Color Mittens**
  Students draw mittens with different colors and label the colored mittens.

Beginning Writers

- **Who Is Hiding in the Mitten?**
  Students draw a creature that might hide in the mitten. Then they copy and complete the sentence.

  _____ *is hiding in the mitten.*

- **Kitten Mittens**
  Have students draw to show part of the story of the three little kittens who lost their mittens. Then have them copy and complete these sentences.

  Three little kittens—
  They lost their mittens
  And they began to cry.

Independent Writers

- **A Mitten Mystery**
  Who took the missing mitten? Students write a tale solving the mystery. Encourage them to include clues that lead to the solution.

- **The Mitten**
  Students write a detailed description that creates a visual image of a mitten. The passage should include details like color, material, texture, condition, and size.

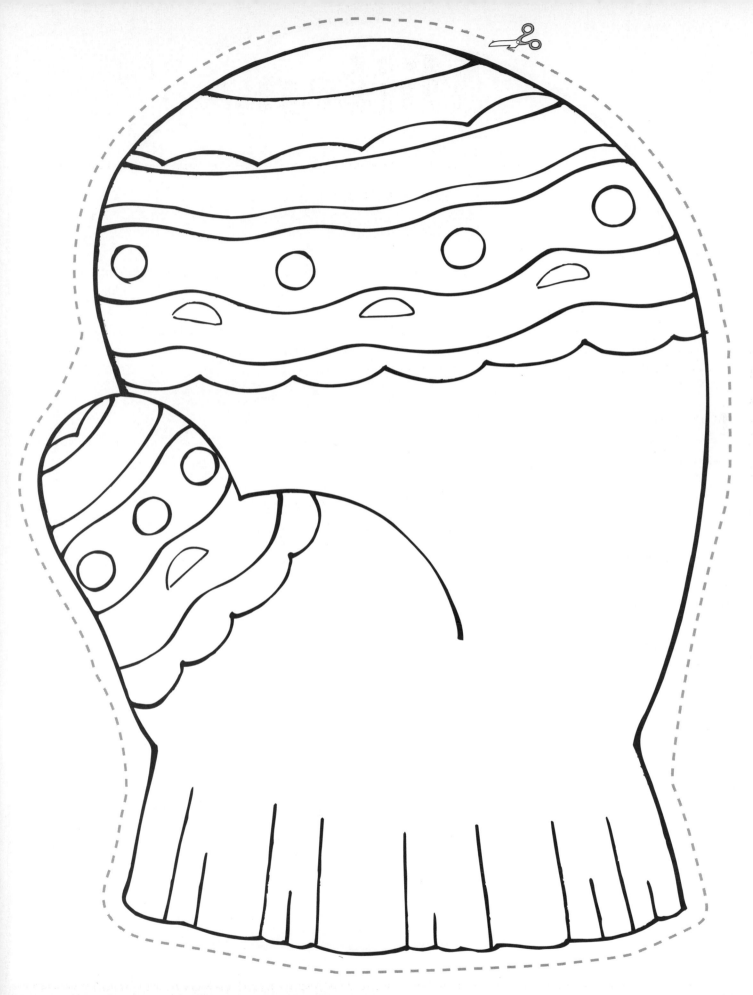

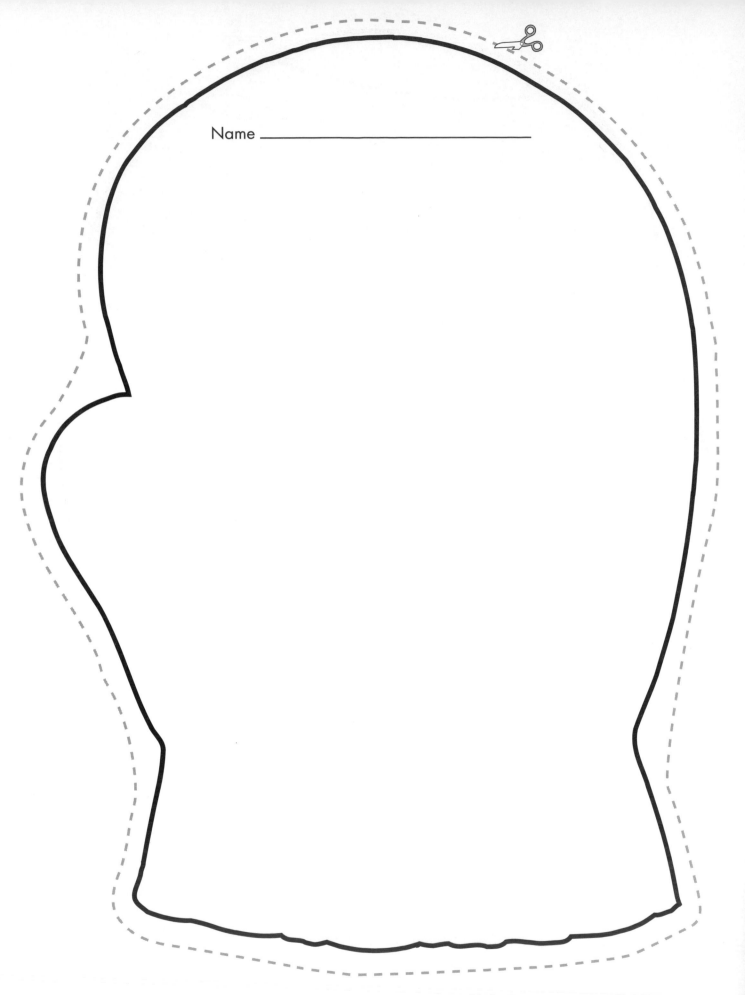

Name _____

On a cold, wintry day with snow in the air

My fuzzy new mittens are just right to wear.

They keep my fingers snuggly warm—

Shielded from the fierce, biting storm.

Dragon

Literature Connections

Down the Dragon's Tongue by Margaret Mahy; Orchard, 2000.
The Dragons Are Singing Tonight by Jack Prelutsky; Greenwillow, 1993.
Dragon Tooth by Cathryn Falwell; Clarion Books, 1996.
The Egg by M.P. Robertson; Phyllis Fogelman Books, 2001.
The Flying Dragon Room by Audrey Wood; Scholastic, 2000.
Raising Dragons by Jerdine Nolen; Silver Whistle, 1998.
Red Eggs and Dragon Boats: Celebrating Chinese Festivals by Carol Stepanchuk; Pacific View Press, 1994.

Concrete Experiences

Talk with students about the difference between real and imaginary. Discuss the question, "Were dragons real animals?" Create a word bank of dragon words.

Let the Writing Begin

Emergent Writers

- **Dragon Says**
  Students draw dragons in different positions. (a dragon sitting down, a dragon standing on one foot, a dragon lying on its back, a dragon flying by) Use the ideas to play a game of Dragon Says (like Simon Says).

- **The Hungry Dragon**
  Students imagine the fire-breathing dragon barbecuing a healthy snack, and draw the snack.

Beginning Writers

- **Baby Dragon**
  Students draw a broken egg and the dragon that has just hatched from it. Then they copy and complete the sentences.

  Look at Baby Dragon.
  See its _____.

- **The Dragon Who Could Not Fly**
  Students draw a picture showing how a dragon that couldn't fly moved around. Then they copy and complete the sentences.

  This dragon could not fly.
  It had to _____.

Independent Writers

- **Dragon Exterminator**
  Students pretend that they have been assigned the job of ridding a kingdom of all dragons. They write about the plans they will make and how they will carry them out.

- **Dragon Power**
  Knights and kings were always killing dragons. Students write a more positive solution to the "dragon problem" by putting dragons to productive use.

Front Cover   239

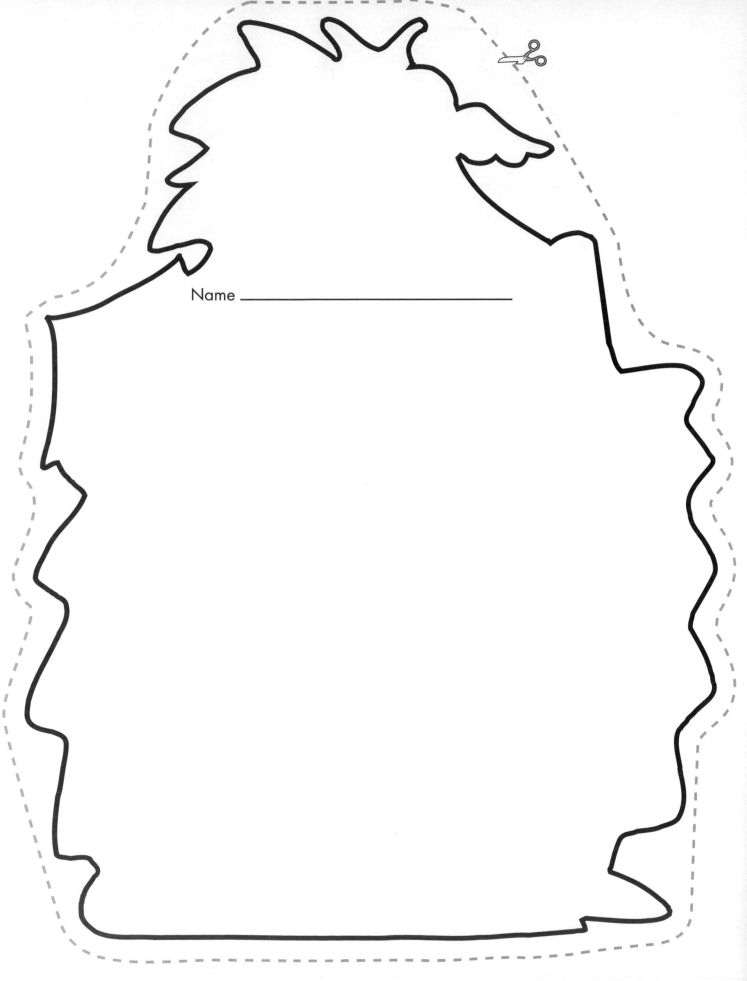

Name _____

The Ultimate Shape Book • EMC 6000 • ©2002 by Evan-Moor Corp

Fiery breath,
Flashing eye—
The dragon soars
Across the sky.

Groundhog

Literature Connections

Geoffrey Groundhog Predicts the Weather by Bruce Koscielniak; Houghton Mifflin Company, 1995.

Gregory's Shadow by Don Freeman; Viking, 2000.

Gretchen Groundhog, It's Your Day! by Abby Levine; Albert Whitman & Co., 1998.

Groundhog Willie's Shadow by Barbara Birenbaum; Peartree, 2001.

It's Groundhog Day! by Steven Kroll; Scholastic, 1989.

Concrete Experiences

Use a brown tube sock with button eyes to reenact the moment when a groundhog sticks its head above the ground after a winter of hibernation. Make sure each student has a chance to think of a response that the groundhog might make.

Let the Writing Begin

Emergent Writers

- **Tunneling Home**
  Students draw what they think the inside of a groundhog's tunnel looks like. They might add directional arrows to show how the groundhog moves from the surface to its home.

- **The First Peek**
  Students draw to show the groundhog's reaction when it first peeks its head out of the hole. Allow time to share the drawings, and have students give the sound the groundhog might have made.

Beginning Writers

- **Afraid of a Shadow**
  Students draw something that they fear and then copy and complete the sentences.

  A groundhog is afraid of its shadow.
  I am afraid of _____.

- **What Will I See?**
  Students draw to show what Groundhog saw as it poked its head above ground. Then they copy and complete the sentence.

  When Groundhog stuck its head up, it saw _____.

Independent Writers

- **"My Journal" by _____ Groundhog**
  Imagine that groundhogs have kept a record of all the Groundhog Days through the years. Students write an entry for this record describing this year's Groundhog Day.

- **Life Underground**
  Students write a story about living underground, highlighting its advantages and disadvantages.

Front Cover 245

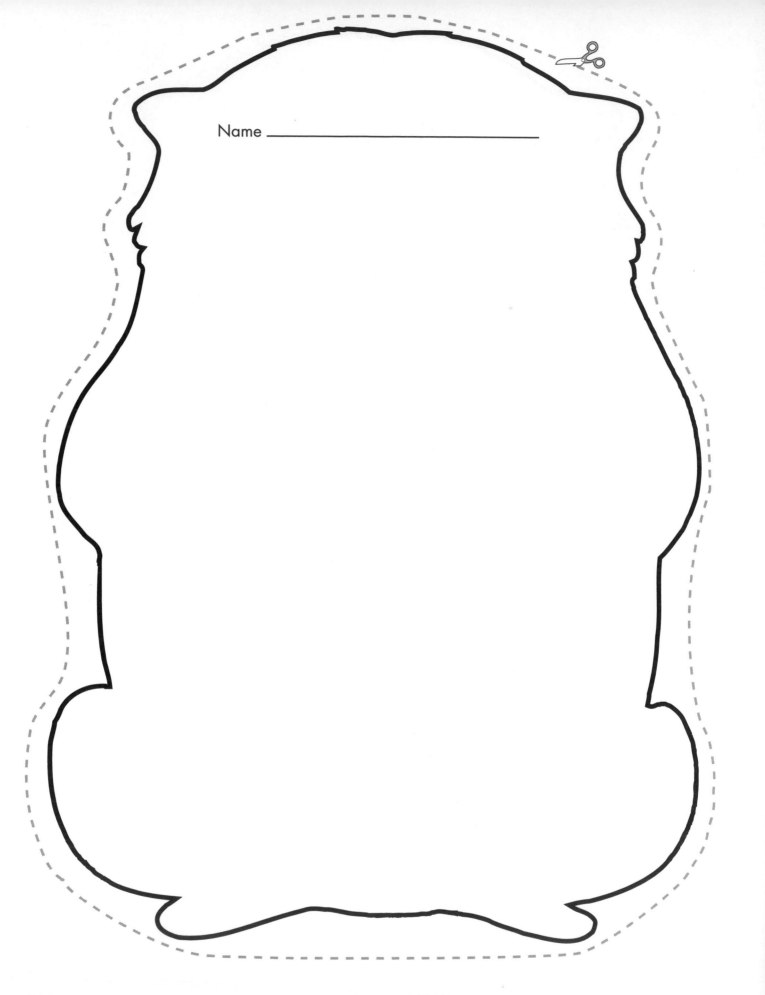

Name _____

The Ultimate Shape Book • EMC 6000 • ©2002 by Evan-Moor Corp.

Spring's warmth calls.

I'll just take a peek.

Let's see now.

What's up here?

A shadow!...EEEEKKKKKKK!

Heart

Prewriting

Literature Connections
Froggy's First Kiss by Jonathan London; Viking, 1998.
Hearts & Crafts by Sheri Brownrigg; Tricycle Press, 1996.
I Love You, Blue Kangaroo! by Emma Chichester Clark; Dragonfly Books, 2001.
I Love You, Stinky Face by Lisa McCourt; BridgeWater Books, 1997.
Love Is a Special Way of Feeling by Joan Walsh Anglund; Harcourt Brace & Co., 1999.
Somebody Loves You, Mr. Hatch by Eileen Spinelli; Simon & Schuster, 1991.

Concrete Experiences
Ask students to explain what the symbol of a heart means. Write words associated with a heart on a chart for reference.

Let the Writing Begin

Emergent Writers

- **My Valentine**
  Students decorate their hearts and draw a picture of their valentines inside.

- **Heart Critters**
  Students cut and paste tiny hearts, then add details to create heart critters. They may give their critters a name.

Beginning Writers

- **A Pet for You**
  Students draw red roses, blue violets, and a pet of their choice. Then they copy the verse and decide to whom they would give the pet.

  To _____:
  Roses are red.
  Violets are blue.
  Here is a pet
  I bought 'specially for you.

- **How to Make a Valentine**
  Students draw a picture of themselves delivering a valentine to a friend. Then they list step-by-step directions for making the valentine, ending with:
  Deliver the valentine to a friend.

Independent Writers

- **The Biggest Valentine**
  Students write a story about a very big valentine.

- **A Valentine for _____**
  Students choose a real person or a character from a story. They describe the valentine they would give to that person and tell what the person did to deserve a valentine.

©2002 by Evan-Moor Corp • The Ultimate Shape Book • EMC 6000

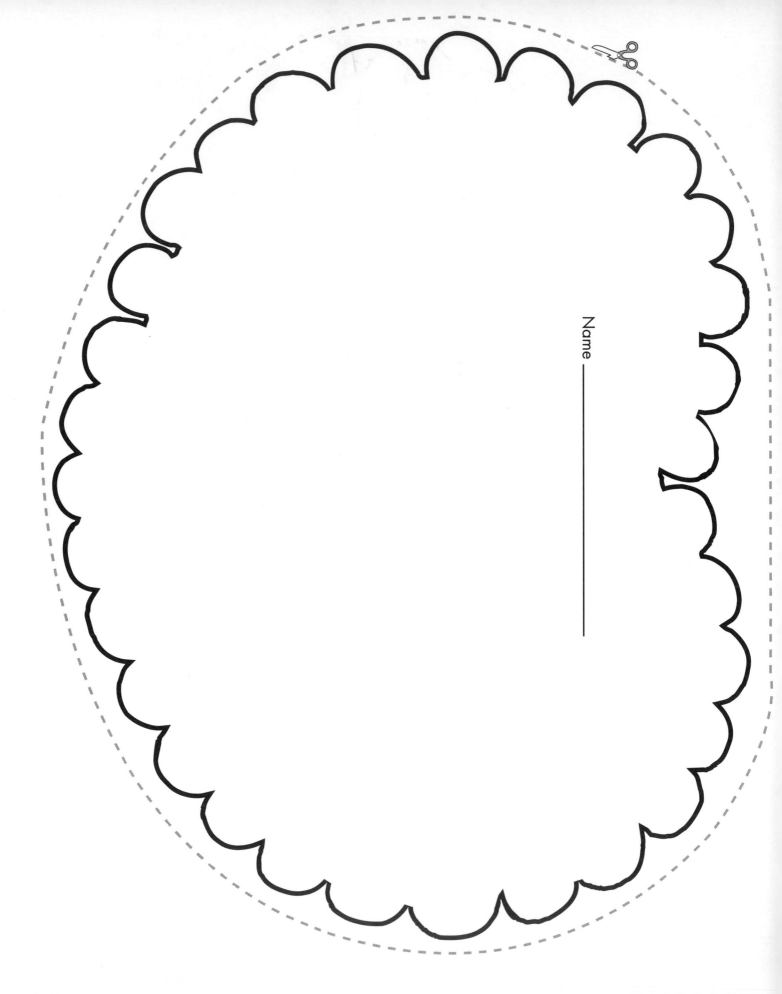

Name _____

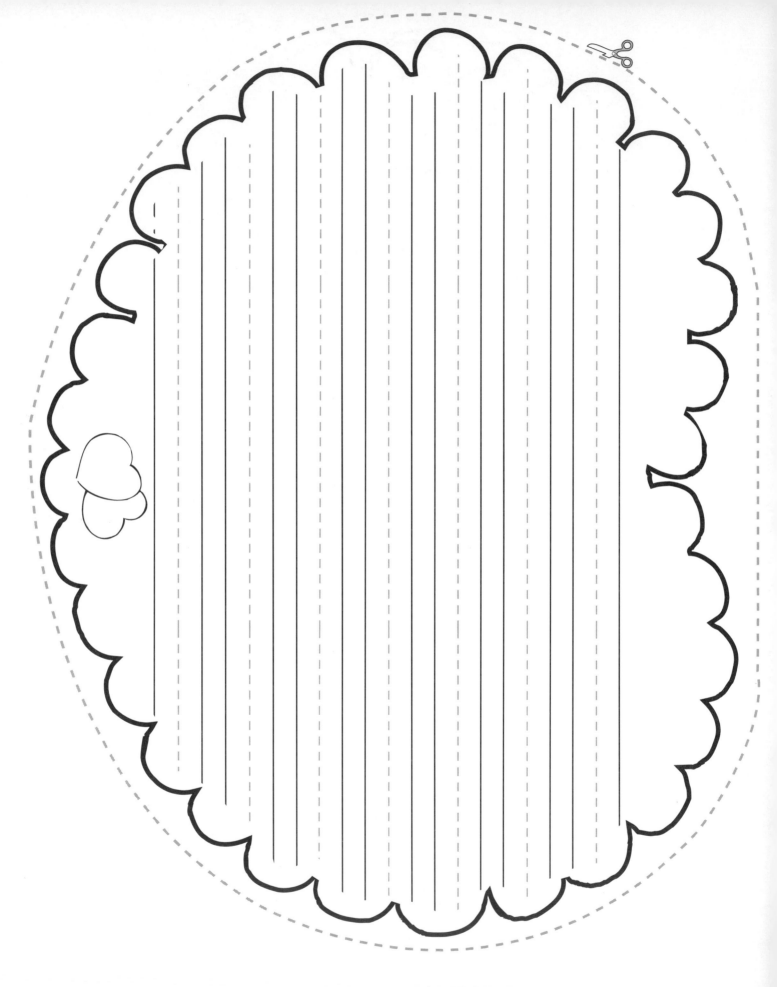

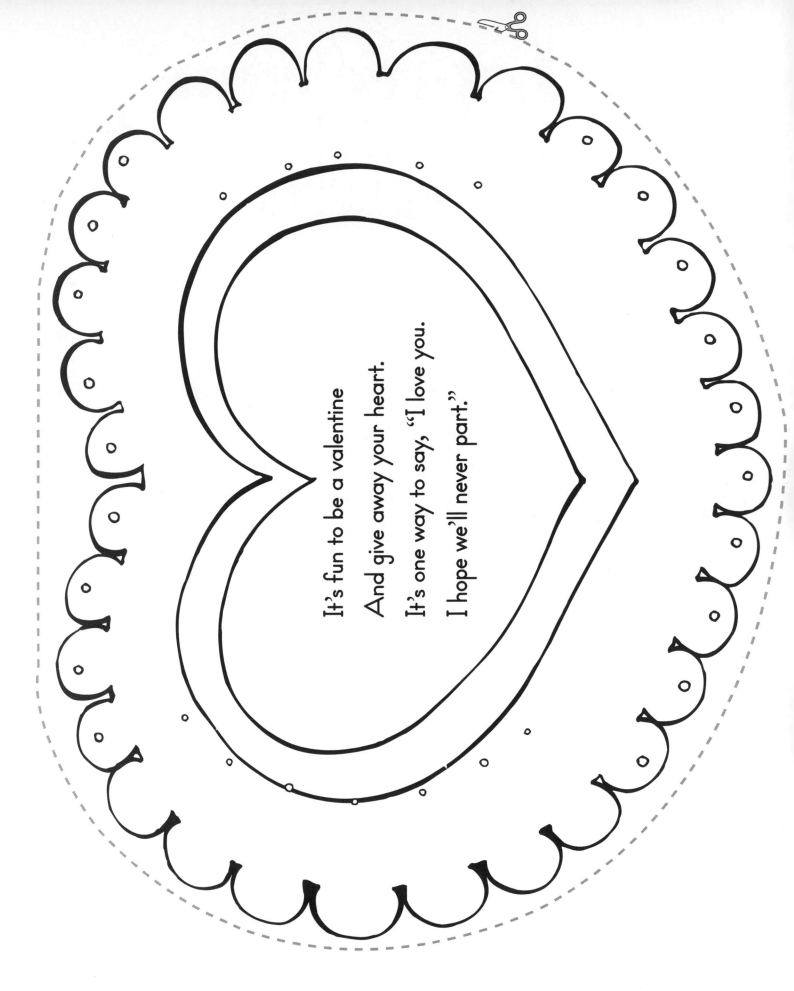

It's fun to be a valentine
And give away your heart.
It's one way to say, "I love you.
I hope we'll never part."

Leprechaun

Literature Connections

Leprechaun Gold by Teresa Bateman; Holiday House, 1998.
The Leprechaun in the Basement by Kathy Tucker; Albert Whitman & Co., 1999.
Lucky O'Leprechaun by Jana Dillon; Pelican, 1998.
The Ring of Truth: An Original Irish Tale by Teresa Bateman; Holiday House, 1997.

Concrete Experiences

Holiday characters are often perceived by young students to be real even though they are imaginary. Spend some time discussing leprechauns. What were they supposed to look like? What were they supposed to do? Were they real?

Let the Writing Begin

Emergent Writers

• **The Leprechaun's Treasure**
Students draw a treasure that might be found in a leprechaun's pot. Then they tell about the treasure.

• **The Wee, Tiny Man**
Students draw a tiny man next to something normal-sized to show a size comparison. Then they make the comparison verbally.

Beginning Writers

• **The Search**
Students draw themselves searching for the leprechaun's pot of treasure. They copy and complete the sentences.

A pot full of _____ is hidden away.
I'm going to try to find it today.

• **A Safe Hiding Place**
Students draw a place where a leprechaun might hide his treasure safely. Then they copy and complete the sentence.

_____ is a safe hiding place.

Independent Writers

• **To the End of the Rainbow**
Students write about a character's quest to find the pot of gold at the end of the rainbow, and explain what the character learned.

• **Why Leprechauns Are So Small**
Students write a tale to tell how leprechauns came to be known as "little people."

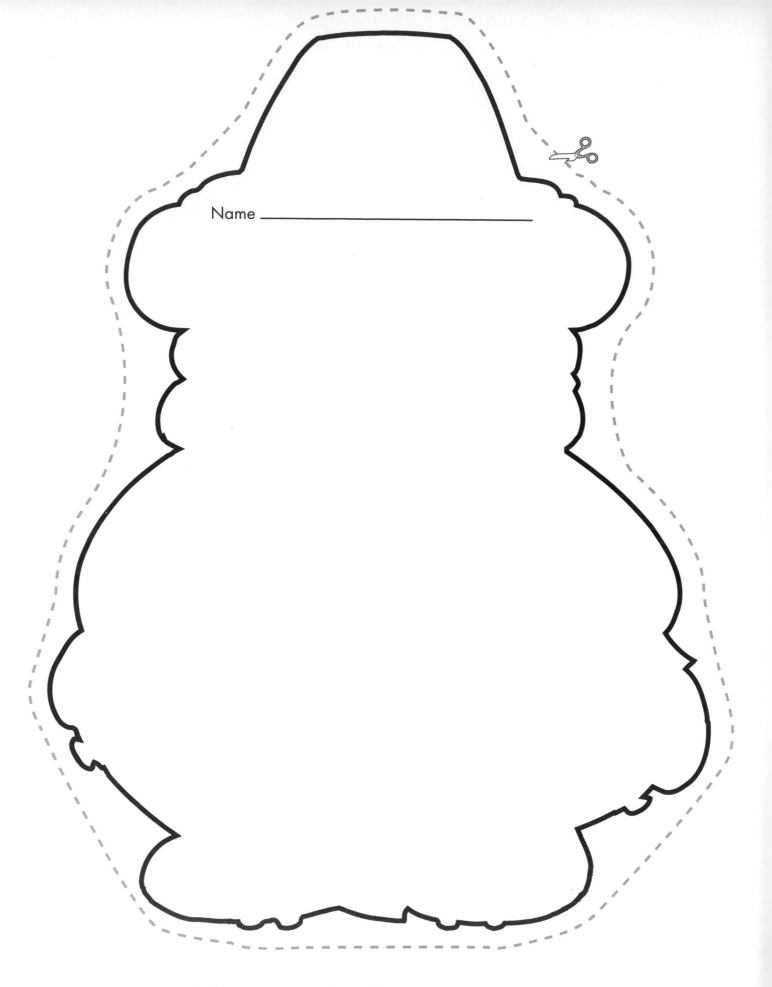

Name _____

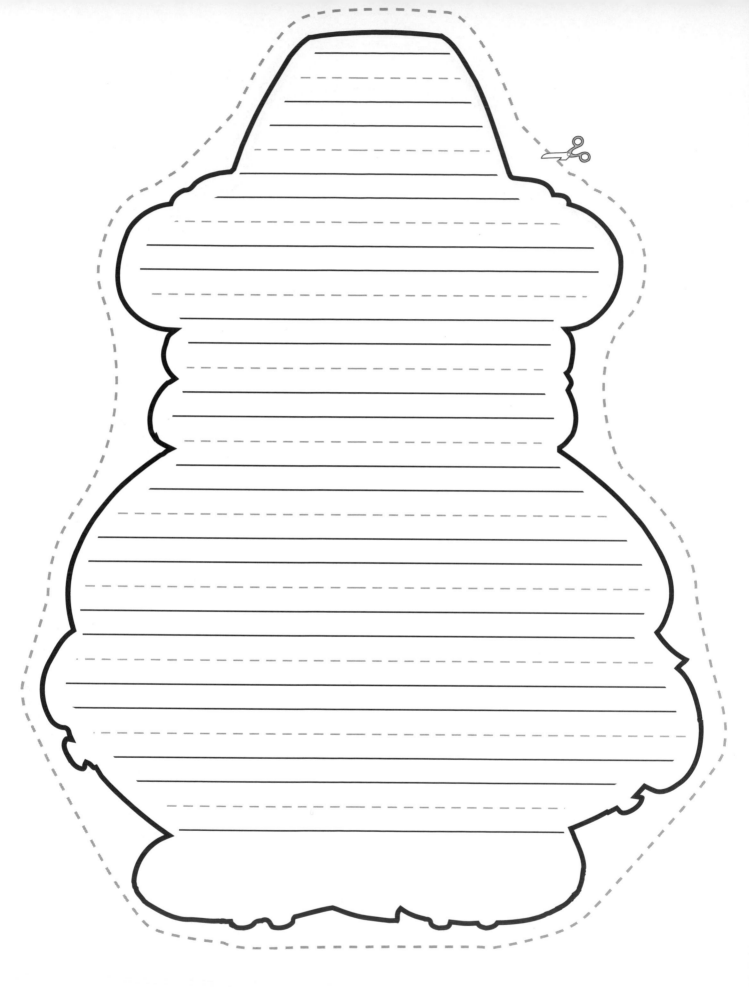

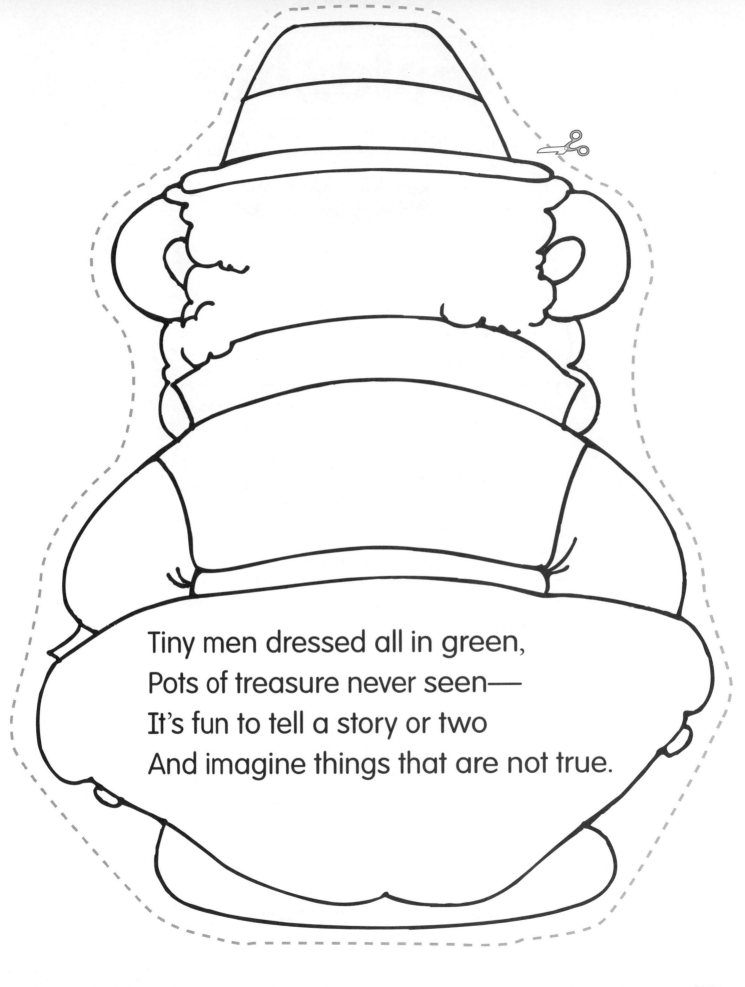

Tiny men dressed all in green,
Pots of treasure never seen—
It's fun to tell a story or two
And imagine things that are not true.

Galoshes

Literature Connections

Johnny Lion's Rubber Boots by Edith Thatcher Hurd; HarperTrophy, 2001.

Puddles by Jonathan London; Puffin, 1999.

Roots, Shoots, Buckets & Boots: Gardening Together with Children by Sharon Lovejoy; Workman, 1999.

Sonny's Beloved Boots by Lisa Stubbs; Barron's, 1997.

Umbrella by Taro Yashima; Puffin, 1977.

Concrete Experiences

Bring a pair of galoshes to class. Talk about other names for these special shoes—boots, overshoes, rubbers, etc. Let students try on the galoshes and walk with them on to get the feel of them.

Let the Writing Begin

Emergent Writers

- **Inside My Boot**
  Students imagine and draw something that has climbed into their boot. Allow time for students to share and tell about their pictures.

- **Splish, Splosh**
  Students draw themselves wearing a pair of galoshes and splashing in the puddle. Write "Splish, Splosh" on the page.

Beginning Writers

- **They Come in Pairs**
  Students draw pictures of things that come in pairs and label the pictures. Then they write the sentence.

  _____ *come in pairs.*

- **The Lost Boot**
  Students draw a picture of a character searching for a lost boot. Then they copy and complete the sentences.

  _____ *lost a boot. Where could it be?*

Independent Writers

- **Walking in the Rain**
  Students write a tale to explain how galoshes were invented.

- **New Galoshes, Please!**
  Students write a plea for new galoshes.

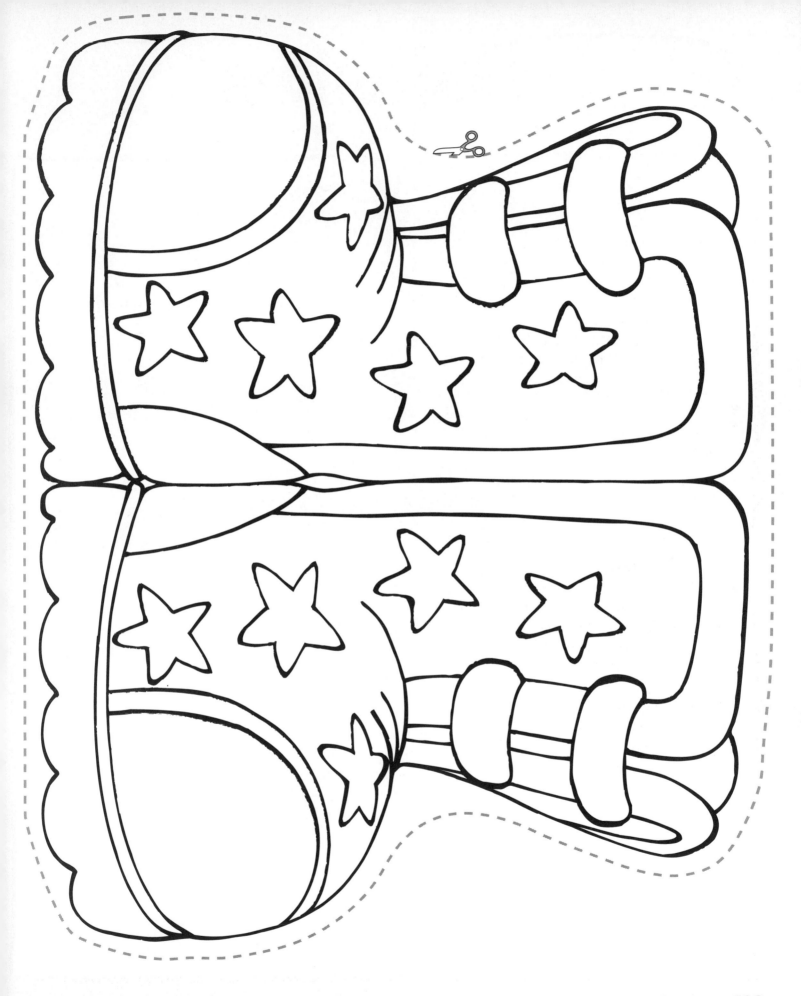

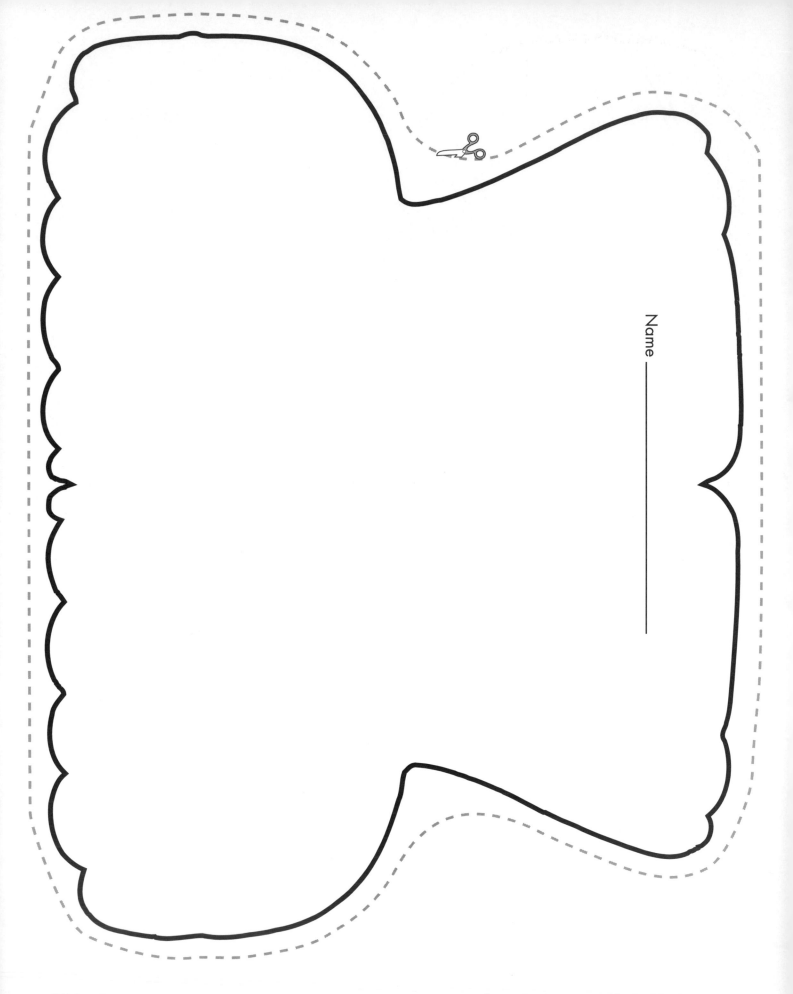

Name

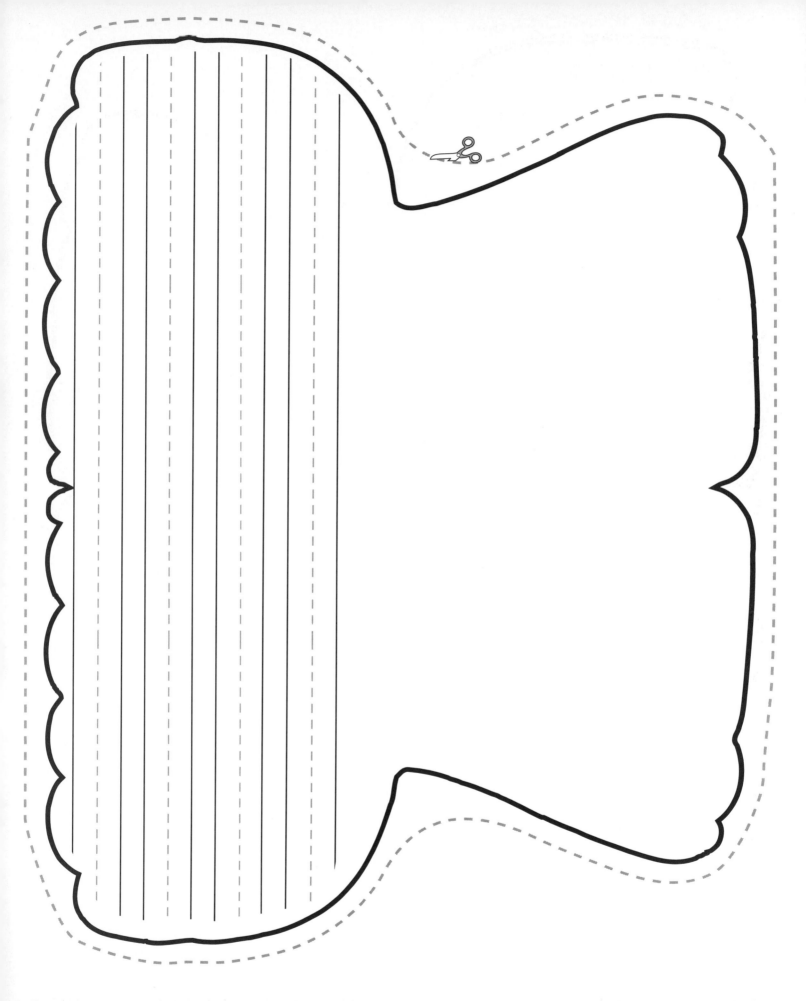

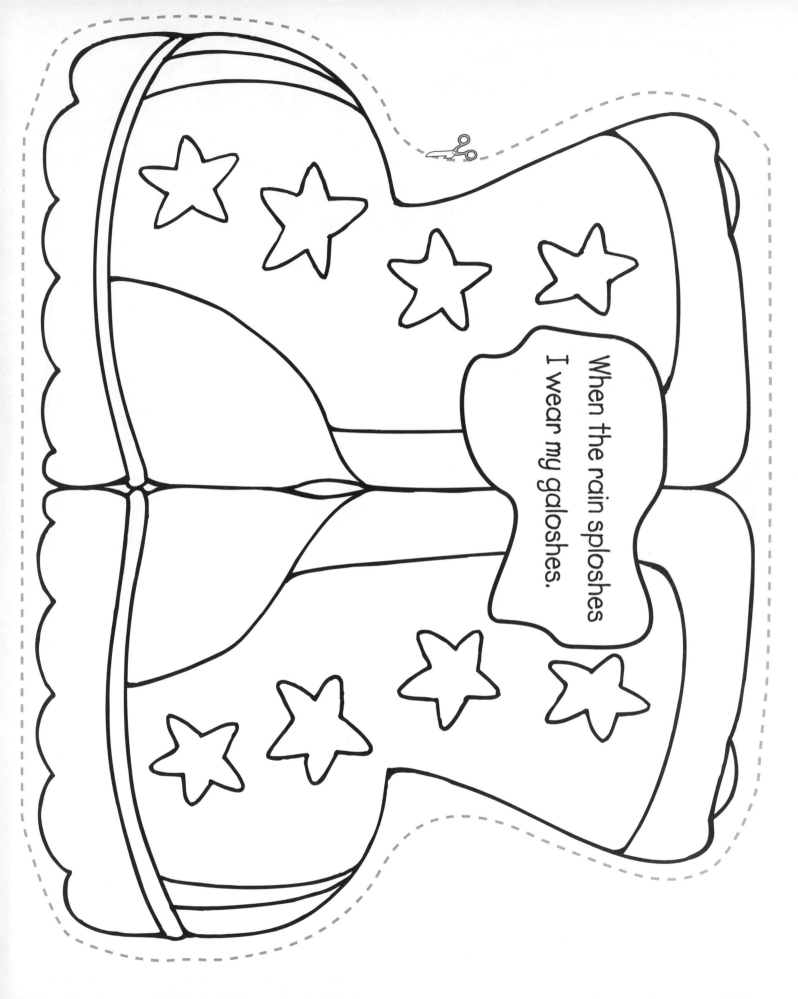

When the rain sploshes
I wear my galoshes.

Flowerpot

Literature Connections

Bulb to Tulip by Oliver S. Owen; Abdo & Daughters Publishing, 1996.
The Empty Pot by Demi; Henry Holt, 1990.
The Flower Alphabet Book by Jerry Pallotta; Charlesbridge Publishing, 1988.
Flower Garden by Eve Bunting; Voyager Books, 2000.
Fran's Flower by Lisa Bruce; HarperCollins Publishers, 2000.
From Seed to Sunflower by Gerald Legg; F. Watts, 1998.
Glenna's Seeds by Nancy Edwards; Child & Family Press, 2001.

Concrete Experiences

Plant seeds in a flowerpot. Care for them and watch them sprout. Create a word bank for growing words.

Let the Writing Begin

Emergent Writers

• **The Best Flower**
Students draw an amazing flower and tell why it is the best.

• **It Used to Be a Seed**
Students draw something that grew and then repeat, "It used to be a seed. Now it's a _____."

Beginning Writers

• **An Unusual Plant**
Students imagine a plant that is out of the ordinary and draw it. Then they copy and complete the sentences.

An unusual plant grew in my flowerpot.
It was _____.

• **What a Flower Needs to Grow**
Students draw a series of pictures that show what a flower needs to grow, label the pictures, and copy and complete the sentence.

A flower seed needs _____ and _____ and _____.

Independent Writers

• **Just About to Bloom**
Students imagine that they are spring flowers just about to bloom and describe the experience.

• **What Is Beautiful?**
Students answer the question, "What is beautiful?" Encourage the use of metaphors and similies.

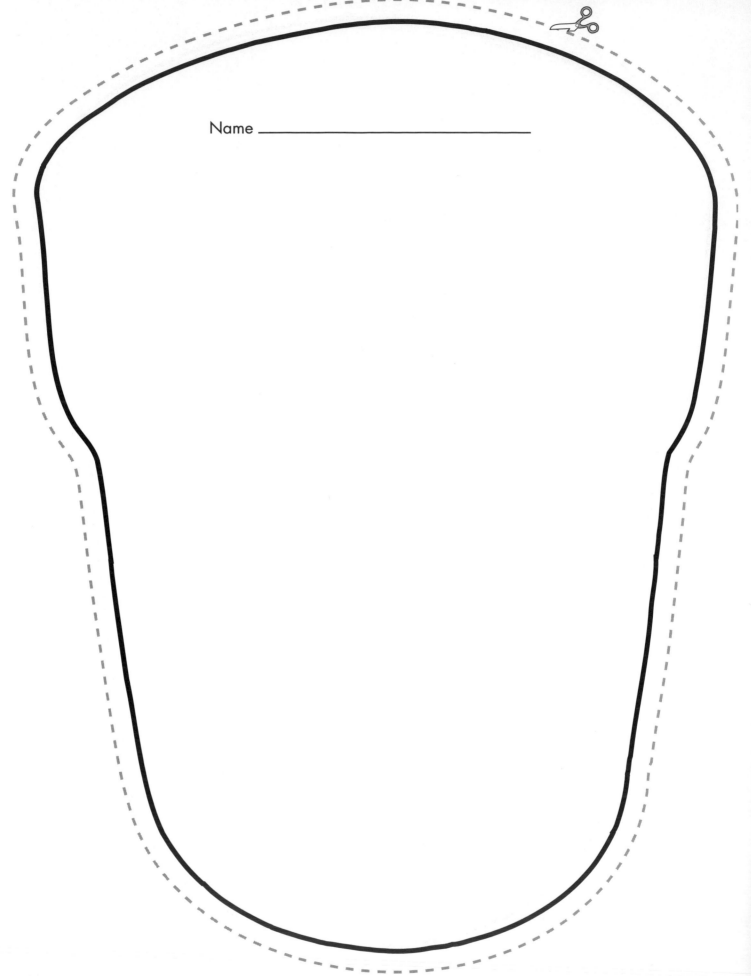

Name _____

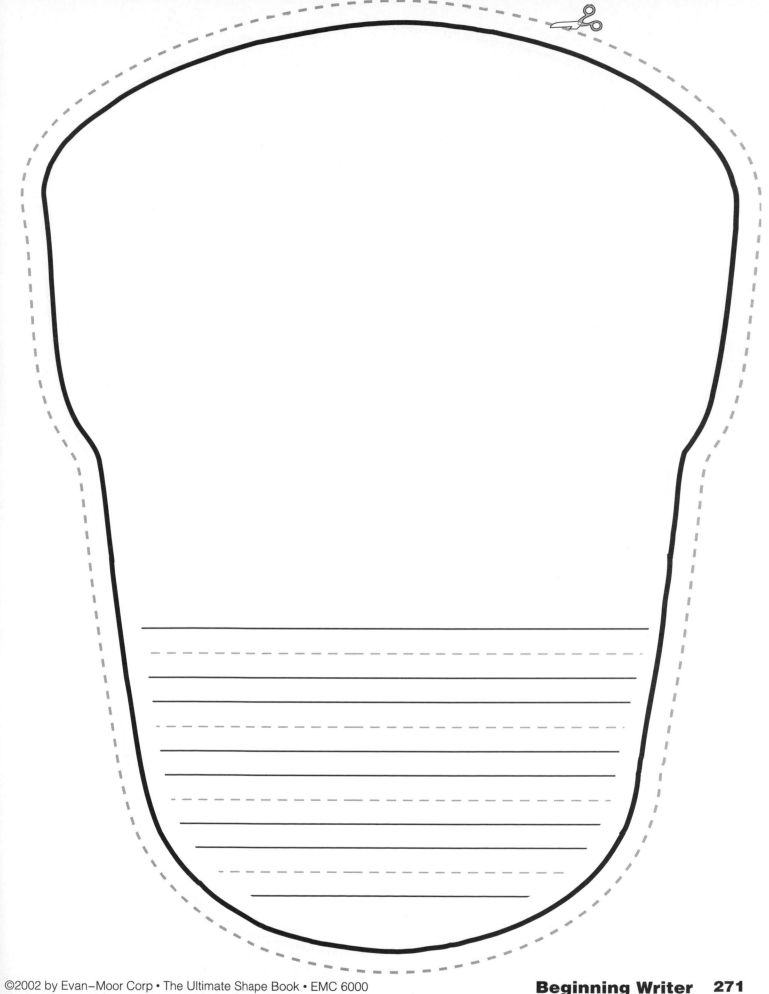

I planted seeds deep in the soil.
I watered them every day.
First came sprouts, a stem, some leaves,
Soon I had grown a bouquet.

Chick

Literature Connections

Egg to Chick by Millicent E. Selsam; HarperTrophy, 1987.
Good Morning, Chick by Mirra Ginsburg; Greenwillow, 1980.
A Number of Animals by Kate Green; Creative Education, 1993.
The Singing Chick by Victoria Stenmark; Henry Holt, 1999.
Super Cluck by Jane O'Connor and Robert O'Connor; HarperCollins Publishers, 1993.

Concrete Experiences

If possible, bring a newly hatched chick into the classroom. Local feed and grain stores may let you borrow several and then return them. Have students describe the way the chicks move, look, and sound. Create a word bank for writing.

Let the Writing Begin

Emergent Writers

- **Hungry Chick**
  Students draw something for a hungry chick to eat and then tell about the meal.

- **Count the Chicks**
  Students make a chart:
  1 egg = 1 chick, 2 eggs = 2 chicks, 3 eggs = 3 chicks. Encourage students to write the numerals as well as the words for each entry.

Beginning Writers

- **Are You My Mother?**
  Students draw a chick talking to another animal, drawing a speech bubble for each. Then they copy and complete this dialog in the speech bubbles.

  Are you my mother?
  No, I am a _____.

- **Cheep, Cheep**
  Students draw a series of chicks. Then they copy and complete the sentences.

  See the little chicks!
  Listen as they talk.

  _____.

  What a noisy flock!

Independent Writers

- **The Early Bird**
  Students write about an experience that supports the proverb "The early bird catches the worm." The experience may be a real one the student has had or a made-up one from the chick's point of view.

- **Life in a Nest**
  Students present the positive and negative aspects of living in a nest from the chick's point of view.

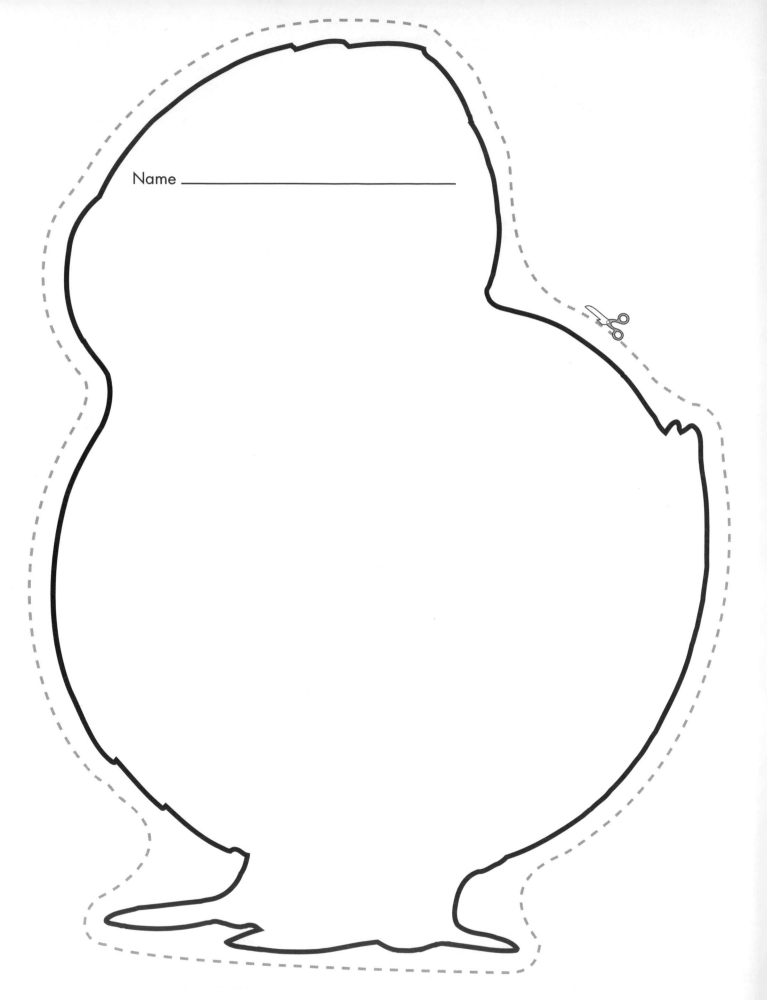

Name _____

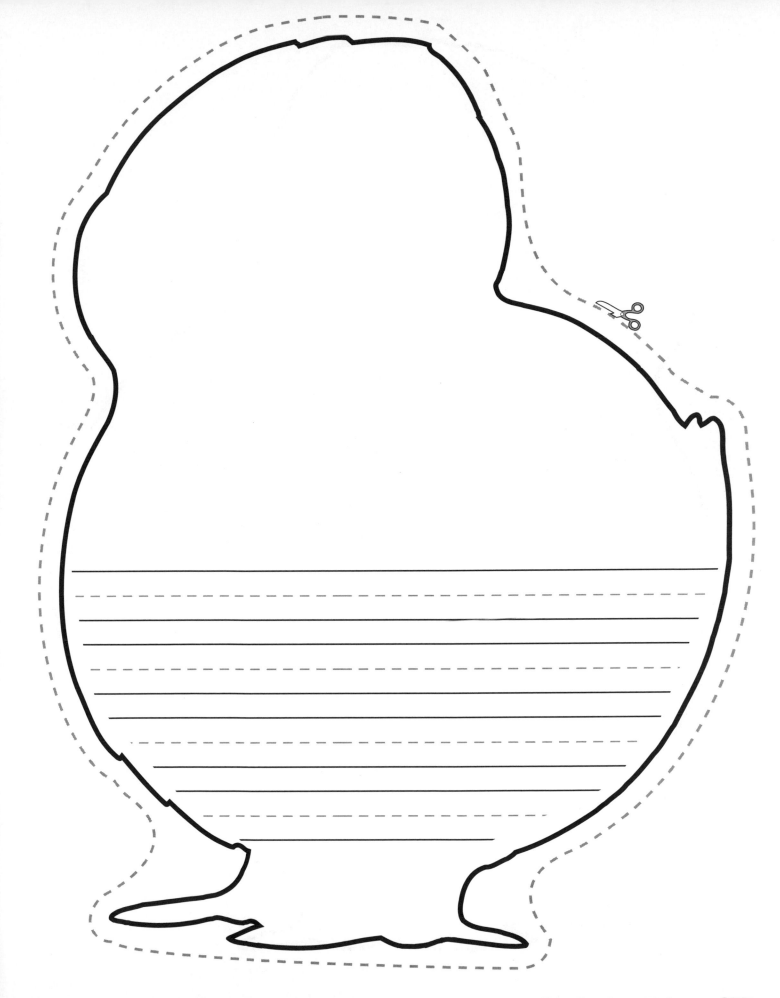

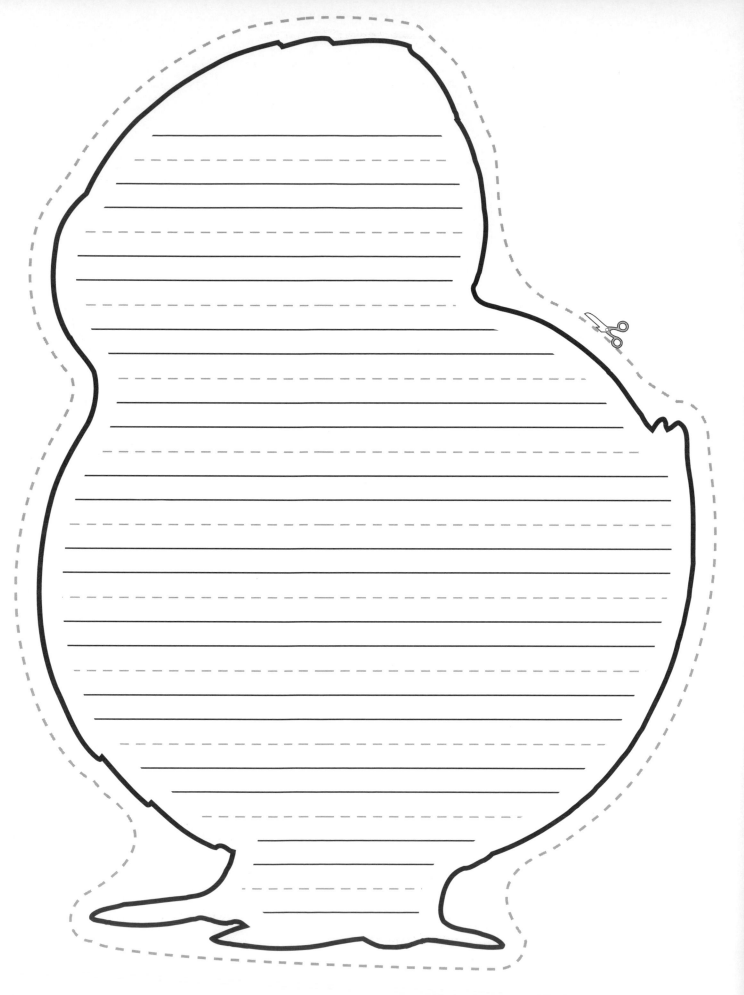

The Ultimate Shape Book • EMC 6000 • ©2002 by Evan-Moor Corp

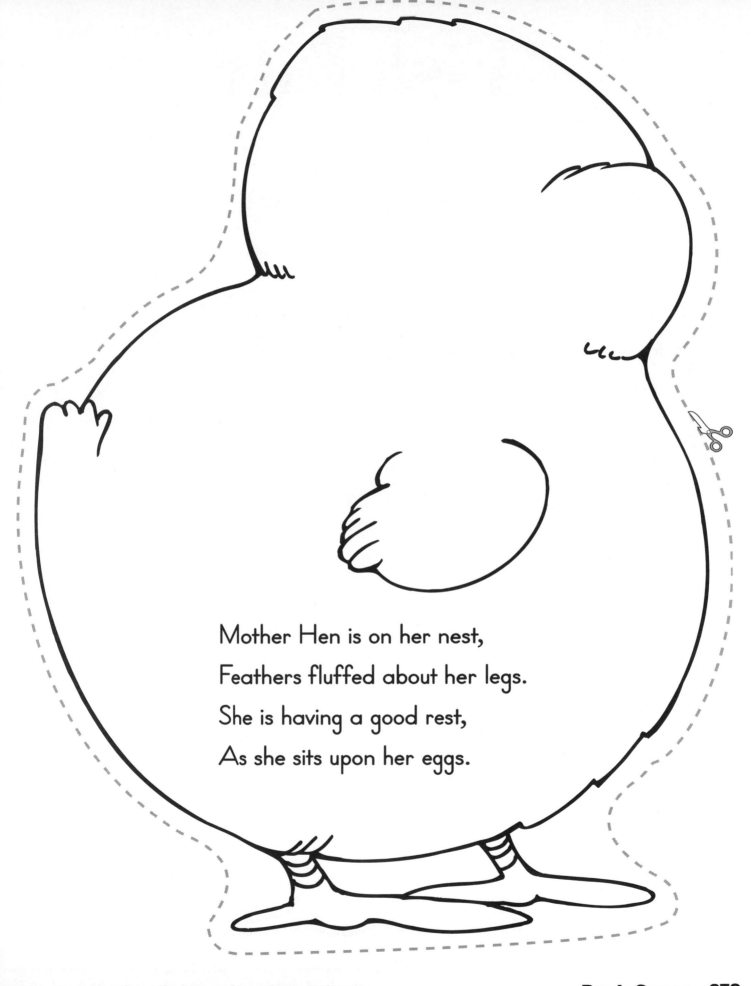

Mother Hen is on her nest,

Feathers fluffed about her legs.

She is having a good rest,

As she sits upon her eggs.

Fish Kite

Literature Connections

A Carp for Kimiko by Virginia L. Kroll; Charlesbridge Publishing, 1993.
Chibi: A True Story from Japan by Barbara Brenner and Julia Takaya; Clarion Books, 1996.
Colors of Japan by Holly Littlefield; Carolrhoda Books, Inc., 1997.
Lucky Song by Vera B. Williams; Greenwillow, 1997.
Moonlight Kite by Helen E. Buckley; Lothrop, Lee & Shepard Books, 1997.
A Sky Full of Kites by Osmond Molarsky; Tricycle Press, 1996.

Concrete Experiences

After reading a nonfiction account of the Japanese tradition of flying fish kites to celebrate their children, have your students make fish kites to fly by your classroom entrance on Children's Day, May 5.

Let the Writing Begin

Emergent Writers

- **Feast of Flags**
  Students draw a long pole with a fish kite for each child in their family. They may label the kites with family members' names.

- **Flying in the Wind**
  Students draw things that fly in the wind and tell about their drawings.

Beginning Writers

- **Kodomo-No-Hi (Children's Day)**
  Students draw a pole with fish kites. Then they copy and complete the sentence.

  On Children's Day, fish kites are flown to _____.

- **Celebrate**
  Students draw a celebration they observe. Then they copy and complete the sentence.

  At my house we always celebrate _____.

Independent Writers

- **Strong and Persistent**
  Fish kites are made in the shape of carp. Carp are strong fish that swim up fast-moving streams. To the Japanese they symbolize courage. Have students write to tell how these fish demonstrate strength and persistence.

- **The Magic Kite**
  Students write a tale about a kite with magical powers.

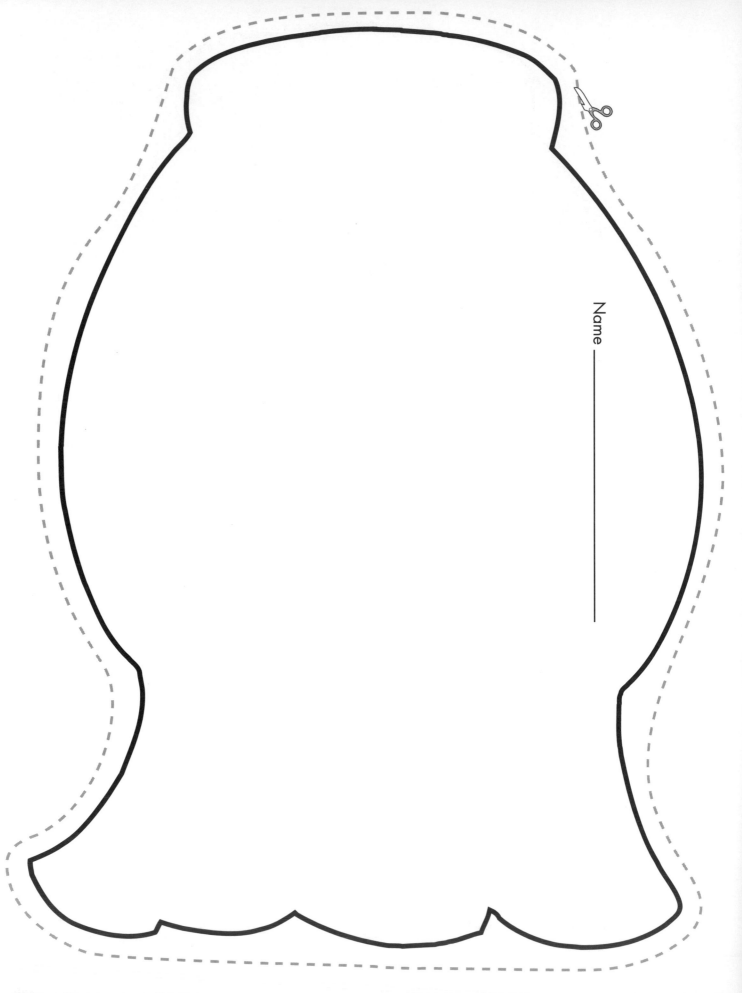

Name _____

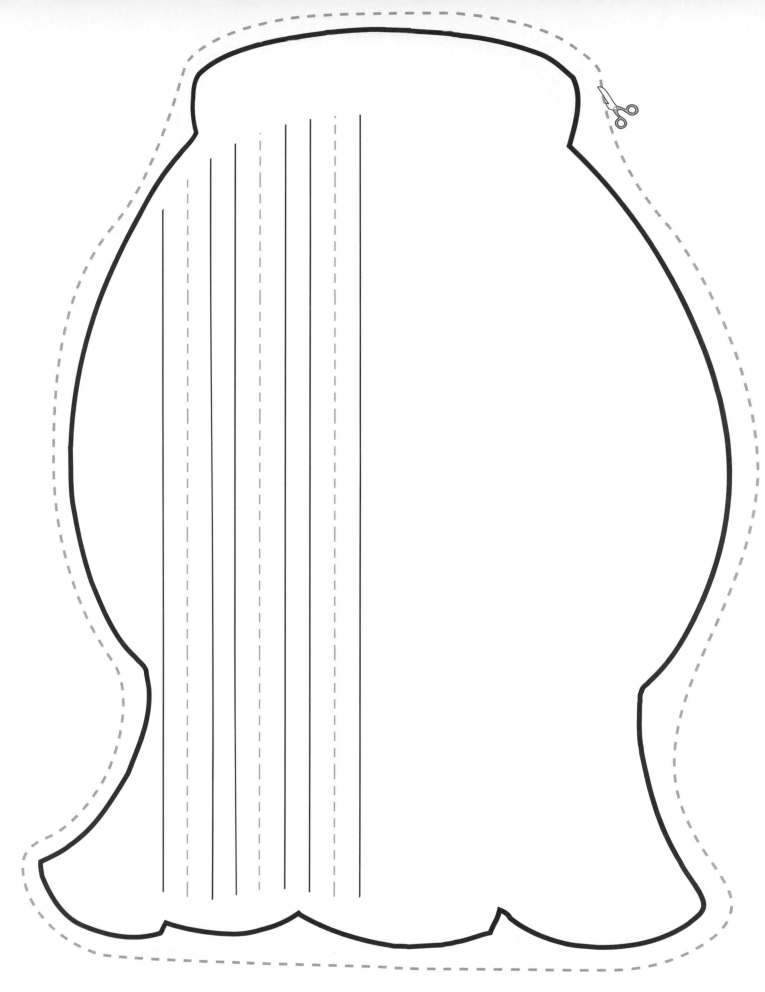

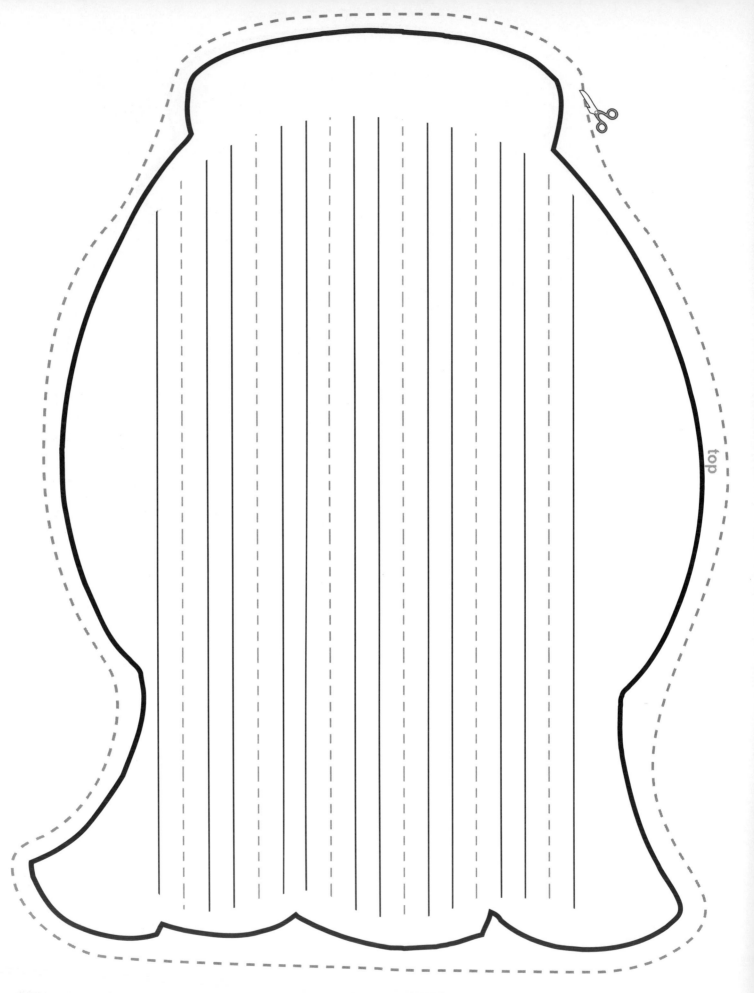

top

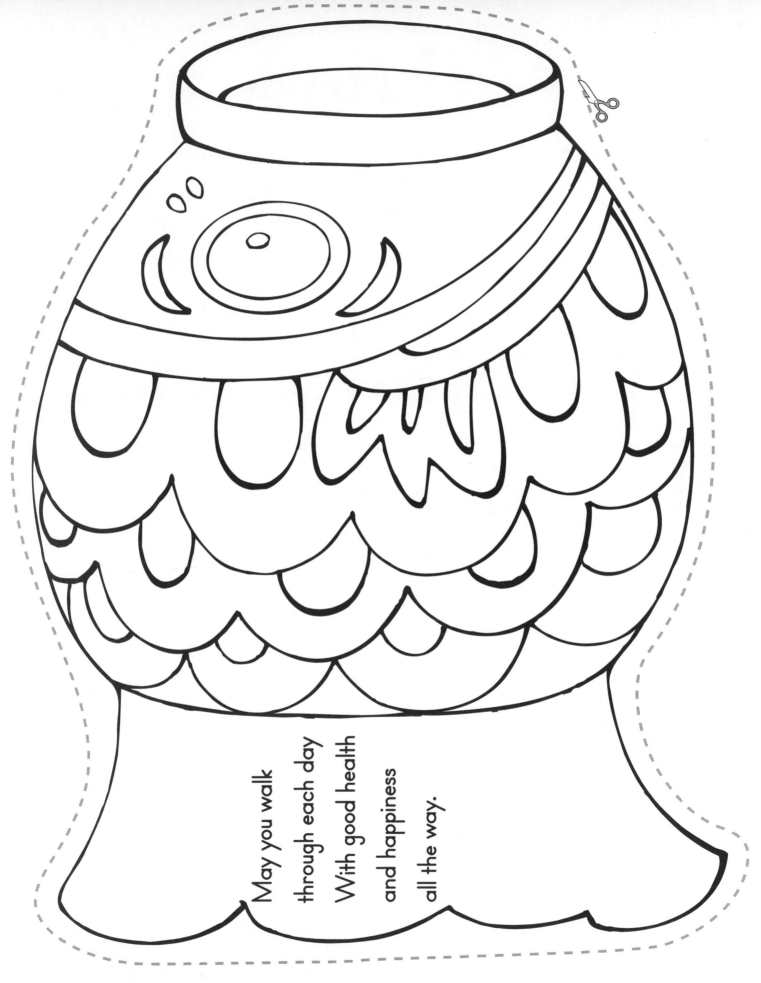

May you walk
through each day
With good health
and happiness
all the way.

Trunk

Literature Connections

Benjamin's Treasure by Garth Williams; HarperCollins Publishers, 2001.
The Dancing Pig by Judy Sierra; Gulliver Books, 1999.
Katie's Trunk by Ann Turner; Aladdin Paperbacks, 1997.
Old Jake's Skirts by C. Anne Scott; Rising Moon, 1998.
Pirates by Dina Anastasio; Grosset & Dunlap Publishers, 1997.
Scholastic's The Magic School Bus Takes a Dive: A Book About Coral Reefs adapted
    by Nancy White; Scholastic, 1998.
The Treasure Chest: A Chinese Tale retold by Rosalind C. Wang; Holiday House, 1995.

Concrete Experiences

Bring a small trunk into the classroom. Have students predict what is inside. Label the parts of the trunk as a resource for writing.

Let the Writing Begin

Emergent Writers

- **What's in the Trunk?**
  Students draw something in the trunk and then tell what it is.

- **A Dress-up Trunk**
  Students draw themselves in clothes that might be found in a dress-up trunk and describe their appearance.

Beginning Writers

- **I'm Going on a Trip**
  Students draw what they would pack for their trip. Then they copy and complete the sentences.

  *I'm going on a trip to _____.
  I will pack _____.*

- **The Old Trunk**
  Students pretend that they found an old trunk. They draw what they imagine would have been in the trunk. Then they copy and complete the sentences.

  I found a very old trunk. When I opened it there was a _____.

Independent Writers

- **An Alphabet in the Trunk**
  Students think of and list things that might be in a trunk that begin with every letter of the alphabet. After the list is made, have them write an introductory paragraph that explains how the things got into the trunk.

- **_____'s Trunk**
  Designate a story character and have students write about what that character would pack into a trunk and why.

Front Cover   287

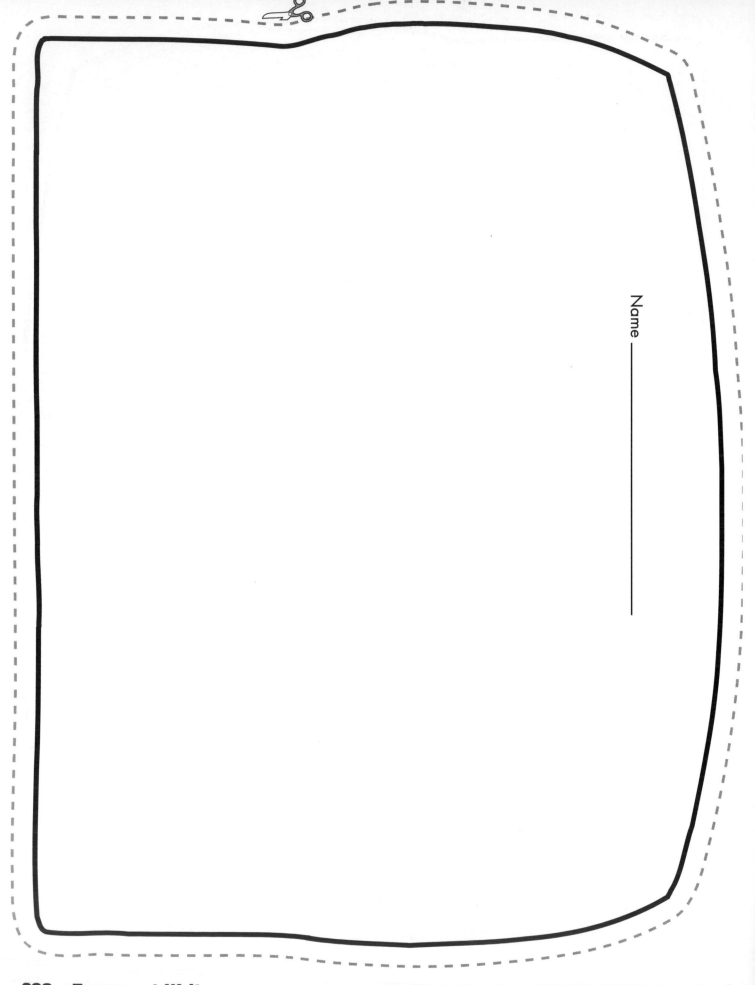

Name _____

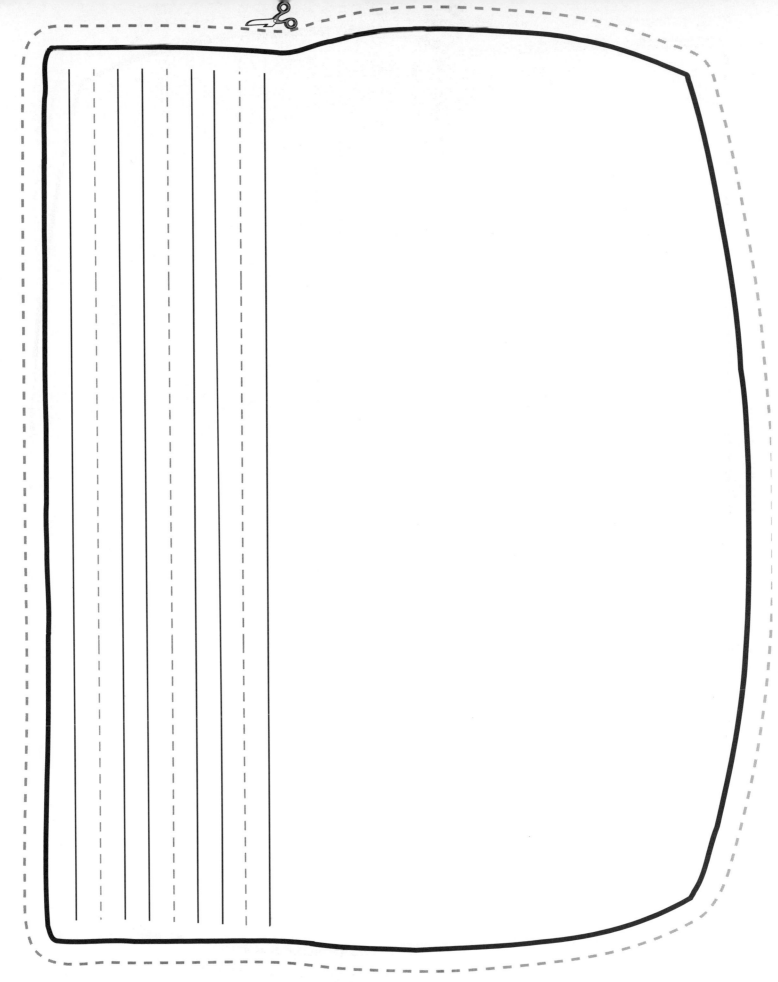

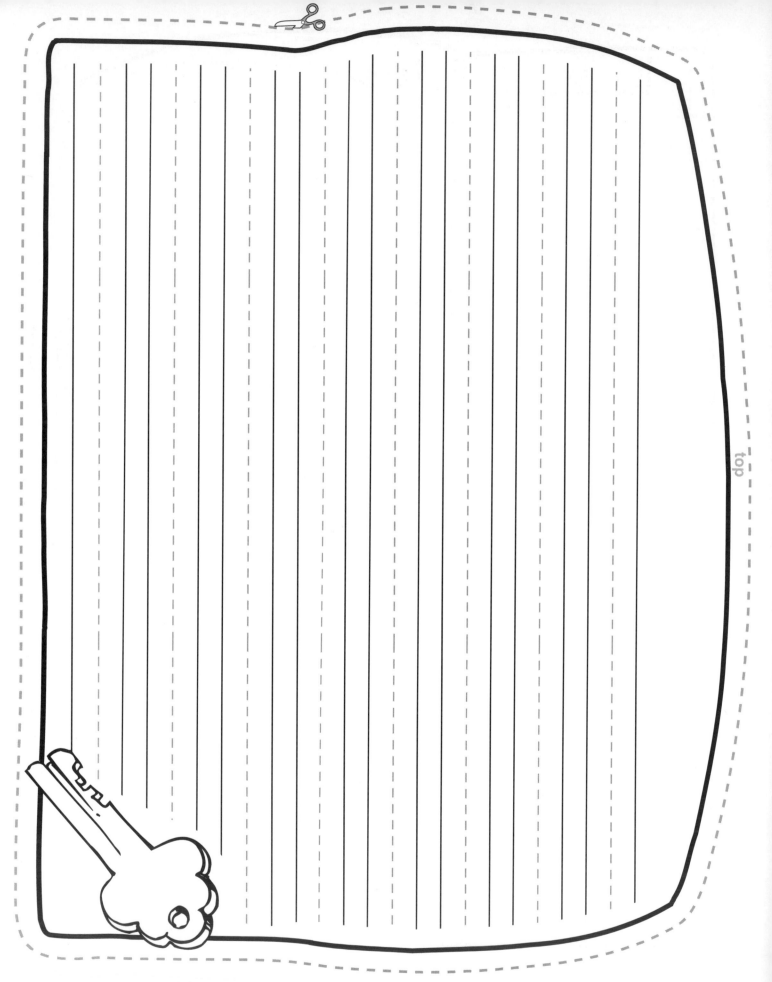

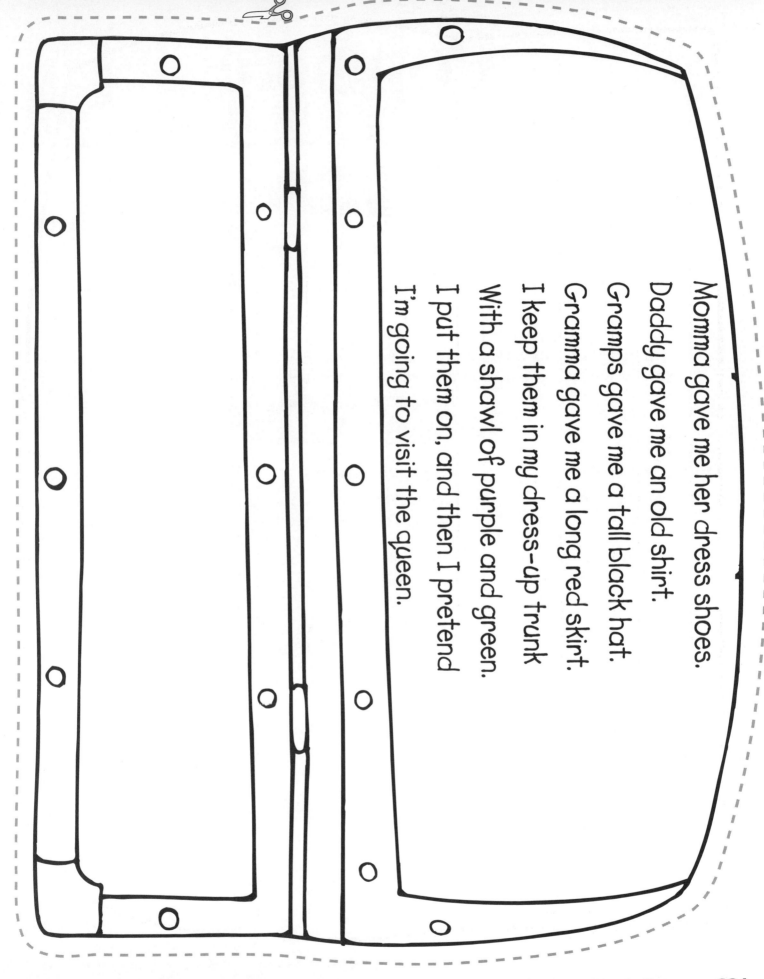

Momma gave me her dress shoes.
Daddy gave me an old shirt.
Gramps gave me a tall black hat.
Gramma gave me a long red skirt.
I keep them in my dress-up trunk
With a shawl of purple and green.
I put them on, and then I pretend
I'm going to visit the queen.

Popsicle

Literature Connections

Big Mama by Tony Crunk; Farrar, Straus & Giroux Inc., 2000.
Isaac the Ice Cream Truck by Scott Santoro; Henry Holt, 1999.
Sweets & Treats: Dessert Poems compiled by Bobbye S. Goldstein; Hyperion Books for Children, 1998.

Concrete Experiences

Enjoy a cool treat. Share Popsicles with students in your class. Have students describe the tastes and sensations. Record the words in a word bank.

Let the Writing Begin

Emergent Writers

- **Yum! My Favorite!**
  Students draw a picture of themselves eating Popsicles of their favorite flavors. Then they tell the name of the flavor and how it tastes.

- **Cold Treat**
  Students draw other cold treats and label each of the pictures.

Beginning Writers

- **A New Flavor**
  Students draw a Popsicle of a new flavor. Then they copy and complete the sentence.

  I invented a great new flavor called _____.

- **Old Popsicle Sticks**
  Students draw three ways to recycle Popsicle sticks. Then they copy and complete the sentences.

  I can recycle my Popsicle sticks.
  I can use them for _____ or _____ or _____.
  It's a cool way to recycle!

Independent Writers

- **My Popsicle Plan**
  Students write a plan for earning money so that they can buy a Popsicle when the ice-cream man visits their house.

- **Popsicle Similes**
  Students write a series of similes comparing cold things and cold feelings to Popsicles. Then they use one of the similes in a descriptive paragraph.

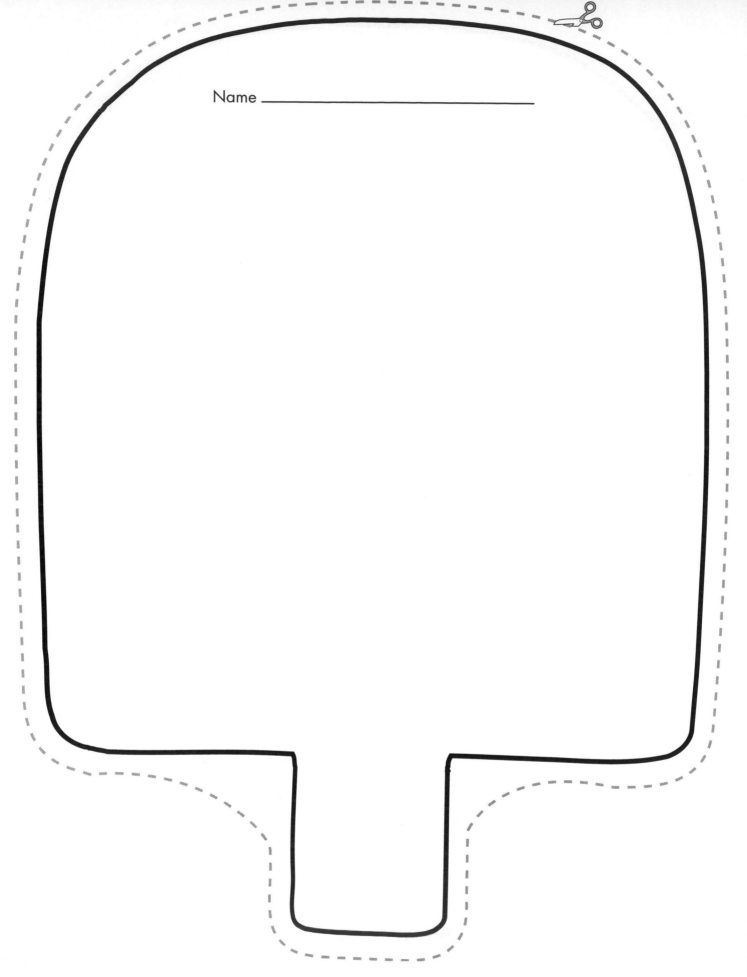

Name _____

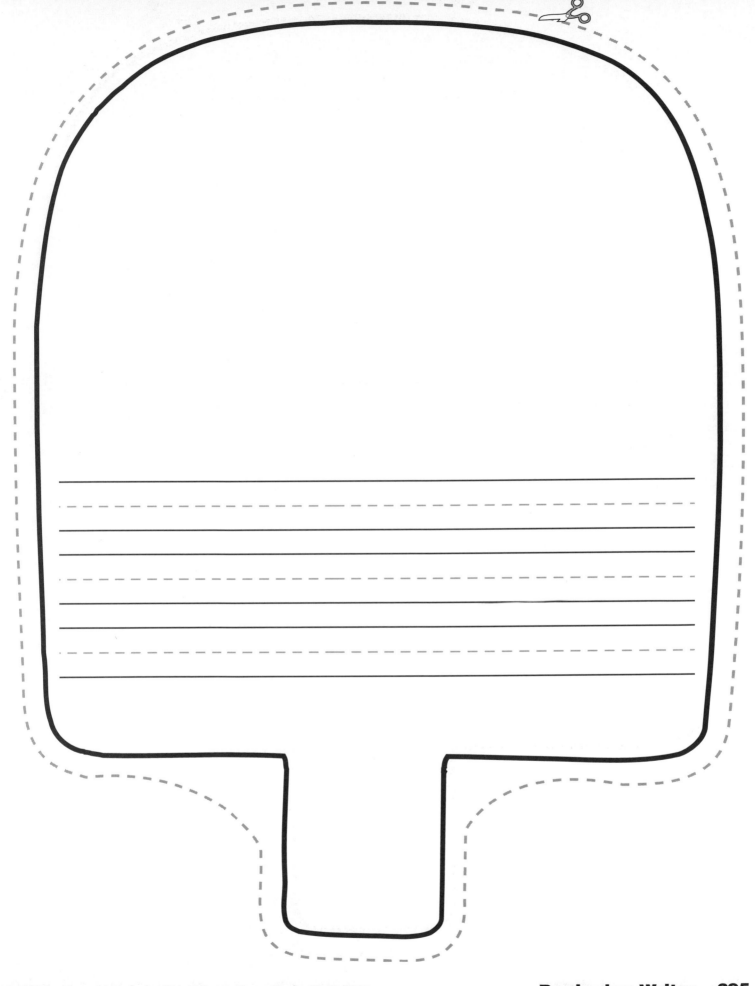

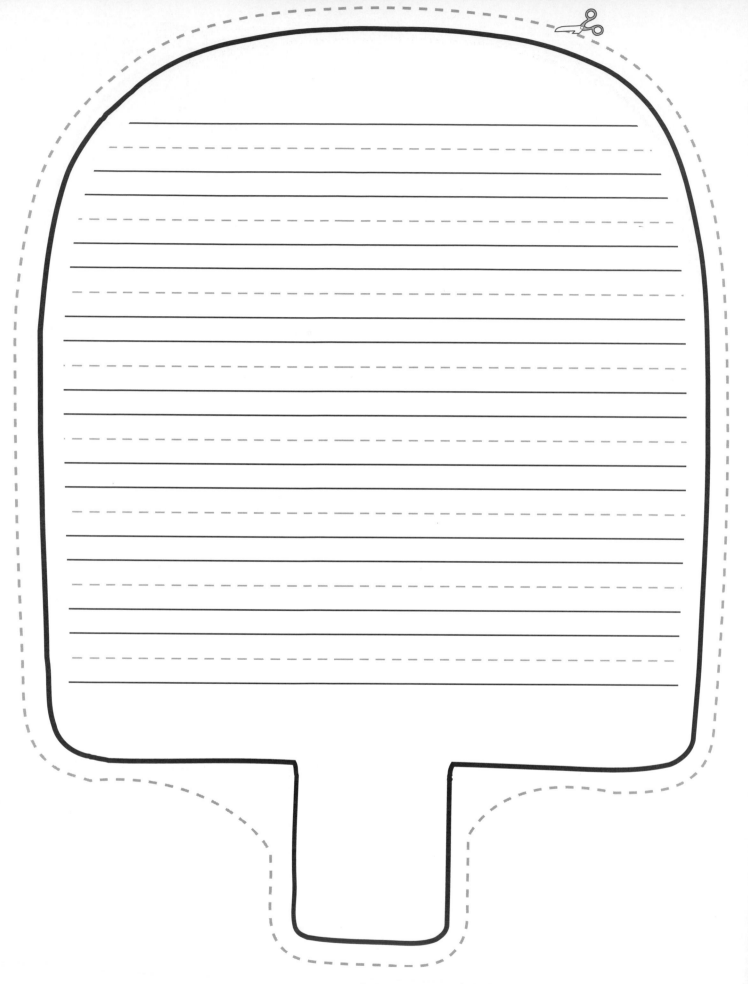

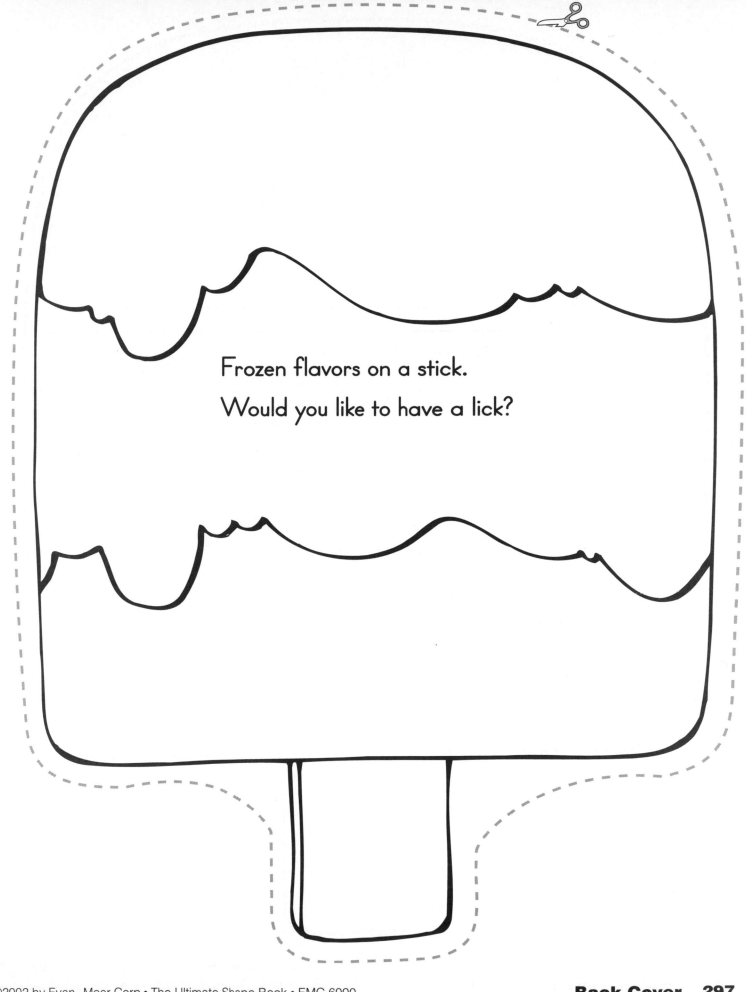

Frozen flavors on a stick.

Would you like to have a lick?

Sun

Literature Connections

Arrow to the Sun: A Pueblo Indian Tale adapted by Gerald McDermott; Viking Press, 1974.
Cock-a-doodle Dudley by Bill Peet; Houghton Mifflin Company, 1990.
Gift of the Sun: A Tale from South Africa by Dianne Stewart; Farrar, Straus & Giroux Inc., 1996.
I Can Hear the Sun: A Modern Myth by Patricia Polacco; Puffin Books, 1999.
Our Big Home: An Earth Poem by Linda Glaser; Millbrook Press, 2000.
A Pizza the Size of the Sun: Poems by Jack Prelutsky; Greenwillow, 1996.
Sun and Moon: A Giant Love Story by Lisa Desimini; Blue Sky Press, 1999.
Walter the Baker by Eric Carle; Simon & Schuster, 1995.
What the Sun Sees; What the Moon Sees by Nancy Tafuri; Greenwillow, 1997.
Who Wakes Rooster? by Clare Hodgson Meeker; Simon & Schuster Children's Books, 1996.

Concrete Experiences

Go outside. Listen to the sounds that you hear when the sun is bright and the world is awake and busy. Make a list of these daytime sounds.

Let the Writing Begin

Emergent Writers

- **Fun in the Sun**
  Students draw themselves enjoying the sun. Then they tell about what they are doing.

- **When the Sun Comes Up**
  Students draw things that happen when the sun comes up. Share the drawings with the class, and then try writing a class poem about the sunrise.

Beginning Writers

- **Picnic in the Sun**
  Students plan a picnic. They draw the picnic scene. They list things they will eat and games they will play. Then they write a simple story about the picnic.

- **Sunny Thoughts**
  Students draw a flower that likes the sun and a flower that doesn't like the sun. Then they copy and complete the sentences.

  I like the sun. It makes me _____.

  I don't like the sun. It makes me _____.

Independent Writers

- **One Day at the Beach**
  Students finish this story:

  The waves crashed against the sand. I plopped my pack down and spread out my towel. The sun was warm on my face. Just then…

- **My Magic Sunglasses**
  Students write a story about a magic pair of sunglasses. When they look through them, they can see into the future.

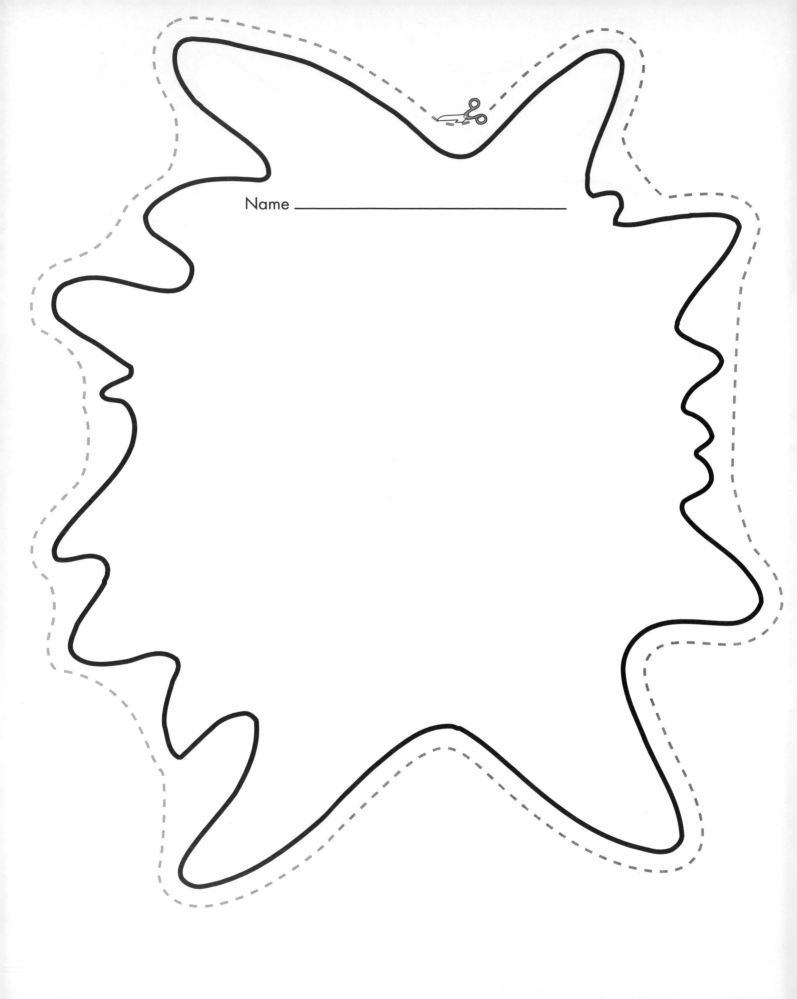

Name _____

Peek-a-boo, Sun
In a cloudy sky—
Shine down on me
As you go by.